P9-CLI-581

nd us.
2.75

13,536

BT
1106
.P5

Pineas
   Thomas More and
   Tudor polemics

DATE DUE

Thomas More And Tudor Polemics
BT1106.P5   13536

Pineas, Rainer
        VRJC/WRIGHT LIBRARY

Thomas More and Tudor Polemics

RAINER PINEAS

Thomas More
and
Tudor Polemics

Indiana University Press

Bloomington · London

VERNON REGIONAL
JUNIOR COLLEGE LIBRARY

Copyright © 1968 by Indiana University Press
ALL RIGHTS RESERVED

No part of this book may be reproduced or utilized in
any form or by any means, electronic or mechanical,
including photocopying and recording, or by any
information storage and retrieval system, without
permission in writing from the publisher. The
Association of American University Presses
Resolution on Permissions constitutes the only
exception to this prohibition.
Library of Congress catalog card number: 68-14610
Manufactured in the United States of America

TO CHARLOTTE

CONTENTS

PREFACE

Although a large proportion of the works published during the Tudor period concern themselves with religious controversy, this huge body of literature has been more often deplored than studied.[1] What scant treatment the subject has received has often been from a theological point of view which usually displays religious bias in favor of one side or the other,[2] while such literary treatments as do exist have not gone into the matter in detail.[3]

It is therefore with the object of providing a fairly detailed and, hopefully, unbiased investigation of early Tudor religious polemics that the present study has been undertaken. No attempt has been made to deal with every work of religious controversy during the period—that is a task for the history books—but my focus is on those controversies which involved Thomas More, the official spokesman for the Catholic position. Therefore the present work examines the polemics of Luther and Bugenhagen insofar as they concerned More, and those of Henry VIII, Tyndale, Barnes, Fish, Frith, Saint-German, and of More himself. Although George Joye wrote against More, he will not be included in this study which deals only with those Reformers whose works More answered.

The specific area on which my study focuses is that of polemical technique. I have given consideration to the polemical use of secular and ecclesiastical history, logic, the Scriptures, humor, and, especially, the figures of rhetoric and of various rhetorical forms, such as the dialogue. Such an emphasis on rhetoric is prompted by the belief that the fiery controversies of the early and middle periods of the sixteenth century played a considerable part in forging the language used so magnificently at its end and in the century following.

To get a clearer view of the Reformers' attacks to which More reacted, I shall consider the entire polemical corpus of each of More's English opponents, and not merely those books to which More replied formally and which were the immediate occasion for his answers. But since More is the pivot around whom the controversies discussed revolve, of necessity greater attention has been paid to his polemics than to those of any other single figure. It is hoped, therefore, that this examination of so important a segment of More's writings—of the 1,458 pages which make up the 1557 edition of his English works, 931 are concerned with religious controversy—will add something to our understanding of this remarkable man.

My analysis of polemical technique is in no way intended to impugn the sincerity or intellectual honesty of any of the polemicists discussed. They were all sincere—whatever their opponents said about them—and Tyndale, Barnes, Frith, and More died for their convictions.

Believing implicitly in the fundamental justice of their respective causes, they sought to advance their cause by all the power at their command. They were advocates in the court of public opinion (More, Fish, and Saint-German being, in fact, advocates by profession)—the Protestants for the prosecution, and More for the defense, and naturally, therefore, they magnified their own case and minimized that of their opposition.

I wish to thank the publishers of the following journals for permitting me to reprint some of the material previously appearing in article form: *Studies in the Renaissance, Studies in Philology, Studies in English Literature, The Harvard Theological Review* (Copyright 1962 by the President and Fellows of Harvard College), *Nederlands Archief voor Kirkgeschiedenis,* and *Bibliothèque d'Humanisme et Renaissance.* Thanks are also due to l'Abbé Germain Marc'hadour of the Université Catholique, Angers, and to Richard S. Sylvester of Yale University, who read the manuscript and made many valuable criticisms, as well as to Richard J. Schoeck of St. Michael's College, University of Toronto, who read parts of the chapter on Christopher Saint-German. Lastly, my thanks go to my wife for her assistance in research and editing and for her encouragement. To her this book is dedicated.

I am, of course, solely responsible for the opinions expressed in this book and any mistakes it may contain.

RAINER PINEAS

York College
City University of New York

Thomas More and Tudor Polemics

I

Lutheran Controversy

On October 6, 1520, Martin Luther published his *De captivitate Babylonica*, in which he attacked the Church's sacramental system, claiming that there were only three sacraments. Among those who wrote in denunciation of Luther was Henry VIII who, in July, 1521, published a defense of the traditional system entitled *Assertio septem sacramentorum.*

Besides defending the seven sacraments, the *Assertio* also proclaimed the supremacy of the Pope and emphasized the importance of ecclesiastical tradition as a source of ritual and dogma, as opposed to Luther's insistence on the Scriptures as the sole authority.

Actually, much of Henry's defense took the form of an attack on Luther's doctrine and—as was common in Renaissance polemics—on Luther himself. A lot has been made of the virulence of Luther's reply to Henry,[1] but the fact that it was the King who first poured abuse on Luther has received less emphasis. Of course, Henry felt he was merely replying in kind to Luther's vituperation against the

3

papacy in the *Babylonian Captivity*, but Luther could hardly be expected to be enthusiastic about hearing himself described by Henry as the devil's servant who spews out the poison of vipers,[2] as a trumpeter of pride and schism, an infernal wolf (sig. *2^v), possessor of a corrupt and rotten heart (sig. A1^r), and a most filthy Antichrist (sig. G3^r).

One of the most notable characteristics of Henry's book is its picture of Lutheranism as an ecclesiastical and social conspiracy which, while pretending to aim at the welfare of church and state, has as its real objective the ultimate destruction of both these institutions. Henry, for example, claims that Luther is devising a series of increasingly radical measures aimed at the abolition of the Sacrament of the Altar (sigs. D2^r-D2^v), and that he is merely waiting for an opportune moment to abolish all of the sacraments (sig. A3^r). According to Henry, the motive for Luther's insistence on communion in both kinds for the laity is to stir up hatred against the clergy (sig. A3^v). Luther's next move, after degrading the priesthood by denying the sacramental character of ordination, will be to abolish the priesthood entirely and reduce priests to the status of the laity (sig. H2^v), for whom Luther has no affection and uses merely to serve his ends (sig. B1^r).

Henry continues his indictment by charging that Luther, not content with stirring up the laity against the clergy, also seeks to breed sedition by inciting the common people against the nobility (sig. C1^r). He claims that Luther's ultimate object is the breakdown of all institutions and of all morality, and that for this task Luther's tool is the doctrine of justification by faith, by means of which he hopes to inculcate immorality (sig. D4^v). Such a projection of Luther's intention serves to picture him as a satanic character who loves evil for its own sake. Henry's charge—in which he was later joined by other Catholic polemicists—that the Reformers were subversive of all religion and government and were ultimately agents of the devil was countered, as we shall see, by a similar charge made by the Reformers that the Catholic clergy had traditionally been a subversive element in every realm.[3]

Another important tactic in Henry's attack is his accusation of inconsistency against the German Reformer, with the object of demonstrating that Luther's beliefs expediently change with the exigencies of the moment, and that therefore his arguments should not be taken seriously. Thus Henry wonders how one can dispute with a man who, as it suits him, would grant what he previously denied or deny what he previously granted (sig. A1^v). That such a question is meant to make a statement about Luther rather than to express any real frustration on Henry's part is indicated by the fact that after asking it the King nevertheless manages to dispute with his opponent at considerable length. Henry thinks it a contradiction that in one place Luther claims that Christ commanded all the faithful to partake of the cup when he said "Drink ye all of this," and that afterward—fearing to offend the laity, whom Luther tries to incite against the clergy, Henry explains—Luther adds that it is not they who communicate in one kind who sin, but that they sin who deny communion in both kinds to those who desire it. What is the need to contradict someone who so often contradicts himself, concludes Henry (sig. A4^r). Henry's accusation in this instance serves a double purpose. Not only does it detract from his opponent's credibility, but it also helps Henry evade the issue Luther had raised, namely, that the laity should receive communion in both kinds.[4] Finally, Henry uses against Luther the latter's own earlier admission that the Church has the power to discern the Word of God from the words of men (*Werke*, VI, 561). How then, asks Henry, can Luther say that the Epistle of James is unworthy of an apostolic spirit, when the Church has accepted it as full of the apostolic spirit? All that is necessary to defeat Luther is to cite Luther against himself, Henry declares (sig. H4^v).

Such a use against his opponent of that opponent's own statements is a deliberate tactic of the *Assertio*. Again and again Henry counters Luther's arguments with Luther's own admission that the Church has the power to discern between authentic and apocryphal Scripture. From this premise Henry develops the position that the Church cannot err in necessary articles of the faith—why else would God have given the Church the powers Luther ascribes to her?—and concludes that he has proved from Luther's own fundamental position that the sacraments of the Church must have been established by God (sigs. G3^r-G4^r). A variation of this technique is the claim that the very biblical texts Luther advances to support his position are the ones which most undermine it.[5]

If we turn to investigate how Henry builds up his own position, we find that his attempt to establish the existence of seven sacraments consists essentially of an appeal to various kinds of authority. As the sixteenth century had great respect for authority generally, some of the deference to authority noted in the works of Tudor religious polemicists may be attributed to a common trend of the time. However, theology and religious practice defer to authority by their very nature, and the frequent reference to authority made by both sides during the religious controversy owes less to the temper of the times than it does to the subject of that controversy itself. There is no question but that both sides leaned to an equal degree on authority. It is merely that the authority was a different one in each case; for the Reformers it was the Scriptures, while for the Catholics it was the dictum of the Church.

Of course, since it was the very authority of the Church to legislate dogma and ritual which was being challenged, it was not good tactics for Catholic apologists to cite that authority against their opponents—although sometimes they did just that. A more effective method of argumentation was to appeal first to mutually respected authorities and then to derive the authority of the Church from these.

Henry's most consistent appeal is to the authority of numbers. Luther's attack on indulgences, transubstantiation, the Mass as a sacrifice, the sacramental character of confirmation and orders is countered by Henry with the argument that these practices and doctrines have been accepted by large numbers of people in many countries over many centuries, and that therefore it is not reasonable to suppose that everyone else is mistaken and only Luther is correct.[6] In other words, concludes Henry, what everybody else believes, Luther alone mocks at, considering himself wiser than all the ancient Doctors of the Church (sig. I2^v).

It is these ancient Doctors who are Henry's second line of defense. Henry calls on Ambrose to refute Luther's denial of the doctrine of transubstantiation (sig. A3^v), and on Ambrose, Gregory, and Augustine to prove that the Mass is a sacrifice (sig. D1^r). To support his view of confession, Henry appeals to Augustine, Bede, and Ambrose: Luther says one thing but, Henry points out to his readers, Augustine contradicts him; Luther says yes, Bede says no; Luther says yes, Ambrose says no—whom will you believe, Luther or the Fathers (sig. E4^r)?

Henry also appeals to reason to support his arguments. He is not content merely to cite authorities, but maintains that the authorities to whom he appeals are more likely to be correct than Luther. For instance, Henry defends the motives of the clergy in denying communion in both kinds to the laity by asserting that if such an action were sinful, it would be unreasonable to suppose that the clergy would have instituted a practice for which they would risk eternal damnation and receive no earthly benefit (sig. A4^r). To Luther's accusation that communion in both kinds was usurped from the laity by the clergy, Henry replies that since Luther can show no record of such a usurpation taking place, it is much more reasonable to suppose that the custom was established with the laity's consent (sig. A4^r).

Finally Henry appeals to the authority of time to bolster his position. He points out for how long a period Christians have considered indulgences effective (sig. A1^v), how long the clergy have administered communion in one kind (sig. A4^r), how long the belief in the Real Presence has lasted (sig. B4^v), and he wonders ironically why Luther's objections to that doctrine have been hidden from past ages (sigs. C3^v-C4^r).

One of the most interesting aspects of Henry's book is the nature of an appeal to history which he—or at least his chief minister, Cromwell, acting on his behalf—was later to repudiate and for which repudiation he was to summon up the evidence he rhetorically demands in the *Assertio*. The question is the authority of the Pope. If Luther is correct, says Henry, in his belief that the Pope achieved his power by force, then let Luther show us from histories when this happened, because so important an event cannot have had an obscure origin. The record of past events shows that right from the beginning all churches in Christendom have obeyed Rome, Henry maintains. How could a defenseless priest without an army obtain power over his fellows, as Luther claims he did, and how, continues Henry, can Luther expect us to believe that nations would yield their sovereignty to a foreigner (sig. A2ᵛ)? As we shall see, the answers to Henry's question were to be provided by Cromwell's protégés Robert Barnes and John Bale, and by William Tyndale, whom Cromwell tried to recruit.[7]

In common with most polemical works on both sides of the religious dispute, Henry's book contains its share of extralogical devices. Whether these were deliberate or whether they merely stemmed from their author's occasional lapses in logic is impossible to ascertain. Naturally, faulty logic was usually regarded as intentional by one's opponent, and reciprocal accusations of the intentional use of sophistry abound in the works of Tudor polemicists. One of the logical fallacies into which Henry falls is that of begging the question—a practice Luther attributes to all controversialists arguing on the orthodox side (*Werke*, X, ii, 182). For instance, Henry supports his contention that the cup should be withheld from the laity partly by the assertion that God must approve of the custom, since He not only receives its supporters into heaven but also wishes to have them venerated on earth (sig. A4ʳ). The truth of these two claims could hardly have been self-evident to the Reformers, who maintained that communion in one kind was ungodly and who opposed the veneration of saints.

Luther's Attack
on Henry

In July, 1522, Luther answered Henry's *Assertio* with his *Contra Henricum regem Angliae*, of which he had previously published a somewhat different German version.[8] Luther's book consists of a defense of himself and of his doctrines, especially those of justification by faith alone and of the primacy of Scripture.

Perhaps the most obvious characteristic of Luther's reply to Henry is its abuse. While, as we shall see, abuse of one's opponent was fairly common in sixteenth-century religious controversy, many polemicists evidently felt that such abuse needed some kind of justification, for their works are full of ingenious excuses for hurling invectives at their antagonists.[9] Of all the justifications for virulence the most common was the citation of scriptural precedent, and to this Luther appeals in defending his conduct. He asserts that while Henry accused him of excessive sharpness toward the Pope, the King should first have proved that the papacy did not deserve such treatment. Did not Christ sharply rebuke the scribes and the Pharisees, calling them hypocrites and murderers, and did not Paul characterize his enemies as dogs, apostles of Satan, and sons of the devil (*Werke*, X, ii, 190)? On one occasion Luther even manages to make polemical capital out of an excuse for virulence by using that excuse to portray himself as a humble man, careless of his own reputation but zealous for the honor of God. He complains that Henry has assaulted him with curses, lies, and sophistry, and says that while he could have forgiven the King of England his errors, he cannot forgive Henry's concocting lies against God; therefore, to uphold God's honor, he concludes, he has every right to cast Henry's filth back into his own teeth (ibid., pp. 184, 189). Often, however, Luther admits less lofty motives and merely claims to be paying Henry back in his own coin (e.g., ibid., pp. 184, 190, 222).

One medium of abuse Luther employs is the derogatory epithet. Throughout his work he ironically refers to Henry as "our lord the king" (e.g., ibid., p. 192), with the implication that Henry expects the whole world to bow to his theological opinions, just as he expects his subjects to obey him in secular matters.[10] Other epithets spell out the implication. Henry is a "new god . . . creator of articles of the faith" (ibid., p. 183), and "the deity recently born in England" (ibid., p. 188). In these epithets the process of denigration has advanced one step, for Henry is pictured not only as demanding credence on the strength of his rank but also as usurping the very office of God. The epithets also make the classic Protestant point that Catholicism is an innovation, a point usually made in reply to the Catholics' charge that the faith of the Reformers dates back no further than Luther's break with Rome.[11] Even Henry's name is pressed into polemical service, when his arguments are labeled "foolish, ridiculous, and truly Henrican" (*Werke*, X, ii, p. 193). Perhaps it was in retaliation for this epithet, which Luther uses frequently, that More dubbed Luther "Luderus."[12]

Another method of abuse Luther employs is general denigration of his opponent's abilities. He speculates that God, as a punishment for

Henry's sins, must have struck him with madness, since it would be impossible to present the King in a worse light than he does himself. Either Henry is mad, Luther tells his readers, or some enemy, in order to disgrace him, has published the *Assertio* in his name (*Werke*, X, ii, p. 210). Here Luther uses the popular polemical technique of claiming that his opponent really needs no confutation—he is his own worst enemy—a device which both Henry and More, incidentally, employ against Luther.[13] Throughout his work Luther laments the fact that he has to waste his time disputing with such a stupid adversary (e.g., *Werke*, X, ii, p. 212). Henry is pictured as a miserable scribbler, at a loss to know how to fill up the pages of his book,[14] and as a silly Thomist who has to be taught the elements of philosophy and theology, a task which, after he has verbally caned Henry for his dullness, Luther offers to undertake (ibid., p. 189).

Much of Luther's attack on Henry is merely vituperation, as when Luther declares that Henry wrote the *Assertio* not out of any real concern for the sacraments but in order to vent the sickness of his spirit; since he could not discharge his hate from a lower area, he took occasion to vomit it forth from his stinking mouth (ibid., pp. 184-185).

The polemical purpose of Luther's abuse of Henry and of his denigration of Henry's abilities is to disqualify the latter's arguments as worthy of serious attention.[15] The technique is a form of *praemunitio*,[16] in that Luther prejudices his readers against Henry before dealing with what he has to say. More formal use of *praemunitio* is made by Luther at the beginning of his work when he rhetorically asks his readers how anyone could believe any part of Henry's book when it contains so many obvious lies (*Werke*, X, ii, p. 185), and at the opening of the section in which he deals with the King's specific arguments, where he says, "Let us now come to the specific points our Henry makes, and let us see how successfully, aided by his renowned Thomistical wisdom, he fits his principles to his conclusions" (ibid., p. 195). It appears that Luther was quite conscious of this technique, for he accuses Henry of using it against him. He comments that Henry seems to have been told by some idiotic orator that if one feels that one's opponent cannot be overcome in any other way, the first thing to do is to jeer at him and to make light of his ability, so that the foolish hearer may believe that the opponent has been beaten before he is even attacked (ibid., pp. 208-209). Thus we can see that Luther is not only a practitioner of *praemunitio*, but that he also has an antidote to its use against him, namely, the assertion that the opponent who employs it thereby reveals his own inadequacy. For although an astute reader would notice the contradiction inherent in deploring in an opponent a technique used by the polemicist himself, Luther and his contemporaries were evidently much more concerned with the immediate emotional impact of a polemical device than with logical consistency. Sixteenth-century controversialists continually accused their opponents of sophistry while themselves employing sophistical arguments, and Thomas More was to accuse one of his adversaries of rhetoric in one of the most rhetorical passages in his own book.[17]

A prominent accusation Luther makes against his opponent is that Henry's position lacks scriptural authority. Luther asserts that the basis on which Henry builds his arguments is not Scripture but human tradition; on this Luther comments that he will oppose anyone who wants to create articles of the faith on the basis of such authority (*Werke*, X, ii, pp. 191, 192), adding that whenever Henry does cite Scripture, he distorts it (ibid., pp. 204, 206).

According to Luther, distortions and lies generally are the hallmark of Henry's book (ibid., p. 183), but Henry's biggest lie is his statement that the Lutheran teachings contain contradictions. Luther comments that this god recently arisen in England thinks that his bare assertion is sufficient proof of truth, and that he gives no examples to substantiate his claims lest he be proved a liar (ibid., p. 188).

It is Luther's contention that, since Henry is unable to answer him by legitimate reasoning, he has to resort to other tactics. Like most polemicists of his day, Luther makes the exposé of his opponent's technique an important element in his own. For instance, Luther charges Henry with begging the question, a practice, he informs his readers, which the Thomists are actually taught in their schools (ibid., p. 182). He maintains that Henry takes as his major premise the very thing that is in dispute, so that when Henry is asked by what authority he does something, he replies that he does it by the mere authority of the fact that he does it and that it has been done for a long time (ibid., pp. 182, 205).

Another accusation is that Henry evades those of Luther's points he is unable to answer—and the polemical corollary that he is unable to answer those of Luther's points he does not specifically discuss (e.g., ibid., pp. 198, 210).

Luther also maintains that Henry is arguing his case maliciously against his better knowledge. The attempt to impugn an opponent's credibility by an accusation of bad faith was, as we have already observed, a common ingredient of sixteenth-century polemics. Luther wonders, for instance, how Henry can accuse him of disparaging good works and condoning evil works, when it is evident that the King has read his books, so that Henry must be aware of not telling the truth (ibid., p. 185). Luther also tells his readers that Henry knows that his charges of inconsistency have no basis in fact, and that this is why he is careful not to adduce even a single example of such alleged inconsistencies (ibid., pp. 184, 188). That this claim was, as we have seen, untrue would not detract from its effectiveness.[18]

To dramatize his opponent's ineptness, Luther on one occasion sets up what might be called an "implied" dialogue, the effect of which is similar to hearing one end of a telephone conversation:

> Where are you, Lord Henry? Produce your illustrious book against Luther. What does your Lordship defend? Seven sacraments? By whose authority? God's or men's? Then let your Thomistical Lordship hear this judgment, not Luther's, but His before Whom the whole world trembles: "Vainly they worship Me with the doctrines of men" (*Werke*, X, ii, p. 192).

As we shall see, More expanded Luther's implied dialogue into a modified dialogue when answering the above passage,[19] so that Luther may have been one of the influences on More's polemical use of the dialogue form in his *Dialogue concernynge heresyes*.[20]

A significant portion of Luther's work is devoted to ridicule of his opponent's method of argumentation, of which we have already observed some examples. Luther's ridicule is usually achieved by exaggeration, as when he claims that there is nothing in Henry's book based on either reason or Scripture, but that everything is argued by means of the Thomistical formula "It appears so to me," "I think so," and "I believe so"; for if the Thomists' major premise is denied, they prove it by saying "It has to be so," and if it is again denied, they retort, "How could it be otherwise? This is how it has to be." Luther says that although in his book he especially attacked this Thomistical principle and set up the Scriptures against human custom and authority, Henry nevertheless parrots only, "It must be this way, it is according to custom, this is how it has been done for a long time." Luther concludes by proclaiming himself convinced that if he were to write a thousand volumes proving the worthlessness of such authorities in matters of faith, Henry would still chant the same refrain, "It has to be this way, usage so dictates, the authority of man says so," and that if he were to ask Henry how he could prove human custom to have any value, the King would merely intone again, "It has to be this way" (*Werke*, X, ii, p. 191). Had Henry really reasoned in such a manner, he would have deserved all the ridicule of which Luther was capable. But Luther has omitted any reference to Henry's scriptural arguments for believing the authority of the Church, used the rhetorical device of putting words into his opponent's mouth to make him sound foolish,[21] and boiled down pages of fairly respectable argument to a ludicrous formula.[22] Another method Luther uses to ridicule his opponent's manner of disputing is that of distortion by means of misplaced emphasis. In an argument about the Mass, for example, he turns Henry's illustration of a point into the major premise of a ridiculous syllogism—which Henry never propounded—and thus saddles him with a series of obvious non sequiturs.[23]

Sometimes Luther goes beyond distortion to outright misstatement of fact, as when he tells his readers that Henry had challenged him to prove that there was no such phenomenon as transubstantiation, and comments that evidently the King has to be taught the elements of disputation, for when he has to prove the affirmative, he insists that his opponent prove the negative. It would be a splendid idea to send such learned men to defend our faith against the Turks, Luther scoffs; we shall no longer have to give a reason for our faith, but we shall merely challenge them to prove the negative (*Werke*, X, ii, p. 204). This is a fine piece of ridicule—except that Henry never did make the statement Luther attributes to him.[24] If we wonder how Luther and his contemporaries could make palpably false statements about what their opponents said, we must remember how difficult it was for readers to check the facts. They would have to have had the energy, the interest, and perhaps the money to acquire both texts in question and compare them, and in England such a course was open only to Protestants and to those Catholics who could read Latin, for Catholics were prohibited from reading vernacular versions of Lutheran literature.[25] The outright lie about an opponent's text was far more difficult to disprove than a mere distortion. In the latter case, one could always cite the correct form of the text in question and hope to be believed, but an alleged quotation or paraphrase manufactured out of thin air was extremely difficult to disprove in a period when texts were scarce. More, for instance, cannot quote anything from the *Assertio* to prove that Henry did not say what Luther claims he did. And it should be realized that a considerable number of More's readers would be Lutherans who, when it came to bare assertions, would rather have believed Luther than More.[26]

More Champions His King

Henry decided not to reply to Luther personally, and the task of refutation was left to others. Among those who resolved to answer Luther or who were asked to do so was Thomas More.[27]

By the time he published his defense of Henry, More had held a succession of positions of increasing importance. Trained as a lawyer, after attending St. Antony's School and Oxford, More was first elected to Parliament in 1504. In 1517 he became a judge in the Court of Requests and a member of the Privy Council. Four years later he was knighted and made Under-Treasurer of the Exchequer, and in 1523, the year of his work against Luther, he was chosen Speaker of the House of Commons. He had achieved literary fame by his *Utopia* of 1516, and had had some experience in both religious and secular controversy, in that he had defended Erasmus' translation of the New Testament against its detractors[28] and had joined battle with the French humanist, Germanus Brixius, on the subject of a French-English naval engagement.[29]

More's *Responsio ad Lutherum,* published early in 1523 under the pseudonym of Ferdinand Baravellus and later in the same year in an expanded version under the name of William Ross, is his first entry into the anti-Lutheran lists. (However, More was later to claim that the *Dialogue concernynge heresyes* was his first work against the Reformers.[30]) Apart from its own merits, the *Responsio* is worthy of note because it contains within it the seeds of most of More's subsequent attitudes and techniques of controversy.[31]

More's work is a defense of the position taken by the *Assertio*. It once again attacks Luther's cardinal doctrines and proclaims them subversive of all good order, both secular and religious.

Characteristically, More has provided his book with a fictional setting,[32] by prefixing to the work a letter from Ross to one John Carcellius and a reply by the latter to Ross. These letters comment on the foul language of Luther's reply to Henry and explain that Henry could easily have answered him, but that Luther was not worthy to have the King reply to him. Lest Luther should remain unanswered and thus appear to have gained the victory, Ross has undertaken to rebut him in Henry's place.[33]

As in his other polemical works which have frame stories or dramatic settings—such as the *Dialogue concernynge heresyes* or the *Supplicacion of soules*[34]—the letters prefixed to the *Responsio* serve not merely to introduce the subject but also to perform a definite polemical function, namely, that of acting as *praemunitio* or prejudicial introduction to the book More is about to attack.

The *Responsio* is cast in the form of quotations from Luther's answer to Henry with appended rebuttal.[35] This was the form of polemic most widely used by both sides in the religious dispute. It can be either extremely monotonous or rather interesting, depending on how it is handled. The trick is to keep both the opponent's quotations and one's own answers short, demolishing the quotation in one or two pithy sentences, and thus achieving the effect of dialogue. As we shall see later, the expert practitioner of this technique was William Tyndale. More's later works, notably his *Confutacyon*, miss this opportunity entirely because of the lengthy and often discursive lectures appended to the quotations, so that the effect of dialogue give-and-take is completely lost. On the whole, More's answers in the *Responsio* are shorter than in his subsequent works, although usually not short enough. Only occasionally does he manage to achieve the effect of dialogue (e.g., *Responsio*, sigs. Z3ʳ-AA1ʳ).

More himself reveals why he chose this particular form in which to answer Luther, and in the very description of his plan of composition he scores a number of polemical points against his opponent. He tells his readers that he decided to cite Luther verbatim so that no one could accuse him of having distorted what his opponent said, for what Luther says is so incredibly stupid that no one would believe that he in fact said such things unless his actual words were quoted. In this way, More adds, it is Luther's own hand which brands him as mad (ibid., sigs. PP4ʳ-PP4ᵛ). In this one brief passage More manages to praise his own fairness, to prejudice his readers against the passage from Luther he is about to cite, and to indicate that Luther has no more redoubtable opponent than Luther himself—all techniques which are characteristic of More's entire conduct of the controversy with the Reformers and which will be discussed more fully later.

Perhaps the most striking feature of the *Responsio* is its similarity to the *Assertio* and the extent to which it depends on that work. Nearly all of More's characteristic attitudes and arguments—though not his style—are in the King's book. The crediting of the Reformers with a diabolic intention of subverting all religion and the conviction that they plan to introduce their schemes gradually at first, so that they will not be recognized for what they are—two of the most pronounced attitudes of More's religious polemics—can already be found in the *Assertio*.[36] An examination of Henry's book also reveals that a number of its polemical techniques closely parallel those used by More. For instance, both Henry and More delight in accusing their opponents of inconsistency and self-contradiction, and both have a penchant for using the very works of their opponent against that opponent himself. While other contemporary polemics occasionally make use of similar arguments and techniques, their concentration in the *Assertio* and in More's polemics is unusual. Fisher's *Defensio Regie Assertionis* (1525) or Eck's *De primatu Petri adversus Ludderum* (1521), for example, give a total impression quite unlike that of the *Assertio* or of More's controversial works. One is left to speculate whether More learned some of his polemical technique from Henry, or whether, when More claimed that he was only "a sorter out and placer of the principal matters"[37] in Henry's book he was being too modest.[38]

Since More is defending the *Assertio,* he constantly quotes from Henry's book. However, even when he does not quote directly, More continually alludes to the *Assertio* and pays his royal master the compliment of adopting most of his arguments.[39] At the end of the first book of the *Responsio* More claims that he has refuted Luther almost entirely by using Henry's arguments (*Responsio,* sig. Q4ʳ).

More's tone in his controversy with Luther is none too gentle. In one of the two prefatory letters to the *Responsio,* More explains that it would be wrong to answer moderately so immoderate a writer as Luther (ibid., sig. A4ʳ), and he says later that it is impossible to answer so evil a wretch with kind words (ibid., sigs. Q1ʳ-Q1ᵛ, XX1ʳ). But More is never so scurrilous as Luther, and the bulk of his answer consists of reasoning rather than invective. It is interesting to note how similar this Latin polemic of More's is to his English works of controversy, as is his Latin letter against Bugenhagen, to be discussed later. While one might expect More to be learned in Latin and popular in English, in fact his Latin and English polemics are very much alike in both content and technique.[40]

One of More's characteristic methods for establishing his case, as was Henry's in the *Assertio,* is reference to the authority of numbers, time, and the Fathers. For instance, to emphasize what he considers to be Luther's presumption in departing from orthodoxy, More enumerates all the nations which, if Luther's view be correct, have erred in obeying the Pope.[41] The list is impressive and serves to cast doubt on the probability that these nations could err and one man be correct. Again, on the question of the Eucharist, More complains that Luther thinks he knows better than all Catholics over the past centuries (*Responsio,* sig. T3ʳ). To support the orthodox view of the Real Presence, More claims the authority of Eusebius, Gregory, Cyril, Jerome, Augustine, and Ambrose (ibid., sig. FF2ʳ).

We can see that More's appeal to the authority of numbers, time, and the Fathers, as was Henry's, is based on the premise that these are reasonable authorities to appeal to and that Luther is unreasonable for opposing them. More's appeal to the authority of reason is another marked characteristic of his religious polemics. He asks Luther, for instance, to explain how God could give the Church the power to distinguish true Scripture from false (see fn. 49) and then allow it to err (ibid., sig. H1ᵛ); and to counter Luther's claim that only the Scriptures are authoritative for doctrine and practice, More wonders what Scriptures Christians read before the Gospels were committed to writing and argues that they must have relied on the spoken word of the Apostles (ibid., sig. L2ᵛ).

But More does not neglect the authority of the Scriptures. Since Luther, and the Reformers generally, claimed to accept no authority but that of the Bible, More realized the importance of supporting his assertions from this source. The most interesting use More makes of scriptural authority in the *Responsio* is his attempt to prove from Scripture itself that the Scriptures should not be regarded as the sole authority for doctrine and practice. More's attempt was probably motivated by Luther's assertion that the Scriptures require that we believe nothing but the Scriptures (*Werke*, X, ii, 195). If only the Scriptures are authoritative, he asks Luther, why does Paul say, "Hold fast the traditions you have learned whether by our word or letter" (II Thess. ii.14), why did Christ say to his disciples that the Holy Spirit would guide them into all truth (John xvi.13), rather than that the Holy Spirit would write the truth, and why did God, through Paul, say that He would put His laws in the minds of His people and inscribe His laws on their hearts (Heb. viii.10), rather than on wood or stone (*Responsio*, sigs. F4ʳ-F4ᵛ)?

As did many of his contemporaries, More uses Old Testament texts to support New Testament theology. For instance, he argues against Luther's assertion that Christ's church cannot consist of sinners mixed with nonsinners by reminding Luther that in Noah's ark—a type of the church—there were mixed both clean and unclean animals (ibid., sigs. H18(a)ᵛ-H18(b)ʳ). But while such use of Old Testament texts was quite common in his time, it was not a use of which More always approved. When it suited him to do so, he was quite capable of criticizing opponents for just such an application.[42] Finally, since Luther leaned so heavily on Scripture, More was at pains to point out that Luther did not really believe the Scriptures as implicitly as he claimed to do, since he distorted the Scriptures to his own convenience. For instance, says More, Luther is selective even in the credence he will give to Paul: He said that on one occasion the Apostle was perhaps speaking only for himself and not for God! Luther also has doubts about whether to believe James, More informs his readers, and he concludes that a man who refuses to believe the scriptural interpretation even of the Apostles who were taught by the Lord must be lying when he boasts that he takes the Scriptures for his guide (*Responsio*, sigs. o2ʳ, o4ʳ).

The use and abuse of logic is another technique which plays an important part in More's polemics. Evidence of More's acquaintance with logic is plentiful, especially in those sections of his works, some of which will be discussed later,[43] in which he attacks the formal validity of an opponent's arguments (e.g., *W**, p. 840).

However, it is not More's adherence to logical form but his use of specious reasoning which is of most interest to the student of his controversial technique, and therefore I shall here indicate some of the devices of doubtful logical validity which More intentionally or unintentionally employs against Luther.

One scholar has assumed More's superiority to his opponents in logic,[44] but I have not been able to find any evidence to support such a view. More's handling of logic is not very different from that of his adversaries; if anything, it is less competent than Frith's.[45]

Frequently More builds up an argument by begging the question, an instance of which can be observed in the following situation: Luther had ridiculed Henry's arguments from time and numbers by pointing out that the Turks' religion has endured for a thousand years, and that the Jews have held their faith longer than Christians. What nonsense, retorts More, to say that because the Jews and the Turks have been so long in error, the Church may also be in error, for the Jews' and Turks' faith comes from the devil, while ours comes from God (*Responsio*, sig. I4ʳ). Here More uses the main point in dispute, whether or not the doctrine of the Catholic Church accords with the will of God, to prove the validity of Henry's argument that the Catholic Church always has carried out the will of God.[46]

Occasionally More evades Luther's main point by fastening onto

---

* *W = The Workes of Sir Thomas More Knyght, sometyme Lord Chauncellour of England, wrytten by him in the Englysh tonge*, ed. William Rastell (London, 1557), *STC* 18,076.

VERNON REGIONAL
JUNIOR COLLEGE LIBRARY

some completely minor portion of Luther's argument and answering only that—a technique, it will be remembered, that Luther used for purposes of ridicule. Thus More gives the impression of having refuted his opponent. This is the method More uses to evade the issue when he answers Luther's main point that the Church has no right to make compulsory such extrascriptural practices as mingling water with the sacramental wine, by noting that in one place Luther had said it was immaterial whether water was added to the wine or not, while in another place he said that such a mingling was not permissible at all. See how Luther contradicts himself, triumphs More (*Responsio*, sig. AA3ᵛ). But what Luther really said was that, to his mind, it was better to omit the water; he never said the mingling was not permissible.[47]

The techniques discussed so far were used by More largely to build up his own case. We turn now to consider some of the techniques More used to attack his opponent's position.

Before attacking one of Luther's arguments, More, as did Henry and Luther himself, characteristically uses *praemunitio* to prejudice his readers against the passage from Luther he is quoting. In his use of this technique More tries to give the impression that he really does not have to refute Luther, claiming that his opponent's arguments are so inept as to be self-defeating. It has already been noted that More's two prefatory letters serve as *praemunitio* for his entire book. Before the reader ever has a chance to find out what Luther actually says in his work, he hears it denigrated by More as a book filled with palpable lies, distortions, and blasphemies, a book which hinders rather than helps its author's cause and is obviously the product of a madman (*Responsio*, sigs. A2ᵛ-A4ʳ). What More does for Luther's entire book, he also does for individual quotations before dealing with them. For instance, he apologizes for Luther's stupidity and comforts his audience by promising them that if by now they are bored with having so many of Luther's remarks quoted to them, the passage from Luther about to be cited is so deliciously absurd that it will relieve their boredom (ibid., sig. M1ʳ). More's apology is also a parody of a similar apology Luther had made to his readers for Henry's stupidity.[48]

An extension of the technique just examined is to use an opponent's

own arguments against him, a favorite practice of More's, characteristic of his entire conduct of the controversy with the Reformers.
Certainly if the polemicist can demonstrate that the very arguments
his opponent advances to strengthen his case—presumably the best
arguments he can find—instead destroy his case, then the polemicist
has succeeded in considerably weakening his opponent's position.
Therefore More declares at the beginning of his work that he intends
to demonstrate to all Lutherans how incompetent their leader is, since
all Luther's efforts serve only to drive deeper into himself with his
own hands the weapon with which he has already been impaled by
his opponent (*Responsio*, sig. B4ᵛ). The statement of Luther's which
serves More best for this purpose is Luther's admission that the
Church has the power to distinguish the Word of God from the
words of men.[49] From this More concludes that Luther is obliged to
agree with the Church when it determines that the Word of God may
be in both written and unwritten form (*Responsio*, sig. L2ʳ). On
another occasion More maintains that Luther has unwittingly proved
the negative of what he had set out to establish (ibid., sig. H13ᵛ).

More also uses *reductio ad absurdum* as a method of ridicule. For
instance, he claims that to Luther all good works are sin and that a
work becomes good only if accompanied by faith. Therefore, concludes More, Luther must believe that evil works such as robbery,
adultery, and blasphemy—so long as they are accompanied by faith—
are meritorious (ibid., sig. H10(c)ʳ).

Another method More uses to ridicule his opponent is that of
dramatic portrayal.[50] A most effective instance of this technique is
used as a reply to Luther's charge that Henry did not write the
Assertio by himself. Employing his favorite tactic of reversing an
opponent's weapon, More assumes that Luther must have received
help in writing his book against Henry—no one man could produce so
much stupidity—and pictures the scene. It is a drunken council of
Pandemonium with Luther as Lucifer. Fortified with drink, the
Lutherans examine Henry's book and find that every word of it is
true. But it has to be answered somehow, and so, in a self-incriminating speech, one of Luther's followers suggests that since all they are
interested in is becoming leaders of a faction and stirring up a tumult,
let them ignore truth and answer the book with insults and mockery.

The plan is approved, and Luther's renegade angels are dispatched over the face of the earth to note whatever expressions they can overhear in taverns, lavatories, and brothels. These they bring back to Luther, and from such material he fashions his book against Henry (*Responsio*, sigs. C4^r-D1^r). It is interesting to note that here More anticipates two of the most important techniques he is to use later against other opponents, the self-incriminatory speech put into the mouth of an adversary, as in his *Dialogue concernynge heresyes,* and the creation of an entire dramatic framework for polemical purposes, as in his *Supplicacion of soules.*[51]

Another important instance of More's use of dramatic portrayal for the sake of ridicule occurs in his answer to Luther's polemical use of implied dialogue against Henry, noted previously.[52] More expands on Luther's use of the technique by substituting direct answers for Luther's implied answers and adding a running commentary to the conversation. Here, More explains, Luther acts like a blind man wishing to be avenged on an enemy. In order to discover in which direction he should strike, Luther first makes his opponent speak to reveal his position. But when the King answers him on the right, Luther strikes on the left, as follows:

> "Where are you, Lord Henry?"
> "Here, right beside you."
> Yet Luther asks him to come closer, so that he can deliver his blow more surely.
> "Produce your distinguished book against Luther."
> "That is what I am doing."
> "Come a little closer. What does your Lordship defend, the seven sacraments?"
> "I do."
> "Come yet closer. By whose teaching, that of God or that of men?"
> "That of God."
> Now sure of his direction, note how unerringly he strikes:
> "Let your Lordship hear this: In vain they worship me with the doctrines of men."

And so, points out More, this blind man, actually nowhere near his opponent, thinks he has struck him a crushing blow (*Responsio,* sig. I3ʳ). A secondary effect of such a technique is to enliven the work in which it appears—a function in later controversies fulfilled by More's "merry tales."[53]

The technique of putting words into an opponent's mouth is another method whereby the polemicist seeks to ridicule his adversary and the position he defends. For the speeches assigned to the opponent are, as in the examples above, always explicitly or implicitly self-condemnatory. The assigning of self-condemnatory speech to the opposition is the basis of polemical dialogue. The combination of polemical dialogue with the creation of a prejudicial dramatic situation for one's opponent is the basis for polemical drama.[54] It should be noted in the first example given above that More has created all the elements of polemical drama except direct dialogue—the self-condemnatory speeches are reported. The situation devised by More is prejudicial because in it Luther initially finds himself unable to answer Henry's book, because he is unable by himself to find a method of answering it, because he accepts the suggestions to answer the *Assertio* by slander, because these suggestions are made at a drunken orgy, and because the slanders are collected in unsavory haunts. The Lutherans' speech is self-condemnatory because they admit that they care nothing for truth and want only to stir up dissension in order to acquire power and riches, because they admit that the King's book is correct and has refuted what they themselves call their heresies, and because they decide to answer it with lies and insults, on the theory that no one could match Luther in that kind of answer since he has the basest of possible characters (*Responsio*, sigs. C4ʳ-D1ʳ). It should also be noted that the technique of putting self-incriminatory speeches into an opponent's mouth is merely an extension of the claim that the opponent really knows he is wrong. By the latter technique the author asserts about his opponent what by the former—and the more effective—technique the opponent asserts about himself.

In the example depicting Luther as Lucifer the reported Lutheran dialogue is purely imaginary. The dialogue set up between Luther and Henry consists mostly of paraphrases of what Luther had said. In the following passage More uses actual quotations from Luther. The ridicule derives from More's arrangement of the quotations;

they are not at all in the sequence of the original. By changing
sequence and context—although using his opponent's actual words—
More makes Luther speak as he, More, wishes him to, and the fact
that Luther's actual words are being used lends credibility to the
process. Let us ask Luther, says More,

> "How do you prove, Father, that you alone are to be believed?"
> To this he answers the following:
> "Because I am certain that I have received my teachings from
> heaven."
> Again we ask:
> "How are you sure you have received your teachings from
> heaven?"
> "Because without any action on my part, God has taken me up
> and placed me in the midst of these disturbances."
> Again we ask:
> "How do you know that it was God who did this?"
> He says:
> "Because I am certain that my teaching is from God."
> "How do you know that?"
> "Because God has taken me up."
> "How do you know that?"
> "Because I am certain."
> "How are you certain?"
> "Because I know."
> "But how do you know?"
> "Because I am certain."   (Ibid., sigs. P3^v–P4^r)

How More has rearranged Luther's words can be seen, for instance,
by the fact that Luther never attempted to prove his assertion that
his teachings were from heaven by his claim that God had taken him
up, as More has him doing, although Luther did make both statements
in separate passages.[55] The technique just described is essentially the
same as the one Luther used to ridicule Henry's alleged "Thomistic
formula,"[56] and it is quite probable that once again More patterned
his technique on that of his opponent, a course of action he followed
consistently in his polemics.

Another of More's weapons is irony. His penchant for irony generally is evidenced by his *Utopia* and by his translating the dialogues

of Lucian. It is the main ingredient of his wit, if not of his entire character. However, More's use of irony against Luther is not nearly so effective as his later use of this weapon against other opponents, and what is most interesting in the present controversy is More's ironic echoing of Luther's phrases. For instance, More says that Luther's chain of reasoning, quoted above, is comparable to an argument between two men, one of whom denies the assumption of his opponent; whereupon the opponent proves his assumption by saying, "It has to be this way." When the assertion is denied, the opponent says again, "And how could it be otherwise? It has to be this way" (*Responsio*, sig. P4^r). More is echoing the words in which Luther had charged that Henry's only and constant argument was: "It has to be this way. How could it be otherwise?"[57] By his ironic echo of Luther's accusation More is seeking to point out that it is really his opponent who uses the question-begging and circular form of reasoning of which he accuses Henry. Other similarly echoed statements of Luther's are his complaint that he has to waste time fighting with fools (*Responsio*, sig. KK2^v), and that Henry plays the fool in matters so sacred and serious.[58] Since the latter complaint is Luther's own ironic echo of Henry's *Assertio*,[59] we have a situation in which Henry makes the original complaint which is ironically echoed by Luther, which in turn is ironically reechoed by More. The use of ironic echo is yet another example of More's fondness for patterning his technique on that of his opponent.

As part of his campaign to discredit Luther and his doctrinal position, More points out a vast number of alleged self-contradictions. For instance, he claims that Luther contradicts himself when in the *De captivitate Babylonica ecclesiae* he says that all should receive the Sacrament of the Altar under both kinds and yet later says that neither kind is essential (*Responsio*, sigs. D2^v-D3^r). Again, More strikes a shrewd blow when he reminds Luther that he cannot say that the Epistle of James is probably not canonical after admitting that the Church, which regards it as canonical, has the ability to determine the canon of Scripture (ibid., sig. O4^r).

Another technique designed to discredit one's opponent, as has been noted previously, is the claim that he really knows that he is wrong and is upholding a position to which his conscience does not assent. For instance, More claims that when Luther interprets the Scriptures contrary to the opinions of the Fathers and the Church, he does so against his own conscience (ibid., sig. P3^r). And when Luther summarizes Henry's position on a certain question, More carries the technique one step further and declares that not only does his opponent know that Henry said hardly any of the things Luther claims he did, but that everyone knows that in making claims of this nature Luther is aware that he is telling lies (ibid., sig. F3^r). Here More adds the "common knowledge" device to his accusation, a weapon more prominent in later controversies.[60]

An opponent who knows he is defending falsehood will have to arm himself with an arsenal of sophistical techniques if he wishes to be successful. It is, therefore, to the exposure of such alleged techniques of Luther's that More devotes considerable attention, with the object of further discrediting his opponent. One of More's charges against Luther is that of evasion. More explains to his readers that because Luther has no confidence in his own position he speaks in generalities and passes over all the specific points he is unable to answer (*Responsio*, sigs. E4^r, I4^v). If he does take up a point, More claims, he will either misquote his opponent's objection or his own previous statement to which the objection was made (ibid., sig. I1^r). More also points out how Luther, in order to give the appearance of being able to vanquish his opponents, makes ridiculous and easily answered objections to his own claims, which purport to represent the objections his opponents would make.[61] In charging Luther with evasion, More is, of course, also paying him back for similar charges he had made against Henry.[62]

One of the accusations More makes most frequently against Luther is that he either lies about what Henry said in the *Assertio* or distorts what the King did say in order to make it appear ridiculous. For instance, to Luther's claim that Henry, unable to prove the affirmative, had challenged him to prove that transubstantiation never takes place—from which Luther makes much capital about Henry's ignorance of the rules of disputation—More replies that Luther's claim is an outright lie; Henry made no such request.[63] The most usual accusation More makes against Luther is that he falsely charges Henry with evasion, whereas in reality Henry has answered the point in question.[64] More further alleges that for purposes of ridicule Luther manufactures foolish syllogisms out of Henry's words, which bear no relation to what the King actually said (*Responsio*, sig. NN1^r).

One of the most unintentionally ironic accusations More makes against Luther is that he does not dispute seriously, but rather trifles and plays the fool (ibid., sigs. I2^r-I2^v), that his reply to Henry is full of mocks and jests (ibid., sigs. A2^r-A2^v), and that it is by such means that he tries to answer all his opponents (ibid., sig. D2^r). That is, More objects to Luther's polemical use of humor, and what is ironic about More's objection is that he himself became the foremost exponent of this technique in Tudor religious controversy; many times he was to be accused of the same thing of which he here accuses Luther.[65] More certainly had given evidence of his fondness for humor before his controversy with Luther, but perhaps he learned from the German Reformer how effective humor could be as a weapon in religious polemics. He seems to have been so impressed by Luther's use of humor—and he was so adept in turning situations to his own advantage—that he pressed into service Luther's very name: "Profecto Domine Luthere," he addressed him, "quando nihil serio disseritis: sed tantum tam stulte luditis . . . nomen uestrum ex Luthero fiet Luderus . . ." (*Responsio*, sig. NN2^r). Luther is "Luderus" from that point on in the *Responsio*.

It is More's aim to expose not only his opponent's tactics but also his alleged strategy, which More seeks to characterize as a strategy of conspiracy. He explains that Luther has attracted many to his standard by giving his followers license to sin (ibid., sig. XX2^v), and prophesies that the Lutherans who today oppose the clergy will tomorrow despoil the nobility (ibid., sigs. XX3^r-XX3^v).

Finally, More engages in outright abuse of his opponent, claiming that it is unfortunately necessary to fight Luther on his own terms, since any other kind of answer would be less effective (ibid., sigs. Q1^r-Q1^v, Q3^r, XX1^r). More's deliberate repayment of abuse by abuse —for which he has been criticized[66]—is but another example of the manner in which he adapts his polemical technique to the work he is answering. More's abuse of Luther takes the form of straight invective and of the derogatory epithet. An example of the former occurs when More tells Luther that, in retaliation for his many lies, he is going to have cast back into his filthy mouth all the dung which his foulness deserves, and that over his head will be poured the contents

of sewers and latrines (*Responsio*, sig. Q1r). More's most constant
epithet for Luther is the play on his name, "Luderus," noted previously. Other epithets are either directly abusive or ironic. Among the
former is "lousy little brother," meant to emphasize Luther's insig-
nificance, as well as the fact that he was a renegade friar (ibid., sig.
E2r), and "Father Sot," referring to Luther's alleged habit of excessive drinking (ibid., sig. G3r). Some of More's ironic epithets for
Luther are "Distinguished Doctor" and "Reverend Father" (ibid.,
sigs. E2v, H15r), both mocking Luther's claim to be able to interpret
God's will more correctly than the Fathers and the entire Church.

Whether it is intentional or not, part of More's attack on Luther
in the *Responsio* consists of a misrepresentation of Luther's position.
For instance, More keeps telling his readers that to Luther all good
works are sin and all evil works are virtue. This, however, is
true only in a qualified sense, which More never makes clear. To
Luther good works undertaken to purchase salvation were indeed
sinful, but neither he nor the other Reformers maintained that good
works were in themselves evil or that evil works were good.[67] In this
case there is really no excuse for More, since Luther had made his
position on this point absolutely clear, and since other Catholics did
not share More's confusion, whether actual or pretended.[68] Other
misrepresentations, probably the result of false information, occur in
personal attacks on Luther and his followers. Among these must be
included the charges that Luther had an image of himself carried
about as an object of veneration (*Responsio*, sig. XX2v), that in
Bohemia marriage was regarded no higher than the coupling of dogs
(ibid., sig. I3r), that all Lutherans who had been priests and who
had married were married to prostitutes (ibid., sig. XX3r), and that
Luther's followers participated in riotous feasts every day (ibid., sig.
XX2r).

Henry's Letter
against Luther

Luther did not answer More's work, but in 1525 he did write a
letter to Henry apologizing for the harsh names he had called him.
Luther's letter was prompted by the erroneous information, supplied

by King Christian II of Denmark, that Henry was beginning to favor the cause of the Reformers. Henry answered in August of 1526, rejecting Luther's overtures to peace and once more attacking his theology. Probably in the same year there was issued, on the advice of Wolsey, a book containing English translations of both Luther's letter and Henry's reply.[69]

It is quite possible that Henry's answer to Luther was written by More. We know that the King gave More Luther's letter to read and that it was last known to be in More's possession when Henry wanted to return it to Luther along with his reply.[70]

Henry's answer certainly sounds like More, both in content and manner of presentation. The English version (the assumption being that More would make his own translation) is heavily alliterative—Luther's "frantyke fauourers . . . fall to wracke,"[71] and Luther promotes "a bold lyberte of leude lyueng" (*A copy*, sig. D4^v)—and alliteration is one of More's favorite vehicles of vituperation.[72]

The strongest indication of More's authorship is the letter's characteristic—one which perhaps more than any other can be regarded as More's hallmark—of clinching almost every argument with reference to Luther's marriage. The letter opens by noting that Luther, once an Augustinian friar, is living with a nun and, even worse, has openly married her;[73] declares that Luther's plea for Christian liberty is merely a demand for license to sin (*Literarum*, sig. C3^r); wonders, in More's characteristic fashion, how Luther could boast so much about depending only on Scripture and yet set so little value on his vow, which Scripture regards as sacred (ibid., sigs. C2^v-C3^r); and closes by exhorting Luther to leave his life of lechery (ibid., sig. F8^r).

Finally, the 1526 letter to Luther contains an almost exact parallel to More's letter to Bugenhagen, probably written the same year, in which the German's claim that he teaches only Christ is rebutted by a series of rhetorical questions on the order of: Is encouraging sacrilegious marriage preaching Christ?[74] Similarly, the letter to Luther asks him how he can be so shameless as to say that he teaches nothing but the faith of Christ, when he plainly writes against the sacraments of Christ, condemns clerical chastity, opposes the idea of holy orders, makes women confessors and ministers of the sacraments, holds that there is little difference between the chaste mother of Christ and his shameless whore,[75] and when he blasphemes the Cross of Christ (ibid., sig. E4^v).

Bugenhagen's Epistle
to the English

The Church took a number of steps to halt the spread of Luther's doctrines in England. Some time after Leo X issued his bull commanding the destruction of Luther's books on June 15, 1520, but within the same year, a burning of heretical literature took place at Cambridge and in other parts of the country.[76] In May, 1521, Bishop Fisher preached a sermon in English against Luther at Paul's Cross, after which Luther's works were publicly burned. On October 12, 1524, Cuthbert Tunstal, Bishop of London, summoned the London booksellers and warned them, on pain of prosecution, against importing or selling Luther's books. Before being offered for sale, Tunstal said, new imported books had to be shown either to Wolsey, the Archbishop of Canterbury, Fisher, or himself. However, Tunstal's warning evidently passed unheeded, for he was forced to call the booksellers to him again in the same year. This time he was more severe. He told them that they were not to handle Lutheran works in either Latin or English, nor to sell any imported works before obtaining the approval of either Wolsey, Fisher, or himself. He also said that no new books whatever were to be printed without authority, except books which had always been approved by the Church.[77] Another book burning took place in St. Paul's Churchyard in December of the same year.[78] In February, 1526, Fisher preached another sermon against Luther at St. Paul's Cathedral, followed by yet another book burning, and one more in the autumn.[79]

One of the Lutheran works which slipped through this blockade of fire was a Latin letter by the German John Bugenhagen. Manuscript copies translated into English, probably by Tyndale, were circulating in England in 1525 and 1526.[80]

Bugenhagen's letter, *Epistola Sanctis qui sunt in Anglia*, originally published early in 1525 at Wittenberg, is very brief, its aim evidently being to promote the cause of Lutheranism in England and to answer charges against Lutheranism which Bugenhagen understood to be circulating there.

The methods by which Bugenhagen seeks to accomplish his purpose are the promulgation of the doctrine of justification by faith, the charge that the opponents of Lutheranism base their beliefs only on human traditions, and rebuttal to the anti-Lutheran accusations by the technique of claiming that the preachers of the gospel have traditionally been slandered and reviled.

More's Reply
to Bugenhagen

A copy of the letter found its way into the hands of More,[81] and he decided it was dangerous enough to require an answer.[82] His reply took the form of a fairly long Latin letter (ca. 1526), not published until 1568 at Louvain. It has been suggested that More did not publish his letter himself because, shortly after he wrote it, the ecclesiastical authorities in England decided to abandon Latin as a medium for combating heresy.[83]

More begins his reply to Bugenhagen by stating that he intends to answer the letter section by section, a scheme which he carries out by quoting his opponent and appending commentary, as he had done in the *Responsio*.[84] As was also true of his earlier polemic, the reason More gives for adopting such a scheme must itself be considered part of his controversial technique. He claims that by this method the worth of each of Bugenhagen's sections will become apparent—with the implication that that worth is not very great (*Correspondence*, p. 326). Also, such a method is, as More has explained in the *Responsio*,[85] the fairest to his opponent, who cannot then complain that he has been misquoted or that important points of his were omitted. And in this letter, as in his other polemics, More is at pains to persuade his readers of his fairness in controversy. He claims that he always tries to put the best possible interpretation on what his adversary says—that, in fact, he strains hard to find interpretations favorable to his opponent, and that he is disappointed when he has to come to the reluctant conclusion that no such favorable interpretation can be found. More asserts he does this out of concern for his opponent and also to demonstrate to his readers that he is being more than fair (*Correspondence*, pp. 350-351). However, after having examined More's work, one may be pardoned for not taking these declarations at face value. For in seeking to demonstrate his fairness by recounting his attempt to find a more favorable interpretation of one of Bugenhagen's passages, More mentions the obvious interpretation of that passage and then rejects it as regrettably untenable. Therefore there can be no question of More's really misunderstanding his opponent—especially since in his rejection he manages to score another clever polemical point. In the passage in question, Bugenhagen says that whatever a man may do to try to justify himself before God and to avoid the punishment due to sin will be hypocrisy and a lie, no matter how pious that act may appear to be (ibid., p. 350). More professes to be shocked at this declaration and proclaims that he has come to the reluctant conclusion that Bugenhagen is opposed to good works and favors evil works (ibid., p. 350 ff.), a charge, it will be remembered, he had already made against Luther. More tells us that before arriving at this conclusion he tried very hard to give his antagonist's words a more favorable interpretation. Perhaps, he speculated, Bugenhagen meant that it is hypocrisy to try to substitute works for faith in Christ. But, he informs his readers, he felt himself forced to reject such an interpretation, for he could foresee that he would be immediately attacked on all sides for shamelessly distorting Bugenhagen's position, since it would be clear to everyone against whom he would be trying to defend Bugenhagen that he could not have meant any such thing, as that was exactly the position of the Catholic Church which Bugenhagen was attacking (ibid., p. 351). Here More assumes his favorite role of trying to save his opponent from his own folly—and failing in the attempt.[86] Thus he scores three polemical points at once: He saddles his opponent with supporting evil works, he implies that Bugenhagen is misrepresenting the doctrine of the Catholics when he claims that they preach justification by works apart from Christ, and he manages to portray himself as a most fair and generous opponent.

As is to be expected, More's polemic contains a series of accusations against his opponent and his cause. More opens his own letter by accusing Bugenhagen of having begun his letter in the style of the Pauline epistles, and he comments that it would have been more modest of Bugenhagen to have imitated Paul's character rather than his style (*Correspondence*, p. 326). Lack of modesty, or pride, is also the reason for Bugenhagen's attack on the saints, More claims; he is afraid that their glory will detract from his own (ibid., p. 329). Such accusations of pride, common in More's religious polemics, [87] serve to link Bugenhagen and his cause with that of Satan, the Father of Pride, which identification is strengthened for More's readers by his accusation of evil living against the Lutherans (*Correspondence*, p. 328). That the Lutherans' evil mode of living supports an evil cause, charges More further, is proved by the fact that they cannot concur even among themselves on the nature of the cause they advocate (ibid., pp. 344-345). Nor will More grant that Bugenhagen, any more than Luther, really disputes on the basis of the Scriptures he claims to revere; it is not Scripture but his own twisted interpretation that Bugenhagen uses, More avers (ibid., p. 337). Finally, he accuses his opponent of inconsistency. Such inconsistency More regards as inevitable, since he is of the opinion that the doctrine of Lutheranism is inherently self-contradictory (ibid., pp. 358-359). If you despise good works, why do you recommend them, and if you recommend them, why do you despise them? More demands of his opponent (ibid., p. 356). He claims that the Lutherans continually contradict one another, as when Bugenhagen says faith necessarily brings forth good works, while Luther says faith may be present when evil works are done (ibid., pp. 330, 347). The reader should be cautioned that some of the contradictions More points out arise not so much from what his opponents actually said as from More's distortions of what they said.[88]

A logical consequence of claiming that your opponent contradicts himself is to use his own arguments against him. But in his controversy with Bugenhagen, More gives this common polemical device an unusual twist. In another instance of adapting his tactics to those of the opposition, More takes over a technique from Luther and turns it on his followers, charging that the only proof Lutherans provide for their belief is Luther's formula, "I am certain that I have received my teaching from heaven."[89] Another uncommon use More makes of the technique of opposing an adversary with his own argument is seen when More is belaboring Bugenhagen for allegedly despising good works. He takes the obviously correct interpretation that Bugenhagen opposes good works only when used as a means to salvation and wields it against the German: You are afraid to oppose good works openly, thunders More, and that is why you try to hide the wickedness of your real opinion under the subterfuge that you oppose them only as a means to salvation but favor them otherwise (ibid., p. 354).

Among the more interesting rhetorical devices used by More against Bugenhagen is *rogatio* (rhetorical and "loaded" question).[90] To Bugenhagen's claim that Lutherans preach only the gospel of Christ, More responds by asking his opponent, among other questions, whether destroying the sacraments of Christ, despising the Cross of Christ, defiling the virginity consecrated to Christ, and encouraging monks and nuns to marry—that is, to live in perpetual defilement—is preaching the gospel (*Correspondence*, p. 328). These questions are "loaded" because obviously Bugenhagen had never agreed that the actions of the Lutherans could be characterized in More's manner. Again, to counter Bugenhagen's assertion that the Lutherans teach what Christ proclaimed by his own lips, More asks another series of obviously absurd rhetorical questions: Where did he teach that he who has previously vowed chastity must marry? Where did he teach that Luther's mistress is equal to the mother of Christ? Where did he teach that the Mass could not profit the dead? Where did he teach that there is no purgatory (ibid., p. 345)? To appreciate the nature of these questions it is necessary only to add the obverse to each question: Where did he teach that the Mass could not profit the dead? Or that it could?

The bulk of More's reasoning against Bugenhagen consists of reliance on the authority of numbers, time, and the Fathers, as well as that of Scripture, but as his use of these authorities is common to all his polemical works and is discussed elsewhere, it will be passed over here.

As we have seen, More builds many of his techniques on distortions of his opponent's position. The Lutherans did not, as More claims they did, lay waste a great part of Germany (unless he erroneously equates the German peasants of the Peasants' Revolt with the Lutherans), and to say that those who did, did so under the influence of Luther's doctrine is an oversimplification of the facts, of which, however, More may have been unaware.[91] Again, as pointed out previously, neither Luther nor Bugenhagen nor any of the Reformers ever said that good works are harmful or do not exist, as More maintains (*Correspondence*, pp. 346, 350). What they did say was that no good work availed for salvation, and More himself admits that Bugenhagen commends good works, which he claims to find puzzling (ibid., p. 347).

II

William Tyndale

While Englishmen were writing against German Lutherans, Lutheran doctrines were making headway in England. German merchants in London who traded with the Hanse towns brought Luther's teachings and books back with them from their trade missions to the Continent.[1] At Cambridge, Luther's teachings were eagerly received by a group of young men who wanted to see in England a reformation of clerical morals and church doctrine such as Luther had advocated in Germany.[2] A number of these young men fled to the Continent where they wrote books in English supporting Luther's views. Their writings were then smuggled into England. Thus there were circulating in England not only the works of Luther and his German followers but also books expressing Lutheran views written by Englishmen.

Of all such books coming into England the works of Tyndale must have been particularly alarming to the ecclesiastical authorities.

William Tyndale (ca. 1494–1536),[3] whom More called "the captain of our Englyshe heretikes,"[4] and who was to be More's principal opponent in the religious controversy, attended Oxford University, where he took both a Bachelor (1512) and a Master of Arts degree (1515). While still at the university he was ordained to the priesthood.

In 1519 Tyndale left Oxford and took up residence at Cambridge, where were many of the future leaders of the Reformation, such as Coverdale, Latimer, and Cranmer, as well as John Frith and Robert Barnes who, like Tyndale, later crossed swords with More.

Tyndale left Cambridge in 1521 to serve as tutor in a private family. He remained in this capacity for the next two years, and then, in 1523, gave up his position to devote himself to making an English translation of the New Testament. Such an undertaking demanded money, and it was with the hope of obtaining the patronage of Cuthbert Tunstal, Bishop of London, that Tyndale arrived in the capital within the same year. However, his hopes were disappointed, for Tunstal declared himself unwilling to render assistance.

After a short stay in London, Tyndale decided to leave England and to continue work on his translation in Germany. It took him two years to complete the task, and late in 1525, at Cologne, printing of a quarto edition of Tyndale's New Testament began. The work was interrupted, however, and Tyndale was forced to flee to Worms, having had printed only the first twenty-two chapters of Matthew, with a prologue and annotations. At Worms he began an octavo edition, omitting the quarto's prologue and annotations. This time he was able to finish his work undisturbed, so that early in 1526 the first complete edition of Tyndale's New Testament came off the printing presses. All that was left to do was to ensure that the translation safely reached the public for which it was intended.

This was no easy matter. Tyndale had not received permission from the Church for the work he had undertaken, and ever since the Lollard translations of the preceding century, unauthorized versions of the Scriptures had been prohibited.[5] Consequently, there was no question of open distribution of the book. However, with the cooperation of some London merchants, many of whom subscribed to the Reformed doctrines, first the Cologne fragment and then the complete Worms edition were shipped to England and distributed mainly within the city of London and its environs.

The authorities did everything in their power to stop this illegal importation. As Bishop of London, the city where most copies of the new translation were circulating, Tunstal officially banned the book on October 20, 1526, and on October 28 Tyndale's New Testament was burned in a grand holocaust of heretical literature at St. Paul's. Wolsey's agents were busy in the Netherlands, trying to prevent further printing of the work there,[6] while in England, Archbishop Warham attempted to buy up the entire edition, a procedure which supplied Tyndale with enough money to revise his original version.[7]

Still working on the Continent, Tyndale published two books in 1528 which directly attacked the practices and authority of the Church: *The parable of the wicked mammon* on May 18, and *The obedience of a Christen man* on October 2. They also were smuggled into England, adding to the list of proscribed works.

In an effort to stem the tide of heretical literature inundating London, Tunstal organized house-to-house searches for the contraband publications, while the quarters of the faculty and students at Oxford and Cambridge were subjected to the same investigation.[8]

As we have seen, apart from Fisher's two sermons in the vernacular, attempts to refute the Reformers had been confined to Latin, not a very effective medium for stopping the spread of heresy among an English-speaking population. In 1528 the Church decided to defend itself in English.

One of those who took up cudgels for the Church was John Skelton. Skelton, cleric and poet laureate, had given proof of his skill in vituperation by having written several daring attacks on the all-powerful Wolsey. In 1528 Skelton was an old man, probably longing for a peaceful end to his stormy life in the form of some not too demanding ecclesiastical preferment. Wolsey was looking for someone with Skelton's talent for invective to denounce heresy, and it seems that the dangers confronting the Church drew these two old enemies together.

Some time in 1528 Skelton published *A replycacion agaynst certayne yong scolers abiured of late*,[9] with a most flattering dedication to Wolsey. The language of this dedication indicates that Wolsey asked Skelton to write the work.[10] Thomas Bilney and Thomas Arthur were the two heretical "yong scolers" of Skelton's title.[11] They had been preaching against the worship of images and of the Virgin Mary. In characteristic fashion, Skelton overwhelms the hapless two with alliterative vituperation, marvels at their boldness in gainsaying the old Doctors and, at the same time, manages to squeeze into his elastic prosody a short dissertation on the distinction between the three degrees of worship, *latria*, *dulia*, and *hyperdulia*.

Skelton's rough diatribe was almost at the other extreme from Fisher's Latin writings against the Reformers, in which the Bishop had attempted to refute Luther's doctrines with scholastic theology applied in an awesome series of closely reasoned pages.[12] Much of the power of Skelton's verse lay in its terseness; his lines were forceful and overwhelming, but their very momentum prevented them from pausing to explain just why that opposition was wrong and why Catholic doctrine should be retained in its place.

That someone was deliberately chosen to take the middle way between Fisher and Skelton is improbable, but it does seem that the writer the Church commissioned did take such a way.

On March 7, 1528, Tunstal sent a letter to Thomas More, asking him to write against heresy. Tunstal pointed out that heretical literature of both German and English authorship was coming into England in such quantities that unless good and learned men could be found to confute these heretical books in English, the Catholic faith in England would be in grave danger. Tunstal continued:

> Because you, most dear brother, are able to emulate Demosthenes in our vernacular tongue no less than in Latin, and are wont to be an ardent defender of Catholic truth . . . you cannot spend the occasional hours that you can steal from your official duties better than in composing in our own language such books as may show to simple and unlearned men the cunning malice of the heretics, and fortify them against these impious subverters of the Church.[13]

One of the reasons More was chosen for this task is mentioned in Tunstal's letter, namely, his eloquence not only in Latin but also in

English, the language in which the Church had decided to continue the conflict. As there is no record of More's having written any English controversial work prior to this commission, Tunstal's reference to More's eloquence must have been occasioned by such works as *The history of king Richard the thirde,* or the "Evil May Day" speech More made,[14] or to his English oratory in the House of Commons, for which body he had once been Speaker.

Also, by 1528 More had been appointed Chancellor of the Duchy of Lancaster (1525) and was a man of considerable importance. Furthermore, he was known not only for his service to the state, but also for his authorship of the *Utopia* (1516) and his friendship with such men as Colet, Linacre, Grocyn, and Erasmus, some of the foremost scholars of the day. His record as a scholar with a European reputation, joined to his friendship with the merchants of London,[15] would assure anything he had to say of the widest possible hearing. And since More was a layman, his defense of the Church was less open to the charge of special pleading than would have been that of a cleric. For these reasons it would seem that the Church made a wise choice indeed when it commissioned More to be its champion against the heretics.

As has been said, the most dangerous of these English heretics was Tyndale. Tyndale wanted to establish the Scriptures as the final arbiter in all matters of doctrine. He taught that in God's sight man was justified by faith alone, apart from works, and that none of the ceremonies of the Church availed for salvation.

More's primary aim in attacking Tyndale was to establish the authority of the Church to determine doctrine and conduct, and to identify the Catholic Church with the church of which Christ spoke. He also wanted to prove that works and ceremonies were necessary to salvation and that Tyndale's New Testament was full of errors.

These were the tasks the opposing controversialists set themselves.

Most of Tyndale's *Mammon* is taken up with a discussion of the doctrine of justification by faith. It states that only faith in Christ can redeem man. Good works, according to Tyndale, are not a means of salvation, but the outward manifestation of an inward saving faith. It is in this book, also, that Tyndale states what he believes should be the Christian's attitude toward his earthly rulers: The king supplies the place of God on earth and, whether good or evil, must be obeyed.

In *The obedience of a Christen man*, published a few months after the *Mammon*, Tyndale again states his theory of kingship. In spite of the name he gave to the book, most of the *Obedience* is devoted to a discussion of church practice and doctrine. Tyndale demands that the Scriptures be made available in English, asserts that the literal sense is the most important sense of Scripture, and insists that no point of doctrine should be established merely on the basis of an allegorical interpretation.

Carrying out Tunstal's commission to combat heresy, More published his first work in the field of English religious controversy, the *Dialogue concernynge heresyes*, in June, 1529; his work dealt with all of Tyndale's points mentioned above. The main discussion in the *Dialogue* centers on the nature and authority of the Church, in which context More considers the matter of Tyndale's translation of the New Testament and examines Lutheran doctrine. More claims that the Catholic Church of his day is the direct descendant of the church spoken of in the New Testament, the church which was given the Holy Spirit to guide it into all truth and which, consequently, cannot err. This is the church, More points out, which determined the canon of Scripture and which, therefore, wields authority superior to that of the Scripture which it determined and before which it existed. Therefore More thinks it impossible that the particular version of Scripture which the Church has been using for so many hundreds of years should be deficient on any point vital to the understanding of the Christian faith, for that would have been contrary to God's promise to preserve His church from all error. Consequently, reasons More, Tyndale's translation of the New Testament, which changes the meaning of many of the words on which the sacraments of the Church depend, must be a false translation, for it implies that the Church has been in error for the past 1500 years.

If, then, the Church cannot err on any matter vital to the faith, reasons More, it follows that the Church also has the ability to determine what matters actually are vital to the faith. More concludes that since the present ceremonies and practices of the Church, such as the homage given to images and the custom of going on pilgrimages and invoking the aid of the saints, have been determined to be edifying by the Church, the Reformers are in error when they object to these practices.

More also devotes considerable space to the defense of the Church's handling of two heresy cases, that of Bilney, on which Skelton had written, and that of Richard Hunne. More claims that there is no doubt about the fact that Bilney was a heretic, and that far from having been unjustly treated, he was actually shown too much leniency, in that he was not handed over to the state for execution.[16] As for Hunne, More maintains that he also was a heretic, that the Reformers' charge that he was murdered by the clergy is false, and that Hunne committed suicide.[17]

Tyndale's *An answere vnto Sir Thomas Mores dialoge*[18] was published in July of 1531, more than two years after the original publication of More's work.

Tyndale realizes that the most important point at issue is the identity and nature of the church, and he consequently begins his *Answere* with a very full discussion of this subject. He points out that there are several current uses for the term "church," but that the one given in the Scriptures embraces all those who "receiue the name of Christ to belieue in him." He insists that the term should not be confined to the clergy as, he asserts, is the contemporary practice. He reasons that the Catholics' claim that the Church cannot err does not help them in the least, for whereas they mean that the clergy cannot err, the term "church" has a much wider meaning, and therefore the infallibility claimed for the clergy is really applicable to the entire body of believers in Christ. Tyndale adds that while there is no doubt that the Christian sins daily in his life, it is impossible for him to sin unto damnation.

He contends that it was not the clergy who preserved the Scriptures to his day, but that, on the contrary, they did their best to destroy the Scriptures and to keep them from the people. He also claims that every one of the changes he made from the previously accepted Vulgate version of the New Testament is justified by the Greek text and is in substantial agreement with the version made by Erasmus.

As for the use of ceremonies, Tyndale says that he condemns no ceremony in itself, but only its abuse.

More replied with *The Confutacyon of Tyndales answere*,[19] the first three books of which appeared in the early months of 1532. Most of the work is a reiteration of points More made before in his *Dialogue.*

Before he wrote the last word of the *Confutacyon*, it had run the length of eight books (plus an incompleted ninth), any one of which would stand separately as a fair-sized volume. When More did lay down his pen it was not for lack of material but for lack of time; he had intended to cover three more points,[20] which would have added at least one more book.[21]

In April of 1533, the year in which More published the second part of his *Confutacyon*, there appeared an anonymous treatise entitled *The souper of the Lorde*, possibly also by Tyndale.[22]

This entire work is given over to a discussion of the Eucharist. It claims that the only sense in which one eats Christ's body and drinks his blood is allegorical, and that the words "This is my body" and "This is my blood" are to be understood in the same figurative sense as they were by the disciples who heard them.

Before Christmas of 1533 More replied to the above with *The answere to the fyrst parte of the poysened booke, whych a namelesse heretyke hath named the souper of the lorde.*[23] As the title proclaims, this work of More's, which is divided into five books, concerns itself with only a partial answer to the *Souper*. He evidently never had an opportunity to complete his task.[24]

More himself is not sure of his opponent's identity, although he says he has heard that the work is either by Tyndale or George Joye, a Reformer who assisted Tyndale in his translation of the New Testament (*W*, p. 1037). In the *Answere*, More once again states the opinion that the words Christ spoke at the Last Supper are to be taken in a literal sense, and that consequently the bread and wine, after they have been consecrated by the priest, are changed into the actual body and blood of Christ.

Tyndale's Use of Scripture

In his fight against the English clergy and their defenders, Tyndale made the Scriptures his main weapon.[25] But before considering Tyndale's polemical practice in dealing with Scripture, it is necessary to examine the principle from which his techniques derive. The corner-stone of Tyndale's doctrine is that the Scriptures are absolute and sufficient authority in all matters of church dogma and practice.[26] He draws analogies from the Scriptures themselves to demonstrate that they should be the Christian's final authority. For instance, he reasons that just as the Israelites in the Old Testament were commanded to search the Scriptures to see if their leaders kept to the right way, so Christians of his era have the same obligation to measure church practice and doctrine by scriptural standards (*Ww*,* p. 177). Even Christ himself, Tyndale points out, always referred his actions to the Scriptures for authority (*Ww*, p. 138). Therefore, Tyndale counsels his readers, do nothing without the Scriptures, and "What soeuer is done without the worde of God, that count idolatry" (*Ww*, p. 86).

By his insistence that the Scriptures are the absolute authority on all spiritual matters and that in them alone God has revealed His will to man, Tyndale sought to set up a rival authority to the Church, which claimed for itself the prerogative of deciding what was the will of God.[27] Tyndale's pronouncement concerning the supremacy of Scripture was a severe blow to the power of the clergy; whereas previously they had determined God's will in general councils and announced their decisions to the laity, through Tyndale's efforts many laymen in England were persuaded that God revealed His will not to the Church but only in the Scriptures, which the laity were just as well authorized to interpret as were the clergy. Furthermore, Tyndale's assertions concerning the primacy of Scripture provided laymen with a measuring rod with which to measure the actions of the clergy, which the former were not slow to apply.[28] Tyndale's doctrine of scriptural supremacy is the base from which he launches all his attacks on the clergy. A progression from this doctrine is the thesis that not only does the Church of Rome not have the sole prerogative to determine what is the will of God, but that the Roman Church is actually the very body least competent in this respect. This conclusion Tyndale reaches by the formulation of the doctrine that

* *Ww* = *The Whole workes of W. Tyndall, John Frith, and Doct. Barnes, three worthy Martyrs ... collected and compiled in one Tome togither*, ed. John Foxe (London, 1573), John Daye, *STC* 24,436.

spiritual insight, which he assumes the clergy lack, is a prerequisite for the correct interpretation of Scripture.

For, having enunciated the doctrine of the supremacy of Scripture, Tyndale proceeds to teach his readers how the Scriptures are to be interpreted. The precondition for any attempt at such interpretation is, according to Tyndale, "right fayth" and regeneration, with its consequent indwelling of the Holy Spirit, since only the Spirit of God can lead man to an understanding of the Word of God, which is beyond the grasp of natural reason (*Ww*, p. 66). Tyndale points out that many learned men have erred in attempting to apply worldly wisdom to explain God's Word (*Ww*, p. 67). For, he says, while the Scriptures use the language of men, that language bears a spiritual meaning which requires spiritual insight for comprehension (*Ww*. p. 80). It is not the spirit of Aristotle but the Spirit of God that is needed for correct understanding of the Scriptures, he maintains (*Ww*, p. 88).

Tyndale claims that complete subjection to the arbitration of Scripture will abolish all differences of opinion on theological problems (*Ww*, pp. 102-103). While such complete subjection may have been the ideal Tyndale had in mind for himself as well as for others, as we shall see, he actually made the Scriptures subject to his personal interpretation. This action he justified on the grounds that to a person without "right fayth," the Scriptures are a closed book which he tries to interpret with "blynd reason & folish fantasies" (*Ww*, p. 66). As Tyndale evidently assumes that he possesses "right fayth" and doubtless includes his opponents among those who suffer from "folish fantasies," he is able to fashion the Scriptures into a very pliable and convenient weapon.

And so, having sought to establish the Scriptures as a rival authority to that of the Church, which claimed authority to reveal God's will both independently of Scripture and as the Scriptures' only authorized interpreter, Tyndale attacks even the interpretative power of the Church by his theory of the necessity of "right fayth" for correct scriptural exegesis. But Tyndale's theory goes further than that; it precludes the possibility of dissent from his own particular interpretation. For while Tyndale complains that his opponents, for lack of better arguments, always resort to the convenient formula that their opinion is correct solely because it is the opinion maintained by the Church (*Ww*, p. 297), he himself really uses exactly the same kind of argument when he insists on the necessity of spiritual insight for the understanding of God's will and denies such insight to his opponents. He has merely replaced the infallibility of the Church of Rome with an infallibility of his own.[29]

While Tyndale does usually claim that spiritual insight and faith rather than reason are the basis for correct interpretation of Scripture, he occasionally finds it convenient not to exclude reason entirely from the interpretative process. He maintains, for instance, that the scholastic method of examining isolated texts is unreasonable and that both the preceding and following passages, as well as similar texts elsewhere, should be considered in the process of explication.[30]

Another guiding principle Tyndale enunciates is that the literal meaning of Scripture should take precedence over the figurative. Tyndale recognizes that the Scriptures contain figurative language, but he maintains, against contemporary scholastic opinion, that the most important sense of Scripture—in fact the real sense which the other senses only serve to illustrate—is the literal (*Ww*, pp. 166-167), and warns his readers not to be "begyled with false allegories" (*Ww*, p. 14). Tyndale's ostensible insistence on the primacy of the literal sense of Scripture over its allegoric sense is again intended to embarrass his opponents, since it attacks a method of exegesis which permitted his adversaries to interpret the Scriptures in any fashion they desired while, at the same time, it reserves that right for himself: As we have seen, Tyndale's denunciation of allegorical interpretation in no way prevented him from tacitly resorting to such interpretation when convenient. But Tyndale does not have to rely solely on the allegorical method he has publicly disavowed to interpret the Scriptures in accordance with his theology. For this purpose he also has recourse to a number of other techniques, among them explication by analogy to popular speech.

An example of this technique is provided by Tyndale's attempt to assure his readers that certain passages of Scripture which seem to advocate good works for the sake of reward do not in actuality bear such a meaning. The misunderstanding, he maintains, stems from faulty reasoning, such as we can observe even in our daily conversation. For instance, he goes on to illustrate, we say summer is near, for the trees blossom, and yet the blossoming of the trees is not the cause of summer's approach, but vice versa. So that when Christ said to Peter that he would believe in Peter's faith if he saw his works, continues Tyndale, he was teaching Peter to show his inward faith and love by his outward deeds, not that the faith and love were a product of the deeds but that the deeds were a product of the faith and love. Christ's meaning, maintains Tyndale, can be appreciated by considering the custom of common speech: "As yᵉ maner is to say, do your charitie, shew your charitie, do a deede of charitie, shewe your mercy, do a deede of mercy, meanyng thereby, yᵗ our deedes declare how we loue our neighbours, & how much we haue compassion on the*m* at their neede" (*Ww*, p. 77; see also *Ww*, p. 92 and the 1525 New Testament, sig. D3ʳ).

Such illustrations make us realize Tyndale's great interest in language, which assisted him in his work as a translator. But their polemical value must not be overlooked, for by these appeals to the customs of everyday speech Tyndale attempts to convince his readers that certain portions of Scripture which appear to contradict his particular view of theology are, in fact, quite in accordance with it. That the idiom of the original and the English language might not necessarily be the same—a fact of which other passages indicate he was certainly aware (e.g., *Ww*, pp. 5-6, 11)—he does not inform his readers on those occasions when he does not consider it advisable. Actually, Tyndale's technique of appealing to the habits of popular speech in elucidation of Scripture is merely a variation of the allegorical or figurative method of interpretation to which he professes to object; both methods subject the literal sense to arbitrary interpretation, although Tyndale's has the added polemical advantage of having a specious kind of reasonableness. His technique also has the advantage of using familiar illustrations, which must have gained wider acceptance than the erudite patristic references indulged in by some of his opponents.

How flexible Tyndale's standard of scriptural interpretation really is can be appreciated by considering his final statement on the primacy of the literal sense. "In conclusion," he says, "the scripture speaketh many thynges as the world speaketh. But they may not be worldly vnderstand [*sic*], but ghostly and spiritually . . ." (*Ww*, p. 80). Such a principle of interpretation is, of course, directly contrary to Tyndale's practice of appealing to the usages of popular speech for the elucidation of certain scriptural passages, for the premise behind such exegesis is precisely that the meaning of a passage can be arrived at by applying to it a "worldly" interpretation, i.e., one based on the habits of everyday speech. But, more important, the enunciated principle enabled Tyndale to use sheer arbitrary dictum to interpret the Scriptures favorably to his viewpoint, with the justification that he did it "ghostly and spiritually."

That Tyndale made extensive use of such arbitrary scriptural exegesis in his campaign against the English clerical party can be observed from the following illustrations. In discussing I Corinthians iii.14, Tyndale says, "He [Paul] exhorteth therfore euery man to take hede what he buildeth vpon, and boroweth a similitude of ye goldsmith, which trieth his metalles with fire, saying, that the fire (that is) the iudgement of ye scripture, shall trie euery mans worke, that is, euery mans preaching and doctrine. If any builde vpon the foundation layde of Paule, I meane Iesus Christ, golde, siluer, or precious stone, which are all one thyng, and signifie true doctrine, which when it is examined, the scripture aloweth, then shall he haue his rewarde, that is, he shall be sure that his learning is of God . . ." (*Ww*, p. 92). The context of this passage—and it will be recalled that Tyndale advocated interpretation within context—does not at all lead to the inevitable conclusion that by "fire" Paul meant "the iudgement of ye scripture," especially since the only "scripture" Paul knew was the Old Testament, surely not the yardstick with which he wished the Corinthians to measure their works; that by "euery mans worke" Paul meant "euery mans preaching and doc-trine"; or that by "rewarde" Paul meant the assurance that one's "learning is of God." Perhaps Tyndale's most astounding interpre-tation is of John ix.4 ("The night cometh, when no man can work"), which, according to Tyndale, means that "when the true knowledge of Christ/ how he onlie iustifieth/ is loste: then can noman worke a good worke in the sight of god/ how gloriouse soeuer his workes apere" (New Testament, 1534, sig. R8^v). Here Tyndale has certainly sacrificed his own principle of interpretation within context for polemical advantage, for the words of Jesus, who is the speaker, immediately preceding the sentence commented on by Tyndale ("I must work the works of him that sent me, while it is day"), make it fairly clear that no such meaning as that given by Tyndale is intended.

A somewhat different kind of arbitrary interpretation of Scripture for polemical purposes is to be found in such declarations of Tyndale's that Paul's injunction to the Thessalonians to hold fast the traditions which they were taught "whether by word, or our epistle" (II Thess. ii.15) in no way contradicts the doctrine that everything necessary for salvation and for the conduct of Christ's church was written down in the Scriptures; as proof Tyndale offers the blanket assertion that "Puule [*sic*] taught by mouth such things as he wrote in his epistles" (*Ww*, p. 128). Of a similar nature is Tyndale's assertion that Moses' injunction to the Israelites to study God's word "was commaunded generally vnto all men" (*Ww*, p. 101).

Besides fashioning the Scriptures into a pliable instrument to support his theology—really an inevitable consequence of his thesis of the primacy and sufficiency of Scripture in matters of doctrine—Tyndale draws extensively on the biblical narrative itself for polemical illustrations. Most of these consist of negative and positive comparisons between biblical figures and the contemporary English clergy. For instance, he asserts that while neither Moses in the Old Testament nor the disciples and Apostles in the New Testament served God's people for reward, with today's clergy "it goeth after the common saying, no penny, no Pater noster" (*Ww*, p. 139). Positive comparisons between the clergy and unsavory biblical figures abound. The clergy assert that the Reformers are disturbing the peace of the realm, Tyndale points out; ". . . let this be an aunswere vnto them. Wicked kyng Ahab sayd vnto the Prophet Elias, Art thou he that troublest Israell? And Elias aunswered, it is not I that trouble Israell, but thou and thy fathers houshold, in that ye haue forsaken the commaundementes of the Lord and folow Idoles. Euen so the preachers of the truth which rebuke sinne are not the troublers of Realmes and common wealthes, but they that do wickedly, and namely high Prelates and mighty Princes which walke without the fear of God . . ." (*Ww*, p. 341; see also *Ww*, pp. 140, 263). That

these comparisons of the contemporary clergy to acknowledged
biblical "villains" is a conscious part of Tyndale's polemic technique
is indicated by his concluding remarks on the question of scriptural
allegories: "And likewise do we borow likenesses or allegories of
the Scripture, as of Pharao and Herode and of the Scribes and Phari-
seis, to expresse our miserable captiuitie and persecution vnder Antichrist the Pope" (*Ww*, p. 168). These analogies derive their force
from the same element as did Tyndale's appeals to the customs of
popular speech—the readers' familiarity with the illustrations. In the
Scriptures, Tyndale has ready-made a set of recognized heroes and
villains, and all that remains for him to do is to identify his supporters
with the former and his opponents with the latter.[31]

Two closely related techniques associated with Tyndale's polemical use of the Scriptures must now be considered. These are, on the
one hand, accusations against the clergy of having distorted the sense
of the Scriptures and, on the other hand, claims that the Scriptures
should be in the vernacular. These techniques serve the double
function of justifying Tyndale's action in undertaking a translation
and of indicting the clergy for failing to do so themselves. Furthermore, the charge that the clergy have distorted the meaning of
Scripture is another shrewd blow against that body's spiritual and
secular power, for it connotes the unscriptural nature of Catholic
theology and practice—especially the nonscriptural basis of the
Church's prerogatives. Consequently, Tyndale is especially concerned to prove that it is with the object of attaining power for
themselves that the clergy have distorted the meaning of Scripture.
This charge also provides Tyndale with another justification for
insisting on a vernacular Bible, since such a Bible would enable the
laity to judge the veracity of his accusation for themselves. And so
he claims that the clergy "haue corrupt the pure word of God, to
confirme their Aristotle with all . . . . what so euer they read in
Aristotle, y^t must be first true. And to mainteine that, they rent and
teare the Scriptures with their distinctions, and expounde them violently contrarie to the meanyng of the text . . ." (*Ww*, p. 61). Just as
the Scribes and the Pharisees blinded the Jews with false interpretations, so, alleges Tyndale, have "ye popyshe doctours of dunces darke
learninge/ . . . with their sophistrye/ sarved vs . . ." (New Testament,
1534, sig. *.ii.^{r}).

Tyndale's appeal for a vernacular Bible was meant to provide the instrument for another abrogation of the clergy's power. An open, vernacular Bible would abolish clerical monopoly on the Word of God and subject clerical conduct to the scrutiny of a laity for the first time able to use the exact scriptural text as a standard by which to judge clerical behavior. The clergy's open opposition to such a translation provided Tyndale with the opportunity of charging that such opposition could stem only from the fear that the application of a scriptural standard to their theology and conduct would expose the former as false and the latter as evil. Again using the Scriptures themselves for illustration, Tyndale points out that the Mosaic law, the Psalms, and the books of prophecy were all written in the language of the people, as were doubtless the sermons whose preaching is recorded in Acts (*Ww*, pp. 101-102); also, St. Jerome translated the Bible into his mother tongue, Tyndale points out (*Ww*, p. 102). He rejects the contention that English is too "rude" as a vehicle for God's will, claiming that both Greek and Hebrew agree much more with English than they do with Latin (*Ww*, p. 102). Setting up a startling picture of an ambitious clergy ready to dictate not only to men but even to God Himself, Tyndale asks: "Hath he not made ye English tounge? Why forbidde ye hym to speake in the Englishe tounge then, as well as in the Latine?" (*Ww*, p. 104).

Tyndale does not believe that the clergy will ever allow a vernacular translation to circulate, and he tells his readers what he thinks are the reasons for such clerical reluctance. "They will suffer no man to know Gods word, but burne it and make heresie of it," he declares in a clever piece of what might be termed polemical metathesis, since he tries to give the impression that the clergy have labeled the Scriptures themselves, rather than the act of unauthorized translation, as heresy; "yea and because the people begyn to smell their falsehode they make it treason to the kyng and breakyng of the kynges peace to haue so much as their *Pater noster* in English" (*Ww*, pp. 138-139), he continues, implying that the clergy have something to hide and attempting to excite his readers' suspicions by the technique of saying that many are already suspicious.[32] The clergy have condemned his translation, he asserts, not because they have found so many errors in it, but because "they haue lost their iugglyng and fayned termes . . ." (*Ww*, p. 254). However, says Tyndale, some good has resulted from the clergy's diligent examination of his translation in order to find its faults: some of them, "which in tymes past were wont to looke on no more scripture then they found in theyr Duns," have in this way read the Scriptures (*Ww*, p. 1). But, he asks, why did they not expend some of the energy used in trying to find his mistranslations in putting out a translation of their own (*Ww*, p. 1)? Tyndale's frequent appeals to the clergy to improve the translation they criticized is surely one of his most effective polemical techniques: Let them, he says, "translate it themselues, after their best maner, yea and let them sow to their gloses, as many as they thinke they can make cleaue thereto, and then put other mens translation out of the way" (*Ww*, p. 389). Such a challenge to come to the court of popular opinion must have impressed Tyndale's readers with the translator's confidence in the rightness of his cause, and the fact that the clergy declined to meet such a challenge certainly did not enhance their position. Again and again Tyndale hammers away at this point. "But Sir," he asks Thomas More, the champion of the English clergy, "aunswere me here vnto, how happeneth that ye defenders translate not one your selues, to cease the murmour of the people, & put to your own gloses, to preuent heretikes? ye would no doubt haue done it long sence, if ye could haue made your gloses agree w^t the text in euery place" (*Ww*, pp. 318-319). The challenge was all the more effective since Tyndale had put himself on record with an annotated edition of part of the New Testament in 1525 and of the Pentateuch in 1530.[33]

Closely related to Tyndale's technique of challenging the clergy to produce their own vernacular Bible is his tactic of basing the defence of his translation on the assumption that even his enemies, whatever they might say publicly, must secretly acknowledge its correctness. That his translation is correct must be apparent to More, Tyndale asserts, for in many of the disputed points it gives the same rendering as does the version made by Erasmus, More's "derelyng," against whom More had said nothing (*Ww*, p. 251). Of course, it was well known that not only had More not attacked Erasmus' translation, but that he had, in fact, vehemently defended it.[34] By thus impugning the honesty and consistency of his opponents' criticism, Tyndale considerably strengthens his own case.

Tyndale's
"New" History

Second in importance only to his use of the Scriptures is Tyndale's polemical use of history. The first English Reformer to use history as a weapon of religious controversy,[35] Tyndale tried to prove that for 800 years the Church of Rome had usurped the temporal power of European and English rulers.

In his appeals to history for the purpose of discrediting the Church of Rome, Tyndale claims to be following historical sources. "Read the Chronicles of England," he advises those of his readers who might wish to have a full understanding of the clergy's treachery.[36] In another place, after making a number of accusations against the Church of Rome, he claims, "These thynges to be true our Prelates know by open hystories . . ." (*Ww*, p. 398). The vagueness of these references to the chronicles is typical of Tyndale's practice throughout his polemical works. On only one occasion does he refer to a source of secular history by name.[37]

It is, therefore, impossible to state definitely what sources Tyndale was using for his historical references. What is quite evident is that he did not confine himself to those chronicles printed by Caxton and his followers, for he deals often with material not in print at the time of his death in 1536.[38] But while we cannot be definite about what specific sources Tyndale used, we do have some indication as to what books he probably meant by "hystories" and "the Chronicles of England."[39] For a few years after Tyndale's death, another Reformer, John Bale, began publishing a series of works[40] in which he greatly expanded on Tyndale's polemical use of history. Since Bale was as specific in his citations as Tyndale was general, and since he covered the same ground, with the same polemical purpose, he provides some indication as to Tyndale's probable sources.

Tyndale displays what appears at first sight to be a rather ambiguous attitude toward the chronicles. While he refers to them extensively, he seems to do so almost reluctantly. Believe the Scriptures, he counsels his readers, not "a tale of Robynhode or *Gestus Romanorum* or . . . the Chronicles" (*Ww*, p. 176). He explains his small faith in the chronicles elsewhere. "Consider," he says, "the story of K. *Iohn*, where I dout not but they haue put the best & fayrest for them selues, & the worst of kyng *Iohn*, For I suppose they make the Chronicles them selues" (*Ww*, p. 181). The charge that the clergy have perverted the chronicles appears frequently in Tyndale's works, as does the claim that the clergy have suppressed those chronicles or parts of chronicles which they consider record any of their evil deeds. Actually, by these declarations of small faith in the chronicles, Tyndale scores a polemical point. For what he is saying is that the chronicles were originally written with a clerical bias and were later pruned of any material inimical to the clergy that the original chronicler had inadvertently recorded. When, therefore, Tyndale claims that in spite of this clerical manipulation, even in the expurgated chronicles, he can still find a large number of incidents illustrative of clerical wickedness, he gives his readers the impression that an unbiased, complete record of clerical machinations would have been truly shocking, thus considerably strengthening his case.[41] And so Tyndale's very profession of doubt concerning the historicity of the chronicles is a polemical device, and, as we shall see, in spite of his professed doubt, Tyndale uses the chronicles as an important element in his technique of controversy.

Behind Tyndale's attitude toward history lies a broader attitude toward tradition generally.[42] As has been indicated, his controversy with More centered on the question whether the final authority in matters of church practice and doctrine should be the Scriptures or the tradition of the Church. More championed the latter point of view, while Tyndale maintained that only the Scriptures were authoritative. Not that Tyndale rejected tradition; he merely considered it unimportant, that is, not relative to salvation. It is this belief in the primacy of Scripture and in the secondary place of tradition which causes Tyndale to regard the Scriptures as the only important record of events, while dismissing such nonscriptural narratives as the chronicles as of very doubtful value indeed. However, just as Tyndale is willing to use tradition, although unwilling to be used by it—for instance, he will permit the veneration of images, so long as the image is the servant of man, directing his thoughts to God, and is not man's idol (*Ww*, p. 270)—so he is willing to make use of the record of human events in what he believes to be the service of God. That Tyndale did not consider himself a slave to history will be made clear presently.

And so Tyndale turns to the history of Europe to trace the development of papal power, charging that by a combination of force and guile the Pope and his clergy wrested the government of the European states from the lawful rulers. This process of deposition began with the clergy's murder of Christ, he maintains (*Ww*, p. 127). Thus, by using the common term "clergy," Tyndale holds the Roman clergy responsible for the actions of the "clergy" at the time of Christ.[43] After the clergy had deposed Christ, Tyndale continues, they plotted against the Emperor and against the kings of the various European states, in which intrigues they were so successful that at the time of writing "yᵉ Emperour and kynges are but vayne names and shadowes, as Christ is, hauying nothyng to do in the world" (*Ww*, p. 127). Tyndale particularizes his charge by recounting how Pope Zacharias persuaded Pepin to oust his liege lord Hildericus, King of France, and how thereafter the Pope controlled the Empire through his puppet (*Ww*, p. 348).

Papal domination of Europe is thus shown to have been established by subversion of lawfully constituted authority. Having seized control of the Empire by guile and force, continues Tyndale, the papacy attempted to lend legal color to its actions by the forged Donation of Constantine and by another spurious document which states that the Pope has the right to elect the Emperor (*Ww*, p. 356). Thus secure, the papacy was in a position to manipulate the political and military affairs of Europe to its own advantage, as it did, Tyndale charges, when it sent the kings of Europe on crusades in order to take over their lands in their absence (*Ww*, p. 181). If any king, charges Tyndale, "displeased the Pope neuer so little, he immediatly curssed him, and excommunicate him, and proclaymed him no right enheritour, and that it was not lawfull to holde of him, and absolued his Lordes and subiectes of their allegeaunce, and sent his blessing vnto the French king and remission of sinnes to go and conquere his land, the Pope and French kyng always deuiding the spoyle betwene them . . ." (*Ww*, p. 348). Such a charge of French-papal alliance in an attempt to dominate Europe—no doubt influenced by the contemporary alliance of the Pope and France against the Emperor Charles V—had the double merit of illustrating the ambitions of the papacy while making the patriotic point that in fighting France the English were fighting the instrument of that ambition.

While France has been the main ally of the Pope, all other European countries at some time or another have been pressed into his service, charges Tyndale, so that in the last 800 years, "farre aboue" 4 million men have been killed in his cause (*Ww*, p. 351). The kings of Europe are merely puppets who must jump when Rome pulls the strings:

> When the Pope hath what he desireth in Italy, then must we make peace with the Frenchmen agayn immediatly, that Fraunce be not all to gether troden vnder the foote: but that it remayne alwaye in a meane state, strong inough to match the Emperour and to keepe him downe, but not to mighty for oppressing the Pope. And then our Prelates to bryng the peace about [say] . . . . Alas what will ye do? spare Christen bloud: will ye slea your owne soules? Be not the Frenchmen as wel Christen as ye? (*Ww*, p. 366).

The result of the papacy's control over Europe is, according to Tyndale, the temporal and spiritual decay of Christendom. He asserts that the rulers of Europe had given so much money to the Pope that they were unable to fight off the onslaughts of the Saracens and Turks (*Ww*, p. 346). Also, claims Tyndale, it was only after the Bishop of Rome had made himself supreme among his fellows that there arose a split between the Roman and the Greek Church, thus destroying the unity of Christendom (*Ww*, p. 347).

Since Tyndale is writing in English for an English audience, his main reference to history is to that of his native country. It is his contention that in England, no less than in any other country, the Pope and his clergy have dictated both domestic and foreign policy.

Even before England was united, claims Tyndale, it was the victim of papal policy, for it was only after the Pope usurped the power of the Emperor that the Danes ravaged England, since then there was no power in Europe to restrain them.[44] William I's invasion of England was supported by the Pope because Harold had exiled the

Archbishop of Canterbury, claims Tyndale, and William would not have succeeded in his invasion, "except the spiritualtie had wrought on his side" (*Ww*, p. 374; misnumbered for p. 362). The slightest disobedience by an English king to clerical authority or prerogative brought swift retaliation. Thus when William II appropriated the annual fees the priests paid to their bishops for licenses to keep whores, the Bishop of Chichester forbade all services within his jurisdiction until the king had restored the money (*Ww*, p. 374; misnumbered for p. 362). In the case of King John, who tried to withstand the power of the Pope, continues Tyndale, the King of France was sent by Rome to conquer the realm and restore papal authority (*Ww*, p. 181), after a clerically inspired rebellion in Ireland had failed (*Ww*, p. 374; misnumbered for p. 362). Tyndale proceeds with his indictment of the clergy by charging that because Richard II would not allow them to kill "at their owne lust" the followers of John Wycliffe, they again stirred up a rebellion in Ireland against the King, after which they imprisoned and murdered him, setting up in his place Henry IV (*Ww*, p. 363). He also asserts that when Henry V was about to confiscate the temporalities of the clergy, they incited Henry to invade France, providing him with money for the invasion so that he would leave their lands alone (*Ww*, p. 366), and that the clergy broke off certain marriage arrangements of Henry VI and Edward IV which were not to their liking (*Ww*, p. 366).

And, says Tyndale, if anyone in this realm has tried to withstand their power, they have murdered him either openly or secretly. Richard was not their only victim, Tyndale charges; in Henry VI's day they slew Duke Humphrey of Gloucester, probably because he was able to detect their necromancy and false miracles (*Ww*, p. 364). Even the dead are not safe from their vengeance, Tyndale points out, for "when they be dead, they rage burnyng their bodies, of which some they them selues of lickelyhode killed before secretly."[45]

In the attempt to prove his thesis that the papacy was a worldwide conspiracy, Tyndale did not confine himself to illustrations from the past but also drew extensively on the contemporary political situation in Europe and England. Indeed, his whole purpose in adducing examples of clerical perfidy from history was to bring them to bear on the contemporary situation, which he viewed as the most recent manifestation of the clergy's attempt to manipulate entire nations for the benefit of the papacy. Conversely, it is quite likely that Tyndale's view of history was colored by the events of his own day, and that the very real intrigues of Cardinal Wolsey on behalf of the papacy influenced Tyndale to regard the events of the past 800 years as the product of a carefully planned papal plot to dominate Europe.[46]

Tyndale sees the Pope as the real ruler of contemporary Europe. He charges that Rome bribes the imperial electors to ensure that only a man favorable to the papal cause will become Emperor and that the Pope arranges the entire affairs of Europe to his own advantage. He sets realm against realm, claims Tyndale, fortunes are spent in war, thousands are slain, and "When the pope hath his purpose, then is peace made, no man woteth how, and our most enemy is our most frend."[47] According to Tyndale, emperors and kings are only names and shadows of power, for they have been reduced to the status of "hangmen vnto the Pope and Byshops" (*Ww*, p. 138); it is the Pope who rules (*Ww*, p. 127). Tyndale gives a forceful rejoinder to those, such as More, who claimed that the Reformers' attempts to over-throw the clergy were merely a preliminary to subsequent attempts to overthrow the nobility and king.[48] The clergy are accusing us, he says, of what they have already accomplished: "the kinges and Lordes are downe already, & that so low that they can not go lower, Ye treade them vnder your feete, and lead the*m* captiue and haue made them your bonde seruaunts to waite on your filthy lustes. . . . Ye haue not onely robbed them of their la*n*d, authoritie honour and due obedie*n*ce, which ye owe vnto them, but also of their wittes . . ." (*Ww*, p. 140). Tyndale illustrates the last claim by pointing out that "They haue with falsehode taken from all Kynges and Emperours their right and duties . . . and haue made euery Kyng sweare to defend their falsehode against their own selues" (*Ww*, p. 155). In other words, he asserts that the clergy have so duped the temporal rulers that they do not even realize they have sworn to give up their power to the clergy. And so, concludes Tyndale, if anyone warns the King that his power is being usurped, the King himself is sworn to kill those who are trying to restore his power (*Ww*, p. 155). This argu-ment is, of course, a piece of special pleading on Tyndale's part, an attempt to persuade all rulers—and especially Henry VIII—that their persecution of the Reformers at the instigation of the clergy is in their own worst interests.

The reason the clergy are able to control the affairs of Europe, charges Tyndale, is that they are in the most secret councils of every land, "But of there Councell is no man" (*Ww*, p. 116). "In all Councels and Parlamentes," he continues, "are they the chief. Without them may no kyng be crowned, neither vntil he be sworne to their liberties. All secretes know they, euen the very thoughtes of mens hartes" (*Ww*, p. 141). Another source of information the clergy utilize, asserts Tyndale, is auricular confession, by which they know "all secretes, thereby mocke they all men . . . and beguile Knight, and Squier, Lord, and Kyng, and betray all Realmes. The Byshops with the Pope haue a certaine conspiration and secret treason agaynst the whole world. And by confession know they what Kings and Emperours thinke. If ought be agaynst them . . . then moue they their captiues to warre and to fight. . . ."[49] By placing auricular confession in such a light, Tyndale is not only exposing what he considers a tool of clerical subversion but is also striking a shrewd blow against an institution which he finds repugnant on theological grounds.

Having established that papal policy is paramount in Europe and that, to their own detriment, the temporal rulers are its unwitting agents, Tyndale specifies what he believes that policy to be. It is, he claims, the achievement of such a balance of power in Europe that no single state will be in a position to counter the territorial ambitions of Rome. And to ensure that no one man will rule too much land, says Tyndale, the Pope tries to create as many small states as possible by resurrecting old titles and quarrels and getting nations to fight each other. If the Pope and his clergy see anyone about to inherit too much land and thus get too much power, such as the Emperor Charles V, they try either to hinder his election or to oust him after he has been elected, as they are now doing (*Ww*, p. 135).

As in Europe, so in England the foreign policy of the realm is, as it always has been, the foreign policy of the Pope, asserts Tyndale (*Ww*, pp. 182, 371):

> The kyng ought to count what he hath spent in the Popes quarell sens he was kyng. The first viage[50] cost vpon xiiii. hundred thousand poundes. Reken sens what hath bene spent by

sea and land betwene vs and Frenchmen, and Scottes . . . and
what hath bene sent out of the Realme secretly, and all to mainteine our holy father. . . . For we had no cause to spend one
peny but for our holy father (*Ww*, p. 180).

English domestic policy, too, Tyndale points out, is as much under
the domination of the Pope as it has been at any time in England's
history. Just as the clergy diverted Henry V's attention from affairs
at home to foreign wars, so they do with Henry VIII, lest the King
perceive their machinations against him and see how they suppress
God's truth.[51] The English clergy—and Tyndale, no doubt, has
Wolsey principally in mind—have duped the King into delivering
the entire domestic as well as the foreign policy of the realm into
their hands (*Ww*, p. 98). The reforms enacted by the Parliament of
1529, Tyndale maintains, are sham reforms meant to deceive the laity,
and the clergy will continue to govern England as they have always
done. He thinks that Wolsey's resignation was voluntary and a part
of the scheme to make the King and laity think that the clergy have
lost their power. They are, however, merely biding their time, Tyndale concludes (*Ww*, pp. 373-374). He goes on to tell his readers
that the new Chancellor, More, is the chief instrument of this plot,
having been selected by Wolsey to replace him temporarily as a sop
to the laity who will think that, since More is a layman, he will act in
their interests, while in reality he is taking his orders from Wolsey.
The entire Parliament and change in chancellorship, maintains Tyndale, were "to bleare mens eyes withall" (*Ww*, p. 373). By the accusation that More is the clergy's agent, Tyndale implies what he
elsewhere asserts—that More's works defending the existing clerical
system do not, as they claim, represent the impartial view of a
disinterested layman, but are rather "golden opinions" purchased by
Wolsey's treasury.[52]

Not only are the domestic and foreign policies of England formu-
lated in Rome, Tyndale charges, but even in theory the King rules
over only half his realm; for England is divided into two kingdoms:
the temporal, which the clergy rule by stealth, and the spiritual,
which they rule openly and for which they have their own laws
which supersede the King's law. And while they will not obey the
King's law, complains Tyndale, they impose their laws on the entire
realm without the consent of either the King or his subjects.[53]

Again and again in his works Tyndale meets the clerical charge that the Reformers are disobedient to rulers with the countercharge that a study of history and contemporary events demonstrates that it is rather the clergy who have always been a subversive element within the realm of England (*Ww*, pp. 115, 116, 124): "For if any man wyll obeye neither father nor mother, neither Lord nor maister, neither King nor Prince, the same needeth but onely . . . to shaue himself a Monke, a Fryer, or a priest, and is then immediately free and exempted from all seruice and obedience due vnto man" (*Ww*, p. 109). Thus Tyndale seeks to establish that the very act of taking orders is an act of disobedience and collusion with a foreign power.

As has already been observed, Tyndale viewed both the past and his own time under the influence of his *idée fixe*, which was that there had been in operation for 800 years a huge clerical conspiracy to dominate the territory of Europe and the minds of its rulers. He interpreted this body of history guided by one organizing principle— the conviction that all actions he regarded as evil emanated ultimately from the Pope and his clergy. It is not unlikely that Tyndale was led to this conclusion from observing the activities of Wolsey who, indeed, motivated by ambition to become pope, managed the affairs of England for the benefit of Rome.[54]

When, therefore, Tyndale examines the chronicles of his own country, it is with the above-mentioned preconviction which permits him to find with little difficulty exactly the corroboration he is seeking. Actually, while his appeals to "open hystories" and the "Chronicles of England" imply that his allegations are based on evidence from historical sources, often the sources available to Tyndale give no support whatever to his charges. Sometimes the discrepancy between Tyndale's account and that in the chronicles arises from his misinterpretation of events actually recorded and sometimes from his quite possibly unconscious habit of manufacturing events not recorded at all. Tyndale also indulges in what might be termed historical innuendo, by which he hints darkly at the existence of events he shrinks from recording as actual fact.

For instance, he says that it was only after the Pope had usurped the authority of the Emperor that the Danes ravaged England, since there was then no longer any power to restrain them (*Ww*, p. 351).

Thus, by implication at least, Tyndale makes the papacy responsible
for the Danish invasion of England, in that the papacy had destroyed
the power of England's protector. But Tyndale certainly never read
in any of the chronicles to which he so often appeals that the
Emperor had ever protected England. Instead, almost all the chronicles are unanimous—a unanimity achieved by the common practice
of one chronicler copying his predecessor, often word for word—that
the Danes invaded England because God wanted to punish the
wicked deeds of the English people.[55] Again, "Take an example of
their practise out of our owne stories," says Tyndale. "Kyng *Herold*
exiled or banished *Robert* Archbyshop of Canterbury. For what
cause the English Polychronicon specifieth not. But if the cause were
not somwhat suspect, I thinke they would not haue passed it ouer
with silence" (*Ww*, p. 374; misnumbered for p. 362). The foregoing
is a good example of how Tyndale deals with the chronicles: If a
chronicle has omitted something, he reasons, then, since the clergy
control the chronicles, the omission must be relative to some evil
action of the clergy. The implication in the above case is that the
Archbishop must have been involved in some clerical plot against the
King. But if on this point Tyndale had troubled to consult some of
the other chronicles which he evidently consulted on other points,
he would have found the reason for the Archbishop's banishment,
namely, that Robert was politically suspect as a Norman, and he
would also have found that the primate was only one of a number of
laymen and clerics banished for this reason. Then Tyndale goes on to
state that William would never have been able to conquer England
without the help of the clergy (*Ww*, p. 374; misnumbered for
p. 362), but neither the *Polychronicon* nor any other chronicle says
that William was helped by the clergy in any way other than that the
Pope judged the invasion of England lawful and sent William his
banner. What the chronicles do say is that an English spy thought
William's army was composed of priests because his soldiers were
all clean-shaven, and that Harold told him that these men were not
priests but that it was a custom among Norman knights to shave off
their beards.[56]

Tyndale also charges that there was a dispute between William II
and the Bishop of Chichester over the King's confiscation of the

annual tribute the priests paid their bishops for the privilege of keeping whores, and that the Bishop forbade divine service in his diocese until the King had restored the money (*Ww*, p. 374; misnumbered for p. 362). While it is recorded that the King and the Bishop quarreled, the ground for their quarrel, which is the point of the accusation, is Tyndale's invention.[57] Concerning the rebellion of the Irish against King John, Tyndale says that it was "not without the secret workinge of our Prelates I dare well say" (*Ww*, p. 363). None of the chronicles say that this rebellion was instigated by the clergy; most give no reason for the rebellion, although one gives as its cause John's attempt to impress Irish soliders into his army.[58] In any case, it is evident, just from the language he uses, that Tyndale has no information on this subject and that the charge arises from his preconception that everything he regards as evil is brought about by the clergy.[59] The same charge is made against the clergy of Richard II's day. After the King had exiled the Archbishop of Canterbury, Tyndale records, there was a rebellion in Ireland, "as before agaynst kyng *Iohn:* But not hardly without the inuisible inspiration of the*m* that rule both in the courte and also in the consciences of all men" (*Ww*, p. 363). Again, no chronicle records that this Irish rebellion was instigated by the clergy, and once more the very language Tyndale employs makes it clear that he has no information but is again indulging in his peculiar interpretation of history. Yet Tyndale began the passage containing these charges by claiming he was about to cite examples of "their practise out of our owne stories" (*Ww*, p. 374; misnumbered for p. 362).

On the other hand, the fact that Tyndale makes some assertions with great assurance is no guarantee of their having any basis in the chronicles. For instance, he declares categorically that Richard II was both deposed and murdered by the clergy (*Ww*, p. 363), whereas the chronicles are unanimous in saying that Richard was deposed by Henry of Lancaster and murdered on his instructions.[60] Tyndale knows very well that Henry was responsible for Richard's death, for when it suits his polemical purpose, he says so (*Ww*, p. 338).

In strongly implying that during the reign of Henry VI the clergy murdered the Duke of Gloucester, Tyndale uses some interesting reasoning to supply the deficiencies of the chronicles. Chroniclers, says Tyndale, cannot tell us "wherfore he dyed, nor by what meanes. No maruell verely. For he had neede of other eyes then such as ye worlde seeth withall that should spye out their [i.e., the clergy's] priuy pathes." However, he continues, More records that the Duke of Gloucester could detect false miracles, "a thyng wherfore a man by their lawe I dare well say, is worthy to dye, and that secretly if it be possible" (*Ww*, p. 364). The foregoing is a good example of how Tyndale "creates" history by the use of innuendo; for an analysis of his reasoning reveals the following approach: the clergy are workers of false miracles. More records that the Duke of Gloucester could detect false miracles. The Duke of Gloucester was murdered. Therefore the clergy must have murdered the Duke of Gloucester!

Tyndale also charges, without support from the chronicles, that the clergy interfered in the marriage plans of Henry VI and Edward IV, because these marriages would have been against the interests of the papacy (*Ww*, pp 366-367). In the case of Henry VI, it is again clear from Tyndale's language that his charge is not based on any historical source, for he says that the proposed marriage was broken off, "not without the secret working of our Prelates . . . thou maist be sure" (*Ww*, p. 366). Actually, two chronicles printed within Tyndale's lifetime say that it was broken off by the Earl of Suffolk,[61] but Tyndale's theory that all events of political importance could be traced, if not to the open policy, then to the secret machinations of the clergy, would allow him to regard as naïveté, if not downright malice, the chroniclers' ascription of an act he regarded as evil to anyone but the clergy.[62]

While many of Tyndale's charges dealing with contemporary English events are well founded and similar to charges made by such loyal supporters of the Church as John Skelton,[63] a number of his assertions have no basis in fact as, for instance, his claim that the Reformation Parliament, as it subsequently became known, was merely another clerical trick to make the laity think the clergy had relinquished power which in reality they retained. Tyndale is equally in error in claiming that Wolsey gave up his post temporarily to permit the anticlerical storm to blow over, while retaining control over More, whom Tyndale regards as Wolsey's puppet. It is highly probable that these baseless charges are a result of false information about English affairs reaching Tyndale in Germany, rather than any attempt to deceive his readers. But these charges are interesting in that they derive from the same kind of thinking which led Tyndale to read into the chronicles what simply was not there, that is, the conviction that all politically significant events were the product of clerical instigation and part of a clerical plot. Also significant is the fact that Tyndale can speak so confidently—even to the point of supplying what purports to be the verbatim text of a conversation— on the basis of what at best must have been secondhand information. For he declares categorically that Wolsey

> set vp in his roome to minister forth, & to fight against God as he had begun, the chiefest of all his Secretaries . . . wherewith the Cardinall caught the kinges grace, whome he called vnto the confirmation of al that he entended to persuade, saying: If it like your grace, More is a learned man, and knoweth it: and is also a lay man, wherfore he will not say otherwise then it is, for any parcialitie to vswarde (*Ww*, p. 373).

Wolsey and More between them, claims Tyndale, managed to dupe their gullible King.

Tyndale's history lessons were not meant to be taken academically by Henry VIII, to whom Tyndale constantly addressed himself. Having diagnosed what he regarded as England's disease, Tyndale did not hesitate to suggest the cure.

One of the most important proposals Tyndale makes is that the realm's clerical courts be abolished. The King's law, he argues, should be the only law of the land; the common law should supersede the canon law, and "one kyng, one law, is Gods ordinaunce in euery realme. Therefore ought not the king to suffer them to haue a seuerall lawe by themselues, and to draw hys subiectes thether."[64] Tyndale was most concerned with the practice of trying cases of heresy in clerical courts, by which procedure men were found guilty by clerical judges administering clerical law and were then handed over to the secular authorities for punishment. Under such a system, the clergy could and did claim that they were not really punishing their critics but were merely ascertaining men's theological beliefs, leaving their punishment to the state.[65] However, says Tyndale, "If the king or his officer for him, will slay me, so ought the king or his officer to iudge me. The kyng can not, but vnto his damnation, lend his sword to kill whom he iudgeth not by his owne lawes" (*Ww*, p. 142). Tyndale also objects to the practice, defended by More in his controversy with Saint-German,[66] whereby clerical courts accepted the testimony of secret accusers, so that the accused had no opportunity to face the man who brought the charges against him. "Let hym that is accused stand on the one syde and the accuser on the other syde," says Tyndale, "and let the kynges iudge sit and iudge the cause, if the kyng will kill and not be a murtherer before God" (*Ww*, p. 142).

Tyndale did his utmost to impress Henry with the duty of defending his subjects against the clergy who had for so long oppressed the entire realm (*Ww*, pp. 137, 141). He does not shrink from reminding the temporal rulers of England that just as Pilate did not escape punishment for being an accessory to the crucifixion of Christ, so they will not escape God's vengeance if they allow themselves to become accomplices to the persecution of God's truth (*Ww*, p. 138). ". . . I beseech his grace to haue compassion on his poor subiectes . . . ," pleads Tyndale, "that the realme vtterly perishe not, wyth the wicked counsell of our pestilent prelates" (*Ww*, p. 375).

Tyndale advises Henry that since the clergy have robbed the realm, they should be made to restore some of what they have stolen: "If the tenth part . . . were geuen the kyng yearely . . . what would it grow to in certayne yeares?" (*Ww*, p. 137). They should be forced, counsels Tyndale, to repay the realm not only the money spent recently in the Pope's wars but also what they have extorted from England through the centuries: "Yea the kyng ought to loke in the Chronicles what the Popes haue done to kings in time past and make them restore it also, And ought to take away from them theyr landes whiche they haue gotten with their false prayers, & restore it vnto the right heyres agayne, or with consent & aduisement turne them vnto the maynteinyng of the poore. . . ."[67]

Finally, Tyndale suggests very strongly to Henry and the rulers of England that it is their duty to promote the truth of God as expounded by the Reformers. Those who will not take a stand for the truth, who will "wincke in so open & cleare light," will assuredly be punished by God no matter what their station, he declares (*Ww*, p. 341). The economic ruin of the realm, described by More in the first book of his *Utopia*, Tyndale ascribes to the activities of the clergy and the punishment God is visiting on England for failure to heed His Word (*Ww*, p. 181). Let the King defend the truth before it is too late, Tyndale pleads: "And I besech his grace also to haue mercy of his own soule, and not to suffer Christ, and his holy Testament to be persecuted vnder his name any longer, that the sword of the wrath of god may be put vp againe, which for that cause no doubt is most chiefly drawne" (*Ww*, p. 375).

How effective was Tyndale's use of history as a polemical weapon? A. F. Pollard states that Henry VIII acted on many of the suggestions Tyndale made as a result of his investigation of history and contemporary events (*Wolsey*, p. 228). While there is actually no evidence that it was specifically on Tyndale's suggestions that Henry acted, it does seem that the King was impressed by his arguments.[68] What can be stated definitely is that in some cases Henry adopted a policy similar to that proposed by Tyndale and other Reformers, and that it was Tyndale's interpretation of history and of contemporary events which gave the Reformers' proposals much of their force.[69] Certainly Henry must have welcomed Tyndale's assertions that it is the duty of a ruler to govern his own realm and not to yield his authority to a foreign, ecclesiastical power, for this was the very kind of propaganda the King himself secretly fostered.[70] While Henry would probably have broken in any case with a pope who refused to sanction his marital wishes, the climate facilitating the break with Rome was prepared by polemicists such as Tyndale, who used the chronicles to demonstrate a long record of papal interference in the affairs of England and who advocated a break with the papacy as both a national prerogative and a religious duty.

In view of Tyndale's charge that the clergy have always been the chief ministers of the Crown, and therefore a subversive element within the realm's most secret councils, it is not without significance that after the fall of Wolsey important government posts began to

pass into lay hands. Tyndale's picture of England as a divided kingdom with separate laws for laity and clergy and his contention that
the King's law should be supreme supported the arguments of such
royal propagandists as Saint-German and helped to create a climate
of opinion in which the Crown could deprive the clergy of authority
to make independent legislation.[71]

That Henry's attention had been directed to the chronicles by
someone is evidenced by the language of one of his most important
assertions of supremacy over the clergy, the preamble to the 1533
Act in Restraint of Appeals (24 Henry VIII, c. 12):

> Where by divers sundry old authentick Histories and Chron-
> icles, it is manifestly declared and expressed, that this Realm of
> *England* is an Empire. . . .
> And whereas the King his most noble Progenitors, and the
> Nobility and Commons of this said Realm, at divers and sundry
> Parliaments, as well in the Time of King *Edward* the first, *Ed-
> ward* the third, *Richard* the second, *Henry* the fourth, and other
> noble Kings of this Realm, made sundry Ordinances, Laws,
> Statutes and . . . to keep it from the Annoyance as well of the
> See of *Rome*, as from the authority of other foreign Poten-
> tates. . . .[72]

That it was from polemicists such as Tyndale that the King learned
his history seems to be indicated by Henry's statement that he meant
to repair the errors of King John and Henry II, who had made
England and Ireland tributary to the Pope, and that he intended to
recover for the Crown the lands appropriated by the clergy throughout the centuries.[73] Henry's determination on the latter point resulted
in the dissolution of the monasteries in 1536 and 1539. Tyndale's
careful accounting of the sums Henry had spent in the Pope's wars
and his urging that the recovery of this money would be simple
justice was certainly not calculated to make the Crown's task of
confiscating clerical property a more difficult one. His contention
that the clergy often resorted to secret murder in order to silence
their critics and that the most recent manifestation of this practice
took the form of secret heresy trials with secret accusers also seems
to have had some effect. By an act passed in 1534 (25 Henry VIII,
c. 14), it was made illegal to execute for heresy without the King's

writ, and by the Act of Six Articles common law procedure became operative in heresy trials.

Tyndale's Techniques of Language, Reasoning, Form, and Accusation

We now come to a consideration of Tyndale's controversial techniques of language, reasoning, and form, as well as of some of his accusations against More.

The subject of sixteenth-century interest in language in general and eloquence in particular needs no elaboration here. That controversy was considered a whetstone for wit is evidenced by the flytings staged for the entertainment of the English and Scottish courts at the beginning of the period and the popularity of the Marprelate and Nashe-Harvey controversies at its end.[74]

In the course of his study at Oxford and Cambridge, Tyndale could not have escaped learning the art of rhetoric and disputation as taught from Aristotle, Cicero, and the fifteenth-century Rudolphus Agricola.[75] After he left Cambridge, Tyndale could have refreshed his memory of these subjects by reading Leonard Cox's *The arte or crafte of rhetoryke* (1524?). But, as we shall see, Tyndale disputed little "by the book."

The most striking feature of the language in Tyndale's polemical works is its sarcasm, the use of which is not specifically advocated by any of the rhetoric books he might have studied but which he nevertheless employs continuously throughout his works of controversy.[76] It is directed, for instance, against the clergy, who "do all thing of a good zeale . . . they loue you so well, that they had rather burne you, than y^t you should haue fellowship w^t Christ" (*Ww*, p. 60). Here, as elsewhere, we shall find Tyndale using economy of technique, for he is not only questioning the professions of the clergy but also—almost incidentally, as it were—telling his readers that the clergy is persecuting the true followers of Christ.

Some of Tyndale's sharpest sarcasm is aimed at the belief in purgatory. The Pope claims authority to bind and loose in purgatory, Tyndale points out. "That permit I vnto him: for it is a creature of his owne makyng. He also byndeth the aungels. For we read of

Popes that haue commau*n*ded the aungels to set diuers out of Purgatory. Howbeit I am not yet certified whether they obeyed or no."[77]
The clergy were not content to rule only over the living, Tyndale
explains, and so they created a purgatory that they might rule also
over the dead "and to haue one kyngdome more then God him selfe
hath" (*Ww*, p. 135). Purgatory is merely a money-making device
invented by the clergy, concludes Tyndale: "Shew the Pope a litle
money, and God is so mercifull that there is no Purgatory" (*Ww*,
p. 307). Here again Tyndale's sarcasm fulfills a double function: It
ridicules the concept of purgatory and at the same time implies that,
if they could, the clergy would like to extend their earthly tyranny
to heaven and subjugate God Himself.

Finally, Tyndale trains his sarcasm on More, whom he portrays as
an abject servant of Wolsey, interested only in wealth and promotion.
As Skelton had done, More, in his attempt to defend the practice of
venerating images, had explained that there were three kinds of worship, *doulia*, *hyperdoulia*, and *latria*, and that the last was never ac-
corded to images but reserved for God. Tyndale brushes aside More's
distinctions by saying, ". . . I would fayne wete . . . whether the
worship done to hys Lord the Cardinalles hat were *doulia*, *hyperdoulia*, or *idolatria*" (*Ww*, p. 269).

Closely allied to sarcasm is irony, which is discussed in classical
and Renaissance rhetorics,[78] but which Tyndale uses less frequently
as a polemical device than he uses sarcasm and much less frequently
than does More. The commonest use of irony to be found in Tyndale's polemical works is in his scrupulously polite references to the
Pope as "our most holy father" whenever he is recounting what he
considers the unholy machinations of the papacy (e.g., *Ww*, pp. 116,
123, 125, 129). It is the clergy's manner of living which evokes what
other irony there is in his works. The church is not only the spirituality, says Tyndale, "(as they will be called for their diligent
seruing of God in the spirite, and so sore eschuing to meddle wyth
temporall matters) . . ." (*Ww*, p. 250). Tyndale refers to the prelates
who examined certain Reformers as "so well learned, so holy and so
indifferent [i.e., impartial]" (*Ww*, p. 318), and he remembers how
when he was in London he "behelde the pompe of our Prelates, and
how busie they were (as they yet are) to set peace and vnitie in the
world . . ." (*Ww*, p. 2).

While there is some humor in his sarcasm and irony, Tyndale never made humor such an important part of his polemical technique as we shall find that More did.[79] Tyndale seems to have been much less fond of a joke than was his principal opponent, and he makes it clear that he sees nothing to laugh at in their controversy. More seems to think it amusing that the wild Irish and Welsh pray for success before they go out to steal, says Tyndale, but "I wonder that *M. More* can laugh at it and not rather weep for compassion, to see the soules for which Christ shed hys bloud to perish" (*Ww*, p. 300). However, there is a kind of humorous wordplay in which Tyndale occasionally indulges at the expense of the opposition. For instance, when More cites Nicolas de Lira against him, Tyndale disposes of the matter by opining that "*Nicolous de Lira delirat*" (*Ww*, p. 303). He thinks that *Opera supererogationis* would be more appropriately called *Opera superarrogantia* (*Ww*, p. 78). His opinion of Wolsey's pastoral care causes him to call the cardinal "Wolfsee" (*Ww*, p. 367), on which name he plays such variations as "this wyly wolfe . . . and raging sea, and shipwracke of all England" (*Ww*, p. 368). The Pope has been made into a god on earth, thinks Tyndale, "of the kinde (I suppose) of *Aarons* calfe. For he bringeth forth no other frute but Bulles" (*Ww*, p. 126), and he is convinced that the only purpose of purgatory is "to purge thy purse withall" (*Ww*, p. 165).

The slip-of-the-tongue device Tyndale occasionally uses is a combination of irony and wordplay; it consists of an ostensibly inadvertent revelation of the truth, which is then immediately retracted to give place to a polite fiction.[80] Speaking of Bishop John Fisher, Tyndale refers to "the ende of his first destruction, I would say instruction" (*Ww*, pp. 129-130). When he was in London, Tyndale recalls, he "heard our praters, I would say our Preachers" (*Ww*, p. 2), and he refers to certain clergy as "heretikes, I would say heremites" (*Ww*, p. 165). Tyndale's characterization of the scholastic method of interpreting Scripture as "chopologicall" (*Ww*, p. 166) instead of "tropological" may be regarded as an uncorrected slip of the tongue or a polemical malapropism.

Another important element in Tyndale's controversial technique is his use and abuse of reasoning. The study of logic and the art of reasoning generally was the third part of the trivium (along with grammar and rhetoric) in sixteenth-century Oxford and Cam-

bridge.[81] But the art of disputation was not only a subject of study;
it was also a method of instruction by which the disputants' minds
were sharpened in a variety of subjects other than logic itself.[82]
When, therefore, Tyndale entered the field of religious controversy,
he must have had considerable knowledge of formal syllogistic logic.
However, while he does make some use of this knowledge, it is again
apparent that he does so to a considerably lesser extent than does
More. Tyndale's meager use of syllogistic logic probably can be
partly accounted for by his general distrust of all learning except that
of the Bible,[83] almost everything outside the pages of Scripture he
regarded as "poetry." And so, when Tyndale uses any kind of formal
reasoning, he feels apologetic: "I will talke a worde or two after the
worldly wisdome with them, and make an ende of this matter,"
he says as introduction to a passage in which he attempts to demonstrate the logical absurdity of the Church's view of sacramental grace
(*Ww*, p. 157). One of his rare uses of formal logic occurs in a passage
attempting to prove that the doctrine of the Church cannot be that
of Christ (*Ww*, p. 200); on two occasions Tyndale does follow the
recommendations of the treatises on the art of reasoning and uses his
knowledge of the syllogism when he demands of More "by what
rule hys argument holdeth" (*Ww*, p. 280) and asks "in what figure
that silogismus is made."[84] That Tyndale remembered his university
training in disputation, even if he did not make much use of syllogistic
logic, is made clear by a passage in which he undertakes to deal with
one of More's arguments "after an Oxford fashion, with *concedo
consequentiam & consequens*" (*Ww*, p. 253).

While Tyndale makes little use of the formal syllogism, he does
often attempt proof by analogy, one of the recognized textbook
methods of reasoning.[85] In trying to explain that Christ did not forgive Mary Magdalene because she loved much but that she loved
much because Christ forgave her, Tyndale draws an interesting analogy from the reasoning process itself and the errors attendant on it.
Because of our poor understanding, he explains, we often reason from
the effect to the cause. For instance, when we see that the moon is
dark, we look for the cause and find that the earth's being between
the sun and the moon is the cause of the darkness. Then we reason
backward, saying, the moon is dark; therefore the earth is directly

VERNON REGIONAL
UNIOR COLLEGE LIBRARY

between the sun and the moon. However, the darkness of the moon is not the cause of the earth's being between the sun and the moon, but the effect. Just so, Tyndale reasons, Mary's love was not the cause of her being forgiven, but the effect, and her story is no support for the doctrine of justification by works (*Ww*, p. 67).

Closely related to Tyndale's use of analogies is his use of illustrations from popular speech to support his arguments, some of which we have already noted in discussing his use of the Scriptures. Such illustrations served Tyndale in a double capacity: From the point of view of general strategy, it was effective polemics to illustrate arguments with the common sayings of the people to whom these arguments were directed; from the point of view of specific tactics, there was no better way of demonstrating the existence of clerical shortcomings than to show that these had become proverbial.

Consequently, when Tyndale wishes to impress his readers with the fact that while works do not justify a man, they are nevertheless an outward manifestation of an inward faith, he turns for illustration to the common speech of his day: "We say," Tyndale writes, ". . . he that loueth not my dogge, loueth not me." That is, he explains, we love the dog because we love the master, and so we should love our neighbors, not because we hope thereby to merit the favor of God, but as a manifestation of the love we bear to God (*Ww*, p. 78). Again, Tyndale appeals to the usage of contemporary speech in support of his contention that Christ did not give Peter more authority than any other disciple. As we call Tully chief of orators because of his eloquence, says Tyndale, and Virgil chief of poets because of his learning, and not because they had authority over other orators and poets, so we call Peter chief of the Apostles only because of his special energy and boldness (*Ww*, p. 128).

Tyndale tells his readers that the morality of the clergy is governed by the common lawyers' maxim *"si non caste tamen caute,* that is, if ye liue not chaste, see ye cary cleane, and play the knaue secretly" (*Ww*, p. 134). So far as the clergy's solicitude for souls is concerned, Tyndale comments, "it goeth after the common saying, no penny, no Pater noster" (*Ww*, p. 139) or "no peny no pardon" (*Ww*, p. 395). However, Tyndale points out, some of the proverbial sayings current among the laity demonstrate that the clergy's short-

comings have not passed entirely unnoticed. For when a matter is
going badly, it is customary to say "the bishop hath blessed it, because
that nothing spedeth well that they medle with all. If the porage be
burned to, or the meate ouer rosted, we say, the Bishop hath put his
foote in the potte or the Bishop hath played the Cooke, because the
Bishops burne who they lust & whosoeuer displeaseth them. He is a
pontificall fellow, that is, proud and stately. . . . It is a pastime for a
Prelate. It is a pleasure for a Pope. He would be free & yet will not
haue his head shauen. He would that no man should smite him and yet
hath not the Popes marke" (*Ww*, p. 166).

Reference to authority, which we have observed Henry and More
using extensively, was another method of bolstering an argument recommended by those books treating of the art of reasoning (Wilson,
Rule, F3^r). Tyndale's primary authority was, of course, the Bible.
But second in number only to his scriptural references are Tyndale's
appeals to the authority of Erasmus, the foremost scholar of the day,
who challenged the sanctity of ecclesiastical tradition with his Greek
New Testament, which corrected many of the errors contained in the
centuries-old Vulgate. But it was not only because of Erasmus' international scholarly reputation that Tyndale was so fond of appealing
to his authority. Tyndale was well aware that the Dutch scholar
was revered especially in England—and by those very men most
active in opposing the Reformers, such as Tunstal, who commissioned
More to write against heresy, and by More himself, Erasmus' alter
ego.[86] It is with particular relish that Tyndale opposes to More's
opinions those of his "derelyng" Erasmus. In answer to More's criticism of certain translations in his English New Testament, Tyndale
replies: "But how happeth it that *M. More* hath not contended in
likewise against hys derelyng *Erasmus* all this longe while? Doth not
he chaunge this word *Ecclesia* into congregation and that not seldome
in the new Testament?"[87] This thrust is all the keener because, as
already mentioned, it was well known that More had defended
Erasmus' translation.[88] In the preface to the 1534 edition of his New
Testament, Tyndale again appeals to the authority of Erasmus to
support his translation of the Vulgate's *conuerti* by "to turne or be
conuerted" instead of "to do penance" (sig. **1^r). Tyndale also
uses Erasmus' New Testament annotations to lend authority to his

own theological views. So far as the intercessory power of Mary is concerned, Tyndale tells his readers, look at Erasmus' annotations on Matthew, chapter 12, II Corinthians, chapter 5, John, chapter 2, and Luke, chapter 2 (*Ww*, p. 172), and also see what Erasmus has to say about the correct interpretation of Matthew, chapter 16, "tu es Petrus, et super hanc petram aedificabo Ecclesiam meam."[89] Tyndale also adduces Erasmus against More in support of the contention that the early Fathers did not advocate auricular confession (*Ww*, p. 339), while implying very strongly that Erasmus and he are in agreement on many theological points.[90] It is Erasmus, according to Tyndale, who has exposed the clergy's attempt to pass off as genuine "many false bookes . . . fayned and put forth in the name of *S. Hierom, Augustine, Ciprian, Dionise* and of other," which supported their position.[91] As a postscript to this examination of Tyndale's polemical use of Erasmus—primarily against More—it is interesting to note that Tyndale also used More himself against his fellows as he had used Erasmus against More. The clergy have brought such ruin to England, says Tyndale in his *The exposition of the first Epistle of S. Iohn*, "that *M. More* could say in his *Vtopia*, that as Englishmen were wont to eate shepe, euen so their shepe now eate vp them by whole Parishes at once . . ." (*Ww*, p. 429).

Tyndale's method of argumentation reveals a strongly pragmatic, rather than a theoretical, approach. While his opponents, and especially More, argue about the theory of dogma, Tyndale concentrates on how that dogma is actually applied in contemporary practice. What is the point, asks Tyndale, of arguing whether or not the Pope can err. Look at history and the present situation, Tyndale advises his readers, and judge "whether they haue erred, and not onely whether they can" (*Ww*, p. 248). And what about these beliefs, he asks, to which they tell us we must subscribe because they cannot err—what about purgatory? "What am I the better for the beliefe in Purgatory? to feare men thou wilt say.[92] Christ & his Apostles thought hell inough. And yet . . . what great feare can there be of that terrible fire which thou mayst quench almost for three halfe pence?" (*Ww*, p. 256). You say, Tyndale addresses More, that we may bestow money on images and still give alms to the poor. "May or not may," answers Tyndale, "I see that the one most necessary of

both, is not done . . ." (*Ww*, pp. 271-272). And you say, Tyndale
continues to More, that you have not taught that the Church consists
of the clergy exclusively but that it includes all Christians. I appeal
to my readers' experience to judge whether or not you have taught
this, Tyndale retorts; let them ask themselves and their friends what
is usually understood by the word "church," whether it is all Christians or the clergy only.[93]

Having examined Tyndale's use of various reasoning processes—
analogy, illustration, appeal to authority, and emphasis on the pragmatic—we should now consider what must be called his abuse of
reasoning, that is, his polemical use of sophisms and specious reasoning. We cannot conclude that because Tyndale was alert to fallacies
in his opponents' arguments, that fallacies in his own reasoning are
necessarily conscious attempts to deceive his opponents or his readers;
it may simply be that Tyndale, in common with More and with most
people, could detect in another's work a fault he failed to notice in
his own. But whether Tyndale's use of specious reasoning is intentional or not, it constitutes a significant element in his controversial
technique.

Begging the question, for instance, which Tyndale objects to on
the part of his opponents (*Ww*, p. 420), is something he himself
indulges in on a number of occasions, as when he asserts that Antichrist (i.e., the Roman clergy) "maketh it treason vnto the kyng, to
be acquainted with Christe" (*Ww*, p. 60). This claim rests on the
assumption that he and his followers are the only ones who wish to
be "acquainted with Christe" and that consequently any legislation
against the Reformers is legislation against Christ. Again, Tyndale
counters the Pope's claim to be Peter's successor with the following
argument: "For were they Simon Peters successours, they would
preach Christ as he did, but they are Simon Magus his successours . . ."
(*Ww*, p. 96). That is, Tyndale uses the disputed question as to what
constitutes correct preaching of Christ as the premise with which to
prove that the Pope cannot be Peter's successor. He uses the same
kind of fallacious reasoning on this subject when he asserts that if
the Pope were the rock referred to in the sixteenth chapter of
Matthew,[94] then the gates of hell could not prevail against him, "but
the contrary see we in our Popes. For hell gates haue preuayled
agaynst them many hundred yeares . . ." (*Ww*, p. 173). "And

agayne," says Tyndale in another place, "if the Pope could not erre in his doctrine, he coulde not sinne of purpose and profession, abhominably and ope*n*ly aboue the Turkes and all the heathen that euer were, and defend it so maliciously as he hath viij. hundred yeares long, and maketh them his Saintes and his defenders y^t sinne as he doth" (*Ww*, p. 308). Since Tyndale's key phrase in the argument is "of purpose," his implication seems to be that the popes secretly know that they are sinning not only in their actions but also in holding a doctrine different from Tyndale's.

Non sequiturs, too, can be found in some of Tyndale's arguments. Do not be discouraged, Tyndale comforts his readers, because you are being persecuted for reading the works of the Reformers and the vernacular Scriptures. For, he argues, the very fact that you are being persecuted is a proof that what you are reading is of God, since the Scriptures make plain that the Word of God has never been without persecution. And from this you can see, concludes Tyndale, that the Pope's doctrine is not of God, since the world receives it so well (*Ww*, p. 97). The obvious comment such an argument demands is that it does not follow that because the Word of God is always persecuted, everything which is persecuted must be the Word of God, or that anything which is not persecuted cannot be the Word of God.

Combining some of the aspects of Tyndale's techniques of language and reasoning is his use of the modified dialogue form, on which we have already commented when discussing More's use of dialogue. While the outward structure Tyndale uses for his controversial works is that of either the straight treatise, such as the *Obedience*, or the more or less point-by-point rebuttal, such as the *Answere*, within the frame of the latter work he has developed a kind of dialogue form which he uses as a very effective polemical weapon. This modified dialogue consists of the juxtaposition of a short and usually sarcastic comment to a short quotation from More. It is possible that Tyndale was led to adopt this form from observing More's sporadic use of it in the *Responsio* or from noting More's success with the reported dialogue of the *Dialogue concernynge heresyes*.[95] Tyndale's modifications of the latter form appear to have been made for the sake of maneuverability and to protect himself from such charges of manipulating the interlocutor as he himself made against

More (see *Ww*, pp. 253, 279, 330). For while More never abandons the form of the dialogue in his work, he often loses the spirit of that medium, in that he assigns speeches to himself of such a length that the reader is apt to forget he is reading a conversation rather than a treatise.[96] Tyndale, by keeping both More's quotations and his own answers very short, avoids this pitfall and retains the flavor of debate. Also, by using More's actual words and thus making him the interlocutor, Tyndale leaves himself less open to the charge of distorting his opponent's viewpoint than did More. At the same time, however, Tyndale loses none of the polemical advantages of the medium he observed More enjoying. For while he is committed to quoting More verbatim, he is not obliged to use everything More said on a particular point, nor is he restricted to introducing More's quotations in their original order or context; he can arrange the series of statements and answers to suit himself.[97] From a polemical point of view, Tyndale's use of the dialogue seems to be more effective than his opponent's.

An examination of the following quotations from More will demonstrate that Tyndale certainly did not choose his adversary's strongest arguments to oppose to himself:

> *M. More. The Apostles and Saintes were prayed so when they were aliue and God not dishonoured. Tynd.* What helpeth that your carnal purpose. I haue aunswered you vnto that & many thinges mo in the obedie*n*ce and other places agaynst which ye reply not, but keepe your tune and vnto all thyng syng kokow, kokow, we be the church & can not erre (*Ww*, p. 297).

The sarcasm of the above passage is characteristic of Tyndale's tone when he adopts the modified dialogue form and probably derives from his desire for brevity; he has to demolish his opponent's statement somehow, without engaging in extended argument. Also, the following quotations seem to indicate that it is just when Tyndale wishes to avoid extended argument that he uses this particular form:

> *More. The Church byndeth no man to chastitie. Tyndall.* of a truth, for it geueth licence to who soeuer wil, to kepe whores, and permitteth to abuse mens wiues and suffereth sodomitrie, and doth but onely forbid matrimonie (*Ww*, p. 314).

While there is no denying the wit of Tyndale's rejoinder, the conclusion is equally inescapable that he has permitted himself to be witty by ignoring More's context and, consequently, the meaning of his statement. More's point is that the rule of celibacy can hardly be characterized as the Church's imposition on an unwilling laity, since only priests have to vow celibacy and the Church forces no man to become a priest (More, *W*, p. 232). Another kind of selectivity is apparent in the choice of the following statement of More's:

> *Christes church hath the true doctrine already, and the selfe same that S. Paule woulde not geue an Angell audience vnto the contrary.*
>
> *Tyndall.* But the Popes Church will not heare that doctrine (*Ww*, p. 319).

Here Tyndale is begging the question; he has picked out a statement from More's work which permits him to juxtapose the terms "Christes church" and "the Popes Church," whose lack of identity he assumes in his rejoinder. Other examples in which Tyndale uses the modified dialogue to avoid lengthy discussion or to score easy points against his opponent are numerous (e.g., *Ww*, pp. 298, 323, 324).

Finally, we must consider a series of accusations Tyndale makes against More. The most prominent is the charge of hypocrisy, so popular with polemicists. But Tyndale seems to be sincere and not merely polemical, for he apparently really believes that More's only motive for defending the clergy is a desire for money and advancement (*Ww*, p. 251). Tyndale also claims that More knows the English translation of the New Testament is an accurate one, but will not admit it, "so blynd is couetousnesse & dronken desire of honour,"[98] while More's treatment of the attributes of God is in one place dismissed with the jibe that "He thinketh of God, as he doth of hys Cardinall, that he is a monster, pleased when men flatter him. . . ."[99] When Tyndale recalled More's earlier activities and writings, such as his championship of Erasmus and his satire on certain clerics in his epigrams,[100] and then compared these with the kind of book his opponent was now writing, he came to the conclusion that More was one of those who "at the beginning take Christes parte, but afterward when they fynde eyther losse or no

vauntage, they get them vnto the contrary part, and are by profession the most cruell enemyes, and subtellest persecuters of the
truth. Looke Maister *More* and reade and marke well" (*Ww.* p.
295).

In *The souper of the Lorde*, possibly by Tyndale, the serious
charge is made that More forged an entire work in the name of the
Reformer William Barlowe (*Ww*, p. 473).

Barlowe had written a number of dialogues in support of Lutheranism, but subsequently he returned to the Catholic faith and in
1531[101] produced a work entitled *A dyaloge descrybyng the orygynal ground of these Lutheran faccyons and many of theyr
abusys*.[102] The author of *The souper* evidently had not heard of
Barlowe's change of views and therefore thought him incapable
of producing a work such as the dialogue in question. That he
thought More was the author of the work, an opinion apparently
shared by others,[103] was probably because it was printed by William
Rastell, More's nephew and printer of his controversial writings.
Another explanation of Barlowe's authorship which was circulating
was that Barlowe had been coerced into writing the work.[104]

Tyndale does not share More's opinion that the interlocutor in
the *Dialogue* has been handled fairly[105] but thinks that More "fash-
ioneth his tale as he doth other mens to iest out the truth" (*Ww*, p.
279). In his *Answere*, Tyndale gives a rather complete summary of
what he thinks of More's fairness as a controversialist:

> *M. More* declareth the meanyng of no sentence, hee describ-
> eth the proper signification of no word, nor the difference of
> the significations of any terme, but runneth foorth confusedly
> in vnknowen wordes and generall termes. And where one word
> hath many significations he maketh a man some tyme beleue that
> many thynges are but one thyng, and some tyme he leadeth from
> one signification vnto an other & mocketh a mans wittes (*Ww*,
> p. 330).

More and the
Dialogue Form

When More decided to employ the dialogue form in carrying
out Tunstal's commission to combat heresy, he was not only satis-

fying the predilections for the dramatic he had already evinced in his *Richard the thirde* and *Utopia* but was also availing himself of a weapon proven potent in the art of religious and secular controversy.

For many centuries Catholic apologists used the dialogue form to defend the Church against the attacks of heretics. Augustine, for example, wrote dialogues to refute the views of the skeptics, the Donatists, and the Manichaeans. Augustine himself appears as a speaker in these dialogues, which are written as reports of authentic conversations. In the dialogue *Contra academicos*[106] the opposing side is represented not by the actual opponents themselves but by some of Augustine's pupils who are made to argue against the Catholic faith, while other pupils defend the orthodox views. Most of the time Augustine himself appears as a judge of his pupils' skill in debate, but occasionally he enters the argument on the Catholic side when some particularly difficult point is in dispute. The figure of Augustine in this dialogue, therefore, is not only that of a defender of Catholicism but also that of a teacher who is instructing his pupils in the art of debate while confirming them in the tenets of the Catholic faith.

While the dialogue form was used by a number of religious controversialists during the Middle Ages,[107] it was not until the Reformation that the form became a popular medium of controversy.

Between the publication of Luther's theses in 1517 and More's commission in 1528, there appeared a large number of religious controversial dialogues, of which the majority were written in Germany by the Reformers. The most notable Protestant controversialist in Germany was Ulrich von Hutten. Hutten's dialogues, in common with most controversial dialogues written by both sides during the early stages of the Reformation, do not attempt a reasoned exposition of doctrine. The theology of his opponents is satirized and parodied rather than rebutted, and Hutten's emphasis is on what he considers to be the political and social evils of Catholicism rather than on its doctrinal errors.

His main technique is ridicule of the opposition. He often effects this by having the Catholic spokesmen in his dialogues make absurd claims for the power of the Church, or by arranging their arguments in such a manner that they condemn themselves by their own words. For instance, in *Inspicientes*,[108] the papal legate Cajetan asserts that he has power to loose and bind the sun, which he commands to beg absolution from him for not shining in the correct manner. The sun is told that as a penance it will have to pay a sum of money to help rebuild St. Peter's. Then Cajetan asks the sun to bring a plague on Germany, so that newly elected cardinals like himself will receive the incomes of the livings left vacant by the deceased incumbents.

Another outstanding writer of Protestant dialogues was the Swiss Niklaus Manuel. In his *Krankheit der Messe*[109] a number of well-wishers—representing various Catholic theologians under disguised names—gather around the sickbed of the ailing Mass. On examining the patient's medical history, the physicans find that the Mass has always been sickly, even from its birth. After it has been determined under which astrological sign the Mass was born, various cures are suggested. One of the most interesting is proffered by a physician who remembers the medieval legend that every lion is stillborn and is brought to life only through the roaring of his father. Now, reasons the physician, since the Mass was born of the Roman See, we shall be able to bring it back to life if we stand over it and roar loudly about the authority of the Fathers and the councils, after the manner of the Roman church.

The device of having the opposing side make self-condemnatory statements is again used by Manuel in his *Barbali*.[110] The young girl Barbali is supposed to enter a convent. Consequently, when her priest hears that she has been reading the New Testament, he is very angry, for, as he says, she will never wish to enter the convent now, after reading that book. The priest, however, tries to persuade Barbali by telling her what a hard time she would have in the world as compared to living in the convent, where she would never have to do any work. As authorities for his arguments the priest cites Ovid and Aristotle, only to be rebutted every time by Barbali's quotations from the Scriptures. When the priest calls in five other clerics to argue with Barbali, they, too, are put to rout by this one unlearned girl.

Manuel's *Krankheit* probably inspired the only English Reformation dialogue before More's, Jerome Barlowe's *Rede me and be nott wrothe.*[111] In this work two servants of the clergy discuss the death of the Mass and their masters' morals. One asks leading questions such as "But aren't the clergy good livers?" which allow the other to expound the vices of the clergy.

One of the most famous of the dialogues in which the central character is condemned by his own words is Erasmus' *Julius exclusus.*[112] The dialogue, which was written on the death of Pope Julius II, in 1513, shows the deceased Pope arriving at the gates of heaven and imperiously demanding entrance from Peter. Peter, however, who is ignorant of the respect due a pope, is not interested in hearing about Julius' greatness but cites a list of Christ's commandments and asks the waiting Julius whether or not he has observed these. The answer being in the negative in every case, Julius is denied admission to heaven.

The most outstanding controversial dialogue defending the Catholic viewpoint is Murner's *Von dem Grossen Lutherischen Narren.*[113] Just as Hutten and Manuel attacked the Catholics by having them condemn themselves, so Murner makes Luther hand down his own indictment in this dialogue. On being asked what the articles of Lutheranism are, Luther is made to reply that the articles of his faith declare that a Lutheran need obey no one, neither Emperor nor Pope, and that Christian liberty permits a Lutheran to despise all authority. Lutherans hold that marriage should be completely abolished. In his sermons, a good Lutheran will stress the monks' voluptuousness, being careful to avoid all mention of their deeds of charity. He will gloss over lies, but at the same time praise the truth. Lutherans do not believe in peace, but love to wash their hands in blood and wade in it up to their knees. Luther is made to conclude this summary of his creed by saying that once they have taken away the goods of the bishops, his followers aim to expropriate the merchants—in short, to overturn the established order and to make everything Lutheran.

Turning to the uses of the dialogue form in secular controversy, we find that this form was used by some fifteenth-century Italian humanists to vilify their enemies. In one of his diatribes against Cosmo de' Medici, Filelfo manipulates his opponent to make ridiculous and easily controvertible statements.[114] Filelfo also creates a character for himself and for Cosmo: By what he is made to reveal about himself in the dialogue, Cosmo appears as a complete libertine who does not scruple to practice the most shameful vices. Filelfo, on the other hand, draws a picture of himself as a teacher of morality who is shocked by the excesses committed by his interlocutor. Throughout the dialogue, Filelfo attempts to instill virtue into the profligate Medici and to restore him to an honorable mode of life.

The same humanist wrote another dialogue in which he presents all his enemies as speakers and then has them defame each other: Poggio admits that he drinks too much, but confesses that in this art he has to yield the palm to Niccoli. The same speaker, when pressed to tell what an ox looks like, can think of nothing which fits this description better than the person of Cosmo de' Medici. When he is challenged on this statement by his incredulous audience, Poggio proceeds to defend his comparison by going into detail. He demonstrates that Cosmo's legs, face, body, and manner of walking are similar to those of an ox, and at last Poggio's listeners have to agree that the comparison is just.[115]

Hutten also used the dialogue in secular controversy. In *Phalarismus*[116] he vented his anger on Duke Ulrich of Württemburg, who had murdered Hutten's cousin Hans, again by the device of having the main character condemn himself. A dialogue takes place in the underworld between a figure called the Tyrant (the Duke) and his teacher Phalaris. The Tyrant tells his teacher how he has profited from his instruction and has murdered his friend Hans Hutten. He relates how he has escaped vengeance for this murder by perfidiously signing a treaty which he did not mean to honor. Having made all preparations for war, he wants to find out from his teacher some suitable tortures to inflict on the enemy, should the victory be his.[117]

We can conclude therefore that, at the time of More's commission to combat heresy, the dialogue form was already a popular medium of controversy. While there is no evidence that More knew German and was acquainted with the many dialogues written in that language, he did know Murner,[118] and it is not unreasonable to suppose that in preparing himself to defend the doctrines of the Church he read the Latin dialogues of Reformers such as Hutten. More may have been familiar with the works of Filelfo,[119] and we know that he had read the *Julius exclusus*, for he makes reference to the dialogue in his letters.[120] As for Augustine's dialogues, since More frequently cites passages from the works Augustine wrote against the Manichaeans and the Donatists, it seems likely that he would also be acquainted with the dialogues Augustine wrote during the same controversies.[121]

While More makes sporadic use of the modified dialogue in his *Responsio* and in his *Confutacyon of Tyndales answere*, his chief use of the dialogue form as a weapon of religious controversy occurs in the *Dialogue concernynge heresyes*. A study of this work reveals the importance of the dialogue form to More's controversial technique.

The *Dialogue* presents the following situation: A friend wants to hear More's opinion concerning the claims made by the Reformers, but because he is unable to come to talk with More personally, he sends a servant instead. This servant is to hear More's views and report them to his master, but, lest any of the material might be misreported, More determines to set down the entire conversation in writing. The situation in More's dialogue is therefore similar to that in Augustine's *Contra academicos*, in that More is not arguing directly against those attacking the Church but against a friend voicing their point of view.

More's narration of the circumstances which led him to write the dialogue has an air of such verisimilitude that one scholar was led to the opinion that the events recorded actually took place.[122] Such a conclusion is not mandatory, however, because More was in the habit of giving his works fictional settings.[123]

As a dialogue is ostensibly a conversation, it need not conform to a rigid pattern of subjects, but may, like a conversation, roam from one topic to another, frequently retracing its steps over material already discussed. Subjects may be raised and dropped at will, to be taken up again at some later point in the discussion, without the necessity for logically building premise upon premise to reach the conclusion.

In fact, More's *Dialogue* is as far removed as it could possibly be from Fisher's unsuccessful attempt to halt heresy by means of scholastic logic. In his *Defensio Regie Assertionis* (1525), Fisher sets up twelve points on which he thinks Luther has erred, proving his arguments with copious citations from the Fathers and the Bible. His *Assertionis Lutheranae Confutatio* (1523) opens with a series of nine "truths," each one of which is logically premised upon its predecessor. In order to prove the first of these truths, Fisher feels obliged to trace the history of heresy from the beginning of the Church to the time at which he is writing. Each of these truths is proved by two lists of citations—first a scriptural, then a patristic one. The *Sacri sacerdotii defensio* (1525) is neatly arranged in three parts. The first part consists entirely of patristic citation, the second, of a series of axioms based on Scripture, and the last, of a rebuttal of all of Luther's attacks on the Church to date. To demonstrate the truth of his first axiom, which states that some there must be whose function it is to look after the welfare of the human soul, Fisher thinks it necessary to discuss the six spiritual dangers to the Christian life and to prove the existence of each danger by a string of scriptural quotations.

In contrast to the scholastic method which Fisher employs in his works, More commences the *Dialogue* with a discussion of the Bilney case, a subject very much on the popular mind in 1528-1529. Thomas Bilney was a young Cambridge scholar who, in September, 1527, was forced to do public penance for entertaining and preaching heretical opinions. More discusses this case first at his interlocutor's request. As the messenger is supposed to represent the average Englishman, unsettled by the recent religious upheaval, it may be inferred that More opens his dialogue with the subject which he thinks will attract most public attention.

That More does use the Bilney case as an attention-getting device is indicated by the fact that it is soon dropped for a general consideration of the Reformers' doctrines and is not taken up again and fully discussed until the third book.

On the surface, the *Dialogue* gives the impression of disorder, for More allows the messenger to wander at will from one point to another, and he himself shows no reluctance to follow his puppet's lead. This method is not logical, but, as we have seen, the logical method had not met with much success in the past. It is the method, or rather the lack of method, of actual verbal argument and has the advantages of both avoiding tedium by dramatic devices and allowing its author a free hand. Thus More's use of the dialogue does not force him to exhaust a subject, once broached, but allows him to take it up, drop it, and then reinsert it wherever he thinks it most effective.

More's *Dialogue* is a kind of drama, and in a play a character is judged as much by what he says and by what is said to him as by any of his actions. Besides wanting to proclaim and justify Catholic doctrine, More intends his readers to get a definite picture of the young man with whom he is disputing. It is improbable that More means his interlocutor to represent an out-and-out heretic, but he does portray him as leaning toward the Reformers, whose cause he is, after a fashion, made to defend. If nothing else, the messenger is weak in the Catholic faith. One cannot but wonder if these disputations had as their prototype More's spiritual wrestlings with his son-in-law, William Roper, a young man just like this one, who was finally brought back to the orthodox fold not by More's reasoning but by his prayers.[124]

More's picture of the young man and, by implication, of those who share his beliefs is not a flattering one. His education does not extend beyond a knowledge of some Latin—the basic course of study in the Tudor grammar school. "As for other faculties he rought not of" (*W*, p. 111). Although he has some acquaintance with the text of Scripture, he finds this text hard enough to understand in itself, without bothering with the glosses to it. That is, he does not possess enough intelligence to realize that the purpose of the glosses is elucidation of the text. As for philosophy—which he has never studied, and consequently is in no position to judge—that he thinks the greatest vanity of all (*W*, p. 111).

He will believe nothing but what is contained in Scripture: "But surely [says More] both nature and reason wil declare and tech vs that a god there is. Wel quod he, I wil not stick in this, sith saint Paule saithe so" (*W*, p. 129). More clearly shows his reaction to such an attitude and, incidentally, indicates that his unfavorable depiction of the messenger is a calculated one when he rebukes him for putting no faith in any study but that of the Scriptures. More says that he would never advise any one to study the Scriptures in such a fashion. He claims that there are many who thus feign simplicity, but that it is really pride which causes them to reject all other learning, and that it is because their interpretations of the Scriptures are opposed by the old Doctors that they dispraise these Doctors and, therefore, all learning generally (*W*, p. 150). Thus More uses the character of the messenger himself to depict what he thinks is wrong with the opposing side and, as in so many Renaissance dialogues, the opposition is condemned by its own words.

In his unfavorable delineation of the simple messenger inclined to Protestantism, More is also reversing a tradition. For the simple character was traditionally anticlerical, as in *Piers Plowman* and, more notably, *Pierce the Ploughman's Creed*. He naturally developed during the Reformation into the simple Protestant who, nevertheless, is more than a match for his learned Catholic adversaries, as we have observed in Manuel's *Barbali*.[125] More makes certain that for once the "simple" Protestant will really be simple—and be soundly thrashed by his learned Catholic opponent, More.

For, just as Filelfo did, More creates a very favorable character for himself in the *Dialogue*. It is established right at the beginning of the work that while the messenger's learning is limited to the Scriptures, More is a respected scholar whose opinion will be recognized as the final arbiter of the religious questions in dispute. More reminds his friend who has sent the messenger of the agreement arrived at: "ye had in me and my lernynge, so speciall trust & confidence, that in any of all these thinges, who so euer ye had herde, or shoulde hyre els where, ye were fully determined to geue full credence to me, & take for the trouthe such answere, as he [the messenger] shoulde bringe you from me . . ." (*W*, p. 111).

More uses still other methods to emphasize his own learning. For instance, very often in the *Dialogue*, using a technique reminiscent of Augustine's, he is not so much arguing with his interlocutor as teaching him by the method of question and answer. This is particularly clear in the section where More shows his pupil-antagonist that while we may regard miracles as being against reason, we daily accept without question events which are actually much more wondrous than the miracles of which he is so skeptical (*W*, pp. 126-127).

We are also shown that the messenger is conscious of his inferiority to More, whom he treats with great respect. Before objecting to what More has said, the messenger will usually first ask permission: "Howbeit yf I durst doubt in y^t point, one thing is ther y^t somwhat

sticketh in my mind." And More always graciously gives his permission: "Doubt on . . . & spare not, nor let not to tell me what
moueth you" (*W*, p. 144).

More's graciousness to the messenger stems from the desire to portray himself not only as a scholar but also as a gentleman. Since in an
argument it is the gentleman's part to be fair to his opponent, More
makes certain that the readers of the *Dialogue* will have ample opportunity to observe just how fair he is. After he has refuted some of the
messenger's main points, More asks:

> How thynke you . . . is ther any thyng in this matter amisse?
> I ca*n* not well tell q*uod* he, what I might aunswer therto. But
> yet methi*n*k that I come to this point by some ouersight in
> graunting.
>
> Well q*uod* I, me*n* say sometyme when they would saye or doo
> a thyng and cannot well come thereon, but misse and ouersee
> themselfe in the assaye, it maketh no matter they saye, ye maye
> beginne agayne and mende it, for it is nother masse nor mat-
> tyns. And all be it in this matter, ye haue nothyng granted but
> y^t is in my mind as true as the mattins or the masse either, yet
> if ye reken your self ouer swift in graunting I geue you leue to
> go backe & cal againe what ye wyll (*W*, pp. 145–146).

More even points out to the messenger that his case is not really
so bad as it looks: "Ye haue not yet q*uod* I lost al that labour. For
though ye haue halfe a checke in this pointe, yet haue ye (if ye perceiue it) mated me in an other point . . ." (*W*, p. 148). After some
banter, More reveals the point to his opponent, who was completely
unaware of it.

Not only is More very fair to his adversary, but he also treats him
with great kindness, often appearing to agree with his argument. For
instance, when the messenger claims that some miracles are false,
More momentarily aids him by himself citing various examples of
supposedly false miracles (*W*, p. 128). Frequently, More generously
commends the messenger's skill in argument with remarks such as
"That is in my minde . . . wel taken," or "Verye well saide" (*W*, p.
142).

As becomes the scholar-gentleman, More is modest. Before answering the messenger's charge that priests encourage superstition for

mercenary motives, More belittles his own competence (and, incidentally, the messenger's) to speak on the subject. He asks the messenger whether he has any intention of becoming a priest; the messenger answers in the negative. Then More explains that, since he
himself has been married twice, he cannot become a priest, and adds,
"we two be not the most metely to ponder what might be said in
this matter for the priestes parte" (*W*, p. 120).

Finally, since a gentleman should be pleasant company, More pictures himself throughout the *Dialogue* as the gracious host—although
he keeps his guest engaged in conversation long past Lady More's
call to dinner—one who likes to hear and tell a "merry tale" and who
extends every courtesy to the young man whom he is entertaining
in his garden at Chelsea, where the scene of the *Dialogue* is set.

One of the main facilities the dialogue form offers for the exercise
of controversial technique has already been noted as practiced by
Hutten, Manuel, Murner, and Filelfo. The writer of a dialogue is at
once the author, casting agent, and director of his drama. He determines what is to be said, who is to say it, and the particular sequence
in which it is to be said. The characters are his creations, his puppets;
and while he may allow them to roam seemingly at will at the end
of a long and almost invisible string, that string is, nevertheless,
always there, and there is no question as to who is manipulating it.
In a polemical dialogue there is never any doubt about who is going
to win all the arguments, for the form allows its author to reserve
the strongest points for himself, to make his opponent dispute more
weakly than he would in actual debate, and to put opinions into his
mouth which he does not really entertain.

Of all these opportunities More avails himself fully, and it must be
his keenly developed sense of irony which causes him to compliment
the messenger, his own creation, in these words: "ye haue not faintly
defended your part, as though it wer a corrupted aduocate, y^t would
by collusion handle his clientes matter febly for the pleasure of his
aduersary, but ye haue saide therein I can not tell whether as muche
as any man may saye, but certainly I suppose as much as ye either
haue hard any man say or can your self say" (*W*, p. 141).

For instance, in developing his argument on the nature of the
church More asks his interlocutor: "But ye grant q*uod* I, y^t the

church ca*n* not erre in the right faith necessary to be beleued, whiche is geuen & alway kept in ye church by god. Trouth, q*uod* he" (*W*, p. 145). That Tyndale's reply to this question would not have been a simple "Trouth" can be seen from a passage in his *An answere vnto Sir Thomas Mores dialoge* in which he accuses More of purposely confusing the terms under discussion: "As he iuggleth with this terme *church*, makyng vs in the begynnyng vnderstand all that beleue, and in the conclusion the Priestes onely" (*Ww*, p. 330). By the word "church" More means what Tyndale would call the Roman Church, and More knew well enough that Tyndale would never have granted him that this church could not err.

Again, in one of the debates on the rival claims of Church and Scripture, More asks the messenger how he came to believe that Christ was born of a virgin, to which the messenger replies that he came to this belief by Scripture. More then asks if this matter were not contained in Scripture but only in the creed, would the messenger believe the creed: "The Crede quod he is a thyng by it self . . . And yet I thynke [says More], yf ghospell hadde neuer bene written, ye wold haue beleued your Crede. So thynke I too quod he" (*W*, p. 174). Considering the fact that the Reformers were most emphatic on just this point, that only Scripture was to be taken as authority for what was to be believed, it is clear that none of them would have given the messenger's answer.

On hearing from More that Tyndale's translation rendered *ecclesia* as "congregation" and *caritas* as "love," the messenger shows no hesitation in concluding "y^t it was not wel nor wisely done, there wyl I trowe no good wyse man deny" (*W*, p. 221). Of this, Tyndale was not quite as confident as the messenger who, according to More, had "not faintly defended . . . [his] part."

As a matter of fact, throughout the *Dialogue* the messenger shows less and less opposition to More, until by the fourth book he has become a mere yes-man to More's rhetorical questions, "Very true . . . by my trouthe," being his stock answer. The *Dialogue* ends with More and his opponent engaged in friendly rivalry to see who can most effectively pull apart Tyndale's *Obedience of a Christen man*.

More realizes that even good dialogue, when administered in large doses, can become tedious, and he therefore occasionally intersperses his work with straight narration. He does this very skillfully, making the narrative parts an outgrowth of the dramatic situation. On one occasion More's young companion returns crestfallen from the university, where he has tried to defend the propositions to which More has forced him to assent. He has been badly put down in his attempt, and this provides More with an opportunity to tell him all the arguments he should have presented (*W*, p. 203 ff.).

Another variation More sometimes introduces into his dialogue is the verbatim report of conversations between speakers other than himself and the messenger. Another time More cites the account of a trial he has attended, which contains a lengthy dialogue between the judges and a witness (*W*, pp. 236-237).

More has an additional reason for relating the events of this particular trial; some aspects of it are quite amusing, and the humor relieves the doctrinal discussion which takes up many pages.

"Merry Tales" and More's Humor as a Weapon

Much of the humor[126] in the *Dialogue* takes the form of the "merry tale."[127] More was not certain that these tales were appropriate to a work of religious controversy, and he tells us that this was one of the reasons he submitted his manuscript to the examination of others before he published it (*W*, p. 106). To help ease his mind on this score, he arranges matters so that most of the tales are told by the messenger rather than by himself. In this way he manages to include their substance without incurring the onus of narrating them himself.

Another effect More achieves by having the messenger tell most of the "merry tales" is to lower him in the estimation of the *Dialogue*'s readers. For in this work More manages to achieve an air of such verisimilitude that the reader is apt to forget that More is the author both of his own part and of the messenger's and to regard the statements of the latter as those of a real person. Some of the tales the messenger tells are very bawdy, and if More's reputation as a serious writer can be questioned by Tyndale because More is a poet who has "feigned" matters in his *Utopia* (*Ww*, pp. 318, 330), these tales are not calculated to present the messenger to his Tudor audience as a morally earnest Reformer, righteously indignant at the vices of a corrupt clergy. Following the technique of other controversialists, More thus adds to his unfavorable delineation of the messenger.

The most obvious reason for the introduction of a humorous story is to relieve monotony, and this is very often its purpose in the *Dialogue*—which contains some lengthy passages of doctrinal exposition —and in More's other English controversial works, in all of which he strives for popular appeal. But, as any good writer does, More practices economy in the devices he uses, and rarely does the narration of a humorous anecdote serve a single purpose only.

It appears that one of the functions More assigns to the device of the "merry tale" is to divert his readers' attention from the points at issue. He uses it for this purpose in his discussion of the case of Richard Hunne, who was apprehended on a charge of heresy and was found hanged in the Lollard's Tower a few days after he had been imprisoned there. The clergy maintained that Hunne had committed suicide, but a coroner's inquest brought in a verdict of murder against the chancellor of the Bishop of London, whereupon the Reformers accused "the clergy" of being responsible for Hunne's death.[128]

More defends the clergy and asserts that Hunne committed suicide but gives no evidence to support his claim. Instead he supplies a very humorous, pretended verbatim report of the examination of those witnesses who testified that Hunne had indeed been murdered. At the trial, begins More, the greatest temporal lord who was there turned to one of his servants and asked to be shown the man who could identify Hunne's murderer, whereupon the servant pointed out a man who was in the courtroom. However, this person denied that he had ever made such a claim, but had said that he had a neighbor who could make the identification. When the lord inquired where that neighbor was, another man was brought forward who, in his turn, was asked if he could identify Hunne's murderer. But this man also denied any such ability, saying what he had really said was that he had a friend who told him he could do it, and with this he produced his friend. His friend, on being questioned as to whether he had made such a claim, protested that he had made it not for himself but for an acquaintance of his, a woman. The lord who was pre-

siding over the trial then asked him how he knew that this woman
could tell who had murdered Hunne, to which the man answered
that he had heard her reveal so many wonderful things—for instance,
if anything were stolen she could say who had taken it—that he
thought she could certainly tell such a little thing as who had murdered Richard Hunne.

More continues his account of the trial by telling of another witness
who asserted that he knew definitely that Hunne did not hang himself, whereupon he was asked how he knew that. At this, says More,
the man looked rather frightened, as if he had said too much, and,
in his confusion, his eyes began to bulge out of his head as though
they were about to fall into the laps of the judges. But in spite of the
fact that he was so confused before the judges that he could scarcely
see, he said that he had been able to see very well that Hunne had not
hanged himself, having seen him both before he was cut down and
afterward. To this the judges replied that there had been many people
who had also seen Hunne's body, but, nevertheless, were unable to
say whether he had hanged himself. The man answered that these
people did not have his experience in such matters, since he had been
working for a long time under several of the King's almoners, in
which capacity he had seen many people who had hanged themselves and so could tell whether a man had taken his own life or been
killed by another. When the man was asked by what signs he could
make such a distinction, he answered that he did not bother about
signs but that he could tell well enough by his own sight. But when
the judges, continues More, heard him speak of his own sight and at
the same time saw what kind of sight he had, with his eyes ready to
fall out of his head, few could refrain from laughing and telling each
other that this man had a very special sight indeed.

Then one of the judges asked the man how many men who had
hanged themselves he had seen in his official capacity, to which the
man answered that he had seen many, although he could not tell the
exact number. One of the judges asked him if he had seen a hundred;
the man replied that he had not seen quite so many. When he was
asked if he had seen ninety, he considered deeply for a while as if
unwilling to give false testimony and after some time said that he
thought he had not seen fully that number. Then, More continues
with his account, he was asked whether he had seen twenty, and to

that, without any hesitation, he answered no, he had not seen twenty. That a man who was in doubt whether he had seen ninety could be so sure that he had not seen twenty made all the judges laugh. Then he was asked whether he had seen fifteen, to which he said no, and likewise of ten. At last they came down to five and from five to four, and at that number he thought again for a long time before he admitted he had not seen so many. When they came down to three, the man, to maintain his reputation, said he had seen so many and more too, but when he was asked the circumstances, he was finally forced to admit that in all his life he had seen only one man who had actually hanged himself (*W*, pp. 236-237).

These stories sound a little too humorous to be factual verbatim reports, which is how More presents them, but they do serve the purpose of diverting the reader's attention from the fact that no specific evidence has been presented to support More's contention that Hunne committed suicide. The point at issue is here obscured not only by the humor of these stories but also by their very length.

Throughout the *Dialogue*, More tries to give the impression of being very fair to the Reformers; he claims that he has presented their point of view at least as strongly as they themselves could have done (*W*, p. 141). Consequently he has the messenger make several charges against the clergy, one of which is that many of them lead immoral lives. To substantiate his charge of clerical immorality, the messenger recounts a long tale of obscene practices carried on in what More calls a French abbey. As the account is also very humorous, it serves to enliven the particular portion of the work in which it appears. More conveniently answers the tale by saying that since the place is in France, he will leave the matter to the University of Paris to defend. Thus, while giving the impression he has somehow dealt with the matter, by use of a "merry tale" More avoids replying to the original charge (*W*, p. 198).

One occasion on which More appears to introduce a humorous anecdote merely for the sake of enlivening his book is during the discussion on miracles, which leads to the question of the credibility of witnesses. On this point More tells the messenger that the best witnesses he knows are the messenger's own two eyes; this causes the messenger to remember a funny story, which he begs leave to tell. "A mery tale quod I, commith neuer amysse to me," answers More, and the messenger tells the story of a poor man who saw the parish priest being too familiar with his wife. When he complained to the bishop, he was not believed and was ordered to recant publicly: ". . . than he sett his handys on his mouth, & said, mouth mouth thou lyest. And by and by thereupon he set his hand vpon both his eyen & sayd, but eyen eyen q*uod* he, by ye masse ye lye not a whitte" (*W*, p. 127).

In his controversy with Tyndale, More used other devices besides the "merry tale" for purposes of obscuring the issue or avoiding a point, for instance, the *reductio ad absurdum*. During a discussion of the Reformers' opinion on confession, More tells the messenger that Luther thinks it permissible to confess to women as well as to men. More finds that he need do little to refute this opinion, for on hearing it the messenger expresses the view that if he might be confessed by a beautiful woman he would go to confession weekly, whereas now he feels like going scarcely once in seven years (*W*, p. 249).

We have another instance of humor being substituted for refutation during More's discussion of the practice of giving homage to saints, one of the few occasions on which he allows himself to make the witty comment. When reminded by the messenger that women actually implore St. Wilgefort to relieve them of undesirable husbands, More replies that he cannot see any great harm in that, for their prayers might be answered in more ways than one. For instance, says More, they may be relieved if their husbands change and therefore become desirable, or if the wives themselves learn to curb their undesirable tongues, which are probably the cause of all their trouble. But, More concludes, if they can be relieved only by death, it may be by their own, and so their husbands would still be unharmed.[129] Here again More uses humor to counter the Reformers' charges of abuses.

A classic instance of *reductio* occurs in the *Confutacyon*, where More is dealing with Tyndale's claim that a member of the true church sins and yet has no sin imputed to him, on account of his faith. I suppose, speculates More, this would be the attitude of Tyndale and his followers toward lying with a harlot:

> . . . then al the waye they go, they say to God and the*m* selfes,
> ywys though I go thither with my feete, yet I wyll not agree to

go thither with myne hart lo. Nor I would not come at her at all good Lord, sauing that vpon ye great occasion that I hadde when I sawe her ones, I then lyked her so well, that I am now caried thyther euen in a rage. But yet for all the rage, I wyl not cast of thy yoke good Lorde, but I wyll carye thy yoke styll about my necke to bedde with her, and put it aboute her necke to, and yoke vs both together. And yet after all thys lo, when all the rage is paste that nowe haryeth me forth in an heate thorowe the fruite of synne, which remayning in my flesh, breaketh out of my members, then wyll I repent it good Lorde, and be sory therfore, & retourne agayne from her to thee, or els bryng her yoked with me to. And then wyl I pray thee of pardon. And then thou must nedes good Lord forthwith at the first worde, gyue me full remyssyon of synne, and payne. . . . And thys good minde good Lord will I keepe styll and neuer let it fall out of my hart, so that al the while that I lye bassing with Besse, and I am doying that horrible dede with my body, yet will I neuer agree therto with my hart (*W*, p. 557).

Very closely allied to the above technique is that of irony; of this More is a past master. As an example of the fact that the elect never sin except when tempted far beyond their strength to resist, Tyndale cites the case of David's sin with Bathsheba and his desire to kill Nabal, the husband of Abigail. On this More comments ironically that when David wanted to slay Nabal and all his sons, even to the child in the cradle, it must be understood he did not have this intention without great provocation. For, as Tyndale tells us, the rude fellow had given David a discourteous answer. More asks who would be so unreasonable as to think that a king or any great man had not cause enough to kill twenty of the common people for the uncivil conduct of one of them. Likewise, he continues, when David committed adultery and murder we can see that he again had great provocation beyond his power to resist, so that we must excuse him. For, as Tyndale tells us, he saw a woman as he looked out of his window. Therefore, More concludes with a *reductio ad absurdum*, whoever catches sight of a woman is excusable if he takes her when he can, except a blind man or one who takes a woman in the dark whom he has never seen in the light (*W*, pp. 593-594).

Tyndale calls David's sin a sleep, implying by this that the elect can never sin unto damnation, but that when they awaken out of their sleep of sin they always return to God. More comments sarcastically that David must have been in a very deep sleep indeed if he did all the devilish deeds recorded of him in his sleep. I suppose, says More, that Tyndale lay beside David and heard him snore—and unless he can prove to me that he did this, I shall never believe that David spied Bathsheba, sent for her, talked with her, got her pregnant, sent for her husband, devised his murder, wrote the letter sending him to his death—all of which happened on various days—while he was sleeping (*W*, p. 595).

More was attacked for using humor in religious controversy, and he felt impelled to defend his use of this weapon. In his *Apologye*, he says that although he may tell an occasional humorous story, he is nevertheless very much in earnest in his defense of the Church. He goes on to say that as a layman it becomes him more to speak his mind in his accustomed manner than to assume a false gravity and solemnly preach to his readers (*Apologye*, p. 194).

False gravity never was characteristic of More or of his writings; he delighted in humor. It is their qualities of humor and wit which chiefly distinguish More's epigrams from those of his humanist predecessors and contemporaries.[130] Beatus Rhenanus, in his preface to More's *Epigrammata*, says of him that he is every inch pure jest.[131] More himself tells us that he was prompted to translate certain dialogues of Lucian because of their stinging sarcasm and amusing wit.[132]

More often joked with such a solemn face that it was impossible to tell whether or not he was in earnest.[133] Actually, many of his humorous works do have a serious purpose, and some of his serious works contain much humor. His early *A mery gest how a sergeaunt wolde lerne to be a frere* illustrates the former tendency: It is full of boisterous fun, but makes the serious point that the man who meddles in matters about which he is ignorant will come to no good, including, significantly, the meddler in theology. Again, while the *Utopia* is full of humor in the form of irony, satire, and witty anecdotes, it is also a crushing indictment of Christian Europe and was not regarded by More's contemporaries as a mere exercise in humanist wit.[134] To illustrate the other tendency in More's work, we have his *Richard the thirde*, a serious historical work exposing tyranny but sparkling with satiric asides and ironic comments. There is also his *A dialogue of comfort*, written while More was a prisoner in the Tower awaiting the possibility of a horrible death—a work wherein one might expect him to be most serious—which contains some of the merriest of his "merry tales."[135]

And so it was consistent with his habit of jesting while very much in earnest that, in his determined struggle to preserve the Catholic faith, More made humor one of his main weapons. Commenting on this in More's own day, Frith claimed that More had inserted so many humorous and bawdy tales into his work that if they were taken away, there would be very little else left.[136] Frith somewhat overstated the case, but it is obvious that More felt humor was a useful weapon against those who were attacking the Church.

More's Use of Authority, Logic, Rhetoric, and History

Another of his weapons was reference to authority. One of the forms this particular technique takes is the frequent mention of the great number of people who have believed as the Church does over such a long period of time, as compared with the small number who share the opinions of the Reformers. For instance, in the *Dialogue* More uses the argument from numbers when he reminds the messenger that all the saints and Fathers believed with the Church, while not a single saint or Father ever expressed opinions similar to those held by the Reformers (*W*, p. 199). In the *Confutacyon*, he conjures up a vision of the entire host of Christendom being contradicted by one puny Reformer: Who could be so mad as to think that

> neither Bishoppe, nor Pope, nor whole general counsayle, nor all christen people together, though they were al assembled vppon a playne, were able so to commaunde so much as a general procession vpon any certayne daie, but that any lewde lither losill that liste not to ryse, maye lye styll in his bedde, and saye he is not bounden to obey mannes tradicions . . . (*W*, p. 509).

Although More is careful not to follow Fisher in wearying his readers with long lists of patristic citations, his appeals to the authority of the Fathers are fairly numerous. Augustine, on whom he had lectured in the church of St. Lawrence Jewry, is his particular favorite, although his knowledge of patristic literature in general is surprisingly extensive for a layman.[137]

His favorite reference, which he uses over and over again, is to Augustine's famous letter *Contra Epistolam Manichaei,* in which Augustine states that he would not have believed the gospel had he not been moved thereto by the authority of the Catholic Church.[138] Quoting this against Tyndale in their dispute about the relative authority of Church and Scripture, More comments that Augustine was quite right, for were it not for the Holy Spirit keeping God's truth in the Church, who could be sure whether he had the correct version of the gospel (*W*, p. 175)?

More wonders if the practice of confessing to the priest is so evil as Tyndale claims it is, since none of the holy Fathers discovered this before Tyndale came along (*W*, p. 249). So far as Luther's theology is concerned, More concludes that because so many holy doctors believed as the Church does now, it would be foolish to change and believe such a false heretic as Luther (*W*, p. 313). To support the contention that the bread and wine are changed into the body and blood of Christ, More cites passages from Theophylactus, St. Bede, St. Cyril, and St. Augustine.[139]

More also appeals to custom to justify the practices of the Church. He does not, as Hooker does in the first book of *Of the lawes of ecclesiasticall politie,* suggest that custom embodies the tried wisdom of many generations, and that for this reason the customary way is probably the best. He claims instead that whatever has been practiced for so long by the Church must be correct because God would not allow His Church to remain in error (*W*, pp. 124, 250, 414).

While More is at pains to prove that the authority of the Church is superior to that of the Scriptures, he does not deny himself recourse to the latter. Actually he was well aware of the tactical advantages to be gained by confuting his opponent with the help of the Scriptures, which the Reformers regarded as the only authority for church doctrine. Therefore, whenever he could prove a point by Scripture, he was very pleased to do so.

An interesting example of More's use of Scripture can be seen in the argument in the *Dialogue* by which he establishes that the Catholic Church is the church of Christ and, consequently, infallible. His first approach to this question is not an enumeration of all those who have believed that the Catholic Church is the true one, although he permits himself this argument subsequently, but rather an examination of Scripture for the characteristics of the church of Christ. Once these are derived from Scripture, More sets out to prove their identity with the characteristics of the Catholic Church, and in this manner comes to the conclusion that the Catholic Church is the church of Christ which cannot err (*W*, p. 141 ff.).

Colet's method of biblical exegesis,[140] which takes into consideration the historical background of the scriptural text, is adopted by More only when it suits his purpose. In discussing the question of ceremonies, More makes indiscriminate use of Old Testament history to illustrate New Testament theology.[141] He uses the same technique when he attempts to prove that the Church was before the Scriptures, by applying the term "church" to the "faithful" of the period between Adam and Noah.[142] More establishes the necessity for clerical celibacy on similar ground, namely, that in the old law the priests were ordered to forbear the company of their wives when it was their turn to serve in the Temple (*W*, p. 232), while on the point of clerical vestments and images, he tells his readers that God's will cannot be more clearly seen than in the ornamentation of the Ark of the Covenant and the attire of the priests who served it (*W*, p. 115). He attempts to disprove the doctrine of justification by faith partly on the ground that God said to Cain, "If thou doe wel thou shalt haue well" (*W*, p. 268), and into an argument on the question whether or not one who has placed faith in Christ can ever perish, More introduces as proof for his point of view a text from the prophet Ezekiel (*W*, pp. 544-545).

While such a use of the Old Testament was common in More's day, it is not one of which he himself always approves. When it suits his purpose, he is quite capable of reminding his opponent that the Old and New Testaments cover two different dispensations. For instance, he will not allow Old Testament texts to be used against him on the question of image worship, called idolatry so often by Moses and the prophets, for he maintains that these words have always been

understood as addressed to the Jews under the Law, who were a
people prone to idolatry (*W*, p. 113). Again, when Tyndale cites
the third chapter of I Timothy, which says that a bishop should be
the husband of one wife, and uses this text to attack clerical celibacy,
More, among other arguments, has recourse to Colet's method of
interpretation, explaining that the text is aimed at the custom of
bigamy which was prevalent among heathen converts to Christianity
in the early churches, and that the text means that if a man were
already married when he became a priest, he might retain one wife
only, but that the text does not mean that he had to have a wife to
become a priest (*W*, p. 229).

One authority More's opponent does not share with him is that of
reason. It would be incorrect to state that the Reformers rejected
reason as a weapon of controversy—they could not have carried on
the controversy at all if they had done so—and there are many examples of Tyndale's appealing to reason, for instance, in his insistence
that Scripture must be interpreted within its context (*Ww*, p. 167).
However, they never made reason the basis on which an argument
was to be settled; the position of final authority was reserved for the
Scriptures, and for the Scriptures alone. More draws attention to the
Reformers' attitude when he makes the messenger declare at the outset of the *Dialogue*, "I take reason for playne enmye [*sic*] to faith"
(*W*, p. 148).

More's respect for reason can be seen in all his works of religious
controversy. His appeal to other authorities, such as the opinions of
the Fathers, the customs of the Church, and the number of those
who share his faith, is usually reinforced by the claim that these are
reasonable authorities to which to appeal. Consequently, when More
cites miracles as proof that God favors the Catholics, he is not content
to say that the Church has vouched for the existence of miracles, and
therefore the Church must be believed; he feels obliged to point out
that miracles are no more unreasonable than many events accepted as
the commonplace of everyday life (*W*, p. 132). To the messenger's
objection that many of the miracles are merely impositions on the
credulity of an ignorant laity, More answers that since God has promised to keep the right faith in the Church forever, it would not be
reasonable to suppose that He would permit the devil to work within

it false miracles which would lead it into the wrong faith (*W*, p. 145).
He concludes that miracles are not really against nature, but are above
it (*W*, p. 130).

What has been said of More's respect for reason suggests alterna-
tively an investigation of his abuse of reason in the form of logical
fallacies throughout his controversy with Tyndale. As already noted,
whether some or all of these fallacies are intentional, or whether they
are merely lapses in logic, it is impossible to determine.

On numerous occasions More uses *ad hominem* argument. For
instance, in spite of the fact that he has not read them, he is quite
ready to condemn Tyndale's translations of the five books of Moses,
for they are translated "we nede not doubte in what maner, when we
know by what man & for what purpose" (*W*, p. 341).

The most prominent case of *ad hominem* argument in all of More's
works is his abuse of Luther. The *Dialogue* in particular is riddled
with references to Luther's marriage, and very often this subject is
dragged into a discussion to which it is at first sight irrelevant, as
when More discusses the question of authority:

> Thus quod I, as if Luther late a frere & hauyng now wedded a
> Nonne, were commaunded to amende his lewde lyuynge and
> put away that harlot, whom he abuseth in continuall incest and
> sacrilege vnder the name of a wife . . . (*W*, p. 168).

In another part of the same work More says:

> Forsoth quod I, they can not but knowe hys open lyuyng in
> lechery with hys lewde lemman the nunne. . . . And bi this can
> thei not doute but y^t their doctryne is nought . . . (*W*, p. 262).

These references to Luther's marriage are meant to impugn not
only his sexual morality but also his credibility—at the very least, his
wisdom. For when referring to the subject, More usually includes the
matter of the broken oath of celibacy, implying that Luther is either
a knave for committing perjury or a fool for having taken what he
now claims is a stupid vow (cf. *W*, pp. 247-248).

In the *Confutacyon* More falls into the habit of attempting to
clinch every argument by reminding his opponent of Luther's lechery and broken vows to God. For instance, he ends a discussion on
what the ancient Doctors said about the nature of the true church

by asking Tyndale to show him "which holy doctours of all that longe time before, dyd constre the scripture so, that any of them woulde saye y^t a monke might wedde a nunne" (*W*, p. 472).

Ironically, after he has used so much *ad hominem* argument against Luther, More complains that Tyndale is using this kind of argument to criticize the institution of the papacy, and he advises Tyndale not to judge the office by its evil occupants, of which, More admits, there have been some (*W*, p. 616).

Continuing our investigation of More's use of specious reasoning as part of his controversial technique, we find that one of his favorite devices, cited by Tyndale in his complaint about More's method of conducting the controversy, is to change the meaning of his terms in the middle of an argument. An instance of this occurs during the discussion of the relative authority of Church and Scripture. To the messenger's assertion that we may believe only Scripture, More counters:

> what if neuer scripture had ben writen in this worlde, should there neuer haue bene any churche or congregacion of faithfull and right beleuyng people? . . . were there neuer any folke that beleued in God, & had a true faith betwene Adam & Noe. . . ? And why did any ma*n* tha*n* beleue ye church that is to witte the nombre & co*n*gregacion of good and right beleuyng folke. . . ?

Then More makes his final point, by asking the messenger: "I praye you tell me, what scripture hath taught ye church to know which bookes be the very scripture . . ." (*W*, pp. 205-206)?

More's argument is that the authority of the Church is superior to that of Scripture, and by "the church" he means the Christian church as it has come down to his day. For he makes it very clear at the outset of the discussion that it is the Christian church to which he is referring, and not any other body:

> Mary q*uod* he there might be some churche of heretikes before the church of Christ. For there might bee some amonge the Iewes before the byrthe of Christ. And suche I suppose were the Saduces that beleued not the resurreccion nor the immortalitie of the soule. If we should go q*uod* I to that reckening, we myght

fetche the churche of Christ farre aboue, and begin it at Ada*m*.
. . . But I speke of Christes churche nowe, as of ye congregacio*n*
y^t bering his name . . . shal till his comming to the dreadfull
dome, continue still in this worlde . . . (*W*, p. 180).

And again, a little later on, he repeats that it is the Christian church
he is talking about and none other (*W*, p. 185).

But in the argument he uses to support the claim that the Church's
authority is superior to that of Scripture, More does not assign a
constant meaning to the term being discussed. At the beginning of the
cited passage the word "church" means "the nombre & congregacion
of good and right beleuyng folk," a body which existed in Old Testament times, and which was consequently composed of non-Christians
—and which More said he would exclude from the argument—while
at the close of the argument the term "church" has clearly come to
mean the Christian church, which More identifies with the Catholic.

Not only is More's Old Testament use of the word "church" not
the usual one, but it is actually the use to which he professes to be
most opposed. On two separate occasions he violently attacks Tyndale for comparing the church of Christ to the Old Testament
congregation of the Jews,[143] while one of the main objections More
makes against Tyndale's New Testament is that it has equated the
words "church" and "congregation":

> For he hath mysse translated three woordes of great weighte. . . .
> The one is quod I this worde (priests). The other the Churche. . . .
> For euery manne well seeth that though the church be in dede a
> congregacion, yet is not euery congregacion the church: but a
> congregacion of christe*n* people. . . .[144]

The controversy over the authority of the Church as opposed to
the Scriptures also contains an instance of circular reasoning. More
contends that the Scriptures themselves acknowledge the superior
authority of the Church, but complains that the reason the Reformers
fail to see this is that they do not read the Scriptures in the proper
spirit; before one can really understand the Scriptures, one must

> come well and surely enstructed, in all suche pointes and articles
> as the churche beleueth. . . . And so let him reuerently knowldge

> his ignoraunce, lene and cleue to the faith of the churche as to
> an vndouted trouth . . . (*W*, pp. 151–152).

That is, to find out whether or not the Scriptures acknowledge the
superior authority of the Church, one must first grant that this superior authority already exists, and then there will be no difficulty in
finding it in the Scriptures.

In an age dedicated to the worship of Cicero, the Ciceronian device
of *praeteritio* was a favorite among controversialists.[145] Although
More employed this device quite frequently elsewhere, he uses it only
once in his controversy with Tyndale, during his treatment of the
Bilney case:

> I will not quod I as I tolde you in yᵉ beginnyng go about to
> reproue his lyuyng, sith yᵉ question standeth not but in his tech-
> ing. And yet maye I be bolde with you to tell you what I haue
> harde (*W*, p. 207).

Whereupon More becomes very bold indeed.

As a variation of the above technique, he uses innuendo. It was a
favorite device of the humanists in their altercations with each
other,[146] and More sometimes finds it a more potent weapon for
character assassination than direct accusation. In the *Dialogue*, the
messenger stresses the zeal and devotion of certain Reformers, together with the holy lives they lead, which support their professions
of faith. To this More replies that we should not judge these Reformers by outward appearances, for we

> little also can tell what abhominacions they may doe to some
> of them secretly. Nor yet can know theyr intent and purpose
> that they appoynt vpon, and the cause for whiche they be for
> the whyle content to take all the payn. Very certayne is it that
> pryde is one cause wherfore they take yᵉ payn. For pryde is, as
> saynt Austine sayeth, the verye mother of all heresies (*W*, p.
> 282).

The final deduction is a pretty piece of logic.

More uses the same tactics against Tyndale when he states that the
heretics are of two kinds, those who are wicked openly and those
who, for the present, still maintain an appearance of morality. Luther
and his followers have married and are wicked openly,

and if any do otherwise, it is for some purpose for the while to blinde the people & kepe theym selfe in fauour, while they may fynde the tyme by leisoure to fassion & frame them better to their purpose, which in the beginning if they shewed them self plainly, could happeli not abide to heare them (*W*, p. 262).

However, More does his best to include Tyndale among those heretics who are wicked openly. Some Reformers asserted that I Timothy iii.2[147] gave sanction for priests to be married, to which More replies that it is remarkable that God should have hidden this interpretation of the text from so many holy Fathers,

til now y^t God hath at laste by reuelacion shewed this high secrete misterie to these twoo goodly creatures, Luther and Tyndal, lest that holy freer should haue lost hys maryage of that holy Nonne, and Tindal som good maryage that I think him towarde (*W*, p. 229).

Tyndale never did marry, and there is no evidence that he ever contemplated doing so.

Therefore, as More never does succeed in digging up anything which he considers scandalous about Tyndale's life to use against him as he uses Luther's marriage to refute that Reformer's writings, he is forced to hint at the existence of what cannot be found: "Now wene I that we nede litle to doubte howe he liueth, that thus wryteth. He liueth, of likelihod, as euill as he teacheth, and worse he cannot" (*W*, p. 284).

Quite frequently More indulges in the fallacy of assuming the premise, as when he claims that the Holy Spirit taught many things unwritten and gives for an example the fact that it is the custom to mingle water with the wine at Mass. He points out to Tyndale that this the Church was taught without Scripture: "And now is ye church so well acertened of goddes pleasure therin without any scripture, that thei not only dare put in water, but also dare not leue it out" (*W*, p. 161). More here takes a nonscriptural tradition of the Church, assumes that because the Church holds it the tradition must have been received from the Holy Spirit, and then uses this assumption as a basis for his argument that not everything that was taught was taught by the Scriptures. Confession is justified on the same ground: "Which thing had vndoubtedly neuer been obteined among ye people . . . if god had not broughte it vp hymselfe" (*W*, p. 283).

Sometimes More misinterprets the views of the opposition; probably the most flagrant example of this is his statement that the Lutherans believe that it matters not at all how they live so long as they retain their faith (*W*, pp. 267; cf. p. 511). This is at best an oversimplification of the doctrine of justification by faith. What both Luther and Tyndale say is that, so far as salvation is concerned, the only saving medium is faith which no amount of good works can replace.[148] More's summary of this view implies that Lutheranism condones a dissolute existence, which neither Tyndale nor Luther ever do condone. More is here saddling the entire movement with the views and actions of some of its most extreme adherents—good polemics, of course, and exactly what the opposition did, for instance, in dwelling on the immorality of some Catholic clerics to impugn the morality of all.

A variation of misrepresenting the Reformed position as a whole is deliberately to misunderstand the meaning of an accurately quoted passage such as the following:

Tyndall

And that the Apostles shoulde teache ought by mouth, that they woulde not wryte, I pray you for what purpose.

More

. . . But sith he seeth hymself, that in his reasons for his own part there is so litle pith, and that he can neuer proue nor no man els, the thinges that Tindal must proue, or els proue himself a foole, for falling from the faythe of Chrystes church, y^t is to say, that the apostles left all such necessary poyntes of the faith in writing: he leaueth of now his part him self, and asketh vs why they left aughte vnwritten as though if I that neuer was of counsayle with them, can not tell vnto Tindall playnlye wherfore and why the apostles left aughte vnwritten, he myghte thereuppon conclude, that they wrote all together (*W*, p. 477).

It is reasonably clear that Tyndale is not asking More a point of information and has not forsaken his own position because he sees that it is untenable, but that he is putting a rhetorical question, meant to illustrate the absurdity of More's contention.

In order to have an excuse for twisting his opponent's meaning, More often "misunderstands" or claims that he actually does not understand the passage in question. This he does, for example, in an attempt to answer Tyndale's contention that God is not dependent on a greater or lesser number of witnesses, and that, therefore, More's argument from numbers (which states that the Catholic faith must be correct since so many people have believed in it over such a long period of time) is not valid. More tackles this by asserting that Tyndale, to support his view, has mistranslated John v.34 as "I take no recorde of man," instead of as "I receiue not the record of ma*n*." This is not done out of ignorance, says More, but is a malicious attempt to make it appear that God utterly refuses all human witnesses (*W*, p. 449). The foregoing probably seemed weak even to More, for he embarks on a lengthy grammatical exposition in justification of his version of John v.34 and in condemnation of Tyndale's. However, Tyndale never said that God accepts no kind of human witnesses whatever, and it is clear that he cited the text to confute More's argument from numbers.

Not only does More claim to have difficulty in understanding his opponent's passages, but he also tells his readers that he will be so magnanimous to Tyndale as to put the best possible construction on the words from his opponent's point of view. More then examines various possible meanings—and finds them all faulty:

> Yet would I fayne in good fayth find and bring it furth, if I could any thyng ymagine, that he myght seeme to meane ryghte, nor neuer will I wittinglye for the preferrement of my parte, construe myne aduersaries wordes wrong (*W*, p. 536).

This is of the same order as More's commending the messenger for arguing so skillfully on the other side; More evidently accepts the maxim that if you tell people often enough that you are fair, they eventually will believe you.

The converse of accusing your opponent of mistranslation is to mistranslate yourself, and this More does while advancing the doctrine that the traditions of the Church have as much sanctity as the Scriptures. The traditions we keep, says More, are the traditions of the Apostles, "For which saynte Paule sayth: *Ego enim accepi a domino quod & tradidi vobis*, For I haue received y^t thyng of our Lord by tradicion wythout wryting, the whyche I haue also delyuered vnto you" (*W*, p. 1091). The words "by tradicion wythout wryting" are in neither the letter nor the sense of the Latin,[149] and the Catholic scholars who prepared the Douay Bible translated the passage as, "For I myself have received from the Lord what I also delivered to you."[150]

We come now to an examination of More's general treatment of history as a weapon of controversy.

More frequently uses references to secular history to bolster his position. For instance, he claims that so long as the Reformers forbore violence, no harm was done to them, and had they but remained peaceable they would have been allowed to preach: they preaching to us and we preaching to them, as he put it (*W*, pp. 275-276). Conditions on the Continent, where the Reformed doctrine made greater progress than it did in England, are used by More against his opponent. He asserts that the Hussites, in spite of the fact that they have broken away from the Church, admit that "thei can not haue the sacramentes ministred, but by suche priestes as be made by authoritie deriued and connueied from the Pope which is vnder Christ vycary & the head of our churche" (*W*, p. 179). This claim, which is an oversimplification of the truth,[151] is nevertheless a powerful argument for the authority of the priesthood. Even less accurate is More's charge that Luther was once a preacher of indulgences who turned against that doctrine only when the preachership and its advantages were taken away from him and given to another (*W*, p. 254). Luther originally believed in the theory of indulgences, just as he accepted the other tenets of the Catholic faith, but there is no basis for More's assertion that Luther's change of views was due to economic rather than theological reasons.[152] Nor, as we have seen, is there any basis for More's claim that Luther wrote a book glorifying himself, which he published anonymously.[153]

Again, More ascribes the disturbances in Germany to the Reformed theology (*W*, pp. 257-258), while he sees in the Sack of Rome a direct result of Lutheranism (*W*, pp. 258-259).

More is certainly oversimplifying when he holds Luther and his teaching entirely responsible for the 1524–1525 Peasants' Revolt in

Germany; the basic causes of the revolt were economic and social.[154] It cannot even be seriously maintained that Luther himself stimulated the revolt, whatever irresponsible persons may have done with his teaching. Luther wrote three works in which, in unmistakable language, he warned against insurrection.[155]

So far as the Sack of Rome is concerned, the army which entered the city contained almost as great a number of Spanish and Italian Catholics as it did German Lutherans,[156] but one would never suspect this from reading More's account. Nor can More's version be excused on the grounds that it was only the Germans who did the actual sacking. Von Pastor writes that "all accounts coincide in giving to the Spaniards . . . the palm for ingenuity in unearthing treasure and contriving tortures, although the Italians and especially the Neopolitans were, on the whole, scarcely second to them."[157]

More likes to demonstrate that his opponents are wrong on every point possible, and he carries this technique so far as to criticize Tyndale's grammar and to set about correcting it. Every humanist worth his salt corrected his opponent's grammar, but for More this technique also serves the specific purpose of casting doubt on Tyndale's competence as a translator. For this reason More takes considerable space in the *Confutacyon* to demonstrate that Tyndale has misused "no" and "nay." According to More, the former should be used to answer a question framed in the negative, while the latter should be reserved for an answer to a question framed in the affirmative. "Ye" and "yes" require the same distinction (*W*, p. 448).

Repetition is another technique used by More. He is evidently aware of the fact that one of the simplest and most effective methods of inducing belief is to say something over and over. There are certain points he never tires of hammering home, and for this the dialogue is particularly suitable, as it allows the messenger to return repeatedly to certain questions on which he claims to be unconvinced, thus permitting More to reconvince him just as frequently. This method has the added attraction of demonstrating More's fairness, as well as his ability to refute his imaginary opponent again and again. For instance, in reply to More's claim of infallibility for the Church, the messenger counters that this infallibility holds good only so long as the Church lets herself be guided by Scripture:

> Are ye there yet agayne quod I? We haue sondry wayes proued
> & agreed betwene vs, that this knowledge and faith was before
> scripture and wryting, and many thinges of necessitie, to be both
> beleued and done, that are not in holye scripture. And yet after
> al this to long to bee repeted ye retourne agayne to the firste
> pointe so often confuted, that nothing is learned nor knowen
> but by holy scripture (*W*, p. 172).

One such constantly repeated point is that, since Christ has promised to be with his church, it cannot possibly err. More uses this so
often that one of Tyndale's biographers refers to it as More's *deus ex
machina* for settling all arguments.[158] Another point to which More
constantly returns is Luther's alleged living in lechery and the claim
that many of his followers are doing likewise. Also, that the Fathers
support the view of the Catholics is mentioned again and again.

More adopts this course not only because he realizes that repetition
breeds conviction, but also because he wants to give the impression
that he can refute his opponents on any point they may mention; the
Reformers are wrong on every issue:

> He repeteth here and hepeth vp all his proues together, which
> proues I haue reproued piece mele altogether, and so his con-
> clusion which he deduceth vpon them, is alreadye reproued al-
> together. But yet for hys double confusion can I not forbeare
> to touche one piece agayn . . . (*W*, p. 484).

This practice of More's is one of the main reasons why his works are
as long as they are.[159]

Under points More loves to hammer home there should also be
mentioned his frequent comparison of the unity within the Church to
the disunity among the Reformers. There is actually no such thing
as a Reformed faith, according to More,

> For in Saxony firste and among al the Lutherans there be as
> many heades as many wittes. And all as wise as wilde geese.
> And as late as thei began, yet bee there not onely as many sectes
> almoste as men, but also the maisters them selfe chaunge theyr
> mindes and theyr oppynions euery daye and wote nere where
> to holde them. Boheme is also in ye same case. One faith in the
> towne, another in the fielde. One in Prage, another in the next
> towne. And yet in Prage it self one faith in one strete, another
> in ye next (*W*, p. 179).

Emphasizing the Reformers' lack of unity, More makes it part of his technique to play Luther off against Tyndale by demonstrating the differences in their respective theologies. He keeps reminding Tyndale that not only have all the holy Fathers found auricular confession a beneficial practice, but that even Luther admitted that there was nothing wrong with it (*W*, pp. 249, 380), while, in distinction to Tyndale, "Luther hymselfe was neuer so shameless to say, that these holye fathers helde on hys syde" (*W*, p. 283). Luther's admission that the church can discern between true Scripture and false[160] is repeatedly used as a stick with which to beat Tyndale.[161]

When More is not using Luther against Tyndale, he is making the latter responsible for the theology and conduct of the former. In the *Confutacyon*, Luther's marriage is constantly brought in as an answer to anything Tyndale might say—so much so that even More himself cannot refrain from commenting on it:

> And al these expounded the apostles & euaungelistes agaynst Luther and Tindal, as the catholike church doth nowe. Wherin yf Tindall dare say that I say false, I shal yet ones agayn like a blind harper that harpeth all on one strynge, fal to my rude refraite [refrain], & sing him mine olde song, wherin I haue so often praied him to tel vs then some one of them al y^t euer accompted it lawefull and helde it not abhominable a frere to wed a nunne (*W*, p. 686).

More cannot make the same charge against Tyndale that he makes against Luther, but at least he can in some way connect him with Luther's marriage: "And Tyndall himself (which thing is worse then the deede doing) mayntaineth in hys boke their dede for well done" (*W*, p. 359).

Both sides accuse each other of being subversive, and More adds this accusation to the others which he makes against his opponent. He says in the *Dialogue* that the heretics, to gain authority for their civil disobedience, claim to be under a law higher than that of the land, assert that they are bound by God to preach, and maintain that no one has authority to forbid them (*W*, p. 150). More also claims that the Reformers' doctrine of predestination leads to anarchy: "Wherof should serue all lawes? And where were become al good ordre among men, if euery misordered wretche myght alledge that his mischieuous dede was his desteny" (*W*, p. 274). He will not accept Tyndale's declaration that the Reformers are ready to obey the rulers because they see the benefits God shows to His people through them. No, says More, such talk is more seditious than ever, for God wants us to obey our rulers merely because they are our rulers, and not for any advantage we may hope to obtain through them (*W*, p. 364).

Such language must have pleased Henry VIII, and during his earlier years More did not go out of his way to incur his sovereign's displeasure. He had already written some very flattering epigrams on Henry's accession, which were dedicated to the young monarch and presented to him in a beautiful manuscript.[162] Now, while the fight against the heretics was at its height, it was more important than ever to retain the royal favor, not so much on his own behalf as for the sake of the cause he was defending. Consequently we find numerous references to the very able book Henry wrote against Luther, in which the latter was so utterly and expertly refuted, according to More, that he can find no better words and no better arguments to use than those already employed by the King.[163] It is probably with the same object of remaining in Henry's good graces that More chides Tyndale for exhorting Henry to bestir himself on behalf of the spiritual welfare of the land. It would be preposterous, exclaims More, to think that the King would be unable to see his own faults (*W*, p. 622).

Continuing our investigation of More's technique, we find that the tone he adopts in the present controversy is one of great self-confidence, a quality which also marks his secular disputations.[164] In conformity with his habit of constant repetition, More never tires of reminding his readers how completely he has overcome his opponent. About Tyndale's *Answere* he asserts in the *Confutacyon*:

> And thus in this mine answer to his one chapter . . . I haue in such wyse confounded him & al his whole doctryne vtterly, that if I neuer woulde wryte one word more, yet shoulde he neuer against this alone defend his deuilish doctryne while he liueth, and take al the deuils in hell to helpe him (*W*, p. 459).

This claim is purely for public consumption. Its maker places so little reliance on it himself that he adds some hundreds more of folio pages to his refutation of the one chapter mentioned. Nevertheless, near the conclusion of all the pages that he does write, More reiterates and broadens that claim, saying that of all his works of religious controversy, the heretics "coulde neuer yet ouerthrowe one lyne" (*W*, p. 1126).

Whether or not More actually believes this himself, it is certainly what he wants his readers to believe. Except for a trifling matter of a page reference and an unimportant error in a quotation, he does not once admit to having made a mistake. This stubbornness sometimes gets him into trouble, as the following case will illustrate. In the *Dialogue* More claims that Peter was saved even when he denied Christ, because he was preserved by faith in Our Lady. When Tyndale tells More that there is no mention of Mary in the Gospels' version of this incident, More, rather than admit error, defends his original claim with the following not overly strong argument: "I wene it wil be no very great sotel thyng to perceyue, that the faith whych saynte Peter confessed, may bothe be his owne in that he confessed it, and yet our ladies to in that she belieued it . . ." (*W*, p. 605). It seems as if in this instance More feels that any answer will serve his case better than none.

Excessive humility is not one of the traits distinguishing More's conduct of the controversy. However, one cannot read his noncontroversial writings without coming to the conclusion that he was basically a humble man; the air of superiority, and almost of infallibility, which he adopts toward his opponents is assumed on behalf of the Church he is defending and not with the object of catering to his vanity.[165]

On the other hand, More shows no hesitation in accusing the opposition of pride. As has already been stated,[166] he is convinced that pride is at the root of the entire Reform movement. He feels that while the Reformers may feign simplicity and maintain that all they want to study is God's Word, it is really pride which causes them to reject the interpretations of the old Doctors and to adopt their own. In this, More maintains, they but follow the old heretics, such as Arius and Pelagius, whose pride led them to reject the infallible teachings of the Catholic Church in favor of their own learning. Pride has always been at the root of heresy, charges More.[167]

Conclusions

Having studied the various techniques the two controversialists used against each other, we now have to deal with certain questions concerning their dispute in general. For instance, to what extent did More and Tyndale understand each other's position?

While More sometimes intentionally misunderstands his opponents on individual points, Tyndale's claim that More really agrees with the Reformers but is arguing against them from mercenary motives cannot be supported. More fails to understand Tyndale's position as Tyndale fails to understand More's.

One example of Tyndale's misunderstanding of More has already been mentioned. To him it seems inconceivable that the man who wrote epigrams satirizing certain clerics[168] and who defended Erasmus[169] can later attack works which appear to be similar to the ones which he himself wrote or of which he approved. It evidently does not occur to Tyndale that More's earlier writings might never have had the same intent as his own, and consequently he accuses More of being insincere in his defense of the Catholic Church.

On the other hand, the following argument of Tyndale's seems to More like so much juggling and cant, a "worshipful ridle" and a "wondreful strange paradox" (*W*, pp. 550, 574):

> Thus are we sinners and no sinners. No sinners, if thou looke vnto the profession of our hartes toward the law of God. . . . Sinners are we, if thou loke vnto the frailtie of our flesh. . . . Notwithstanding yet the spirite leaueth vs not, but rebuketh vs & bryngeth vs home agayne vnto our profession . . . (*Ww*, p. 258).

What Tyndale means, as he explains further on in the discussion, is that while God's elect sin daily insofar as they still inhabit the sinful body with its frailties and weaknesses, as regenerate souls they are incapable of sinning unto damnation, being preserved therefrom by the indwelling of the Holy Spirit.[170] But Tyndale's statement seems absurd to More, who makes it the object of one of his most biting pieces of ridicule.[171]

Again, in spite of the fact that Tyndale on a number of occasions

(*Ww*, pp. 270-271, 277) expressed the opinion that there was nothing wrong with images in themselves, but only in their superstitious veneration, More continues to assume that Tyndale objects to images under any circumstances. Actually, More and Tyndale think almost alike on this question, of which More says:

> . . . to al these maters is one euident easye aunswere, that thei nothing touch yᵉ effect of our matter, which standeth in this, whether the thing that we speke of, as prayeng to saintes going in pilgrimage, & worshiping relykes and images, may be done wel: . . . For if it maye bee wel done, then though many wold misseuse it, yet doth al that nothing minishe yᵉ goodnes of the thyng selfe (*W*, p. 198).

How consistent are the opposing controversialists? Although Tyndale thinks More inconsistent and accuses him of this fault, Tyndale himself is not free from inconsistency. In one place he professes to be shocked by More's claim that all heretics are ready to recant when faced with death, and asserts that this is not true. But he merely asserts this, without giving any proof to the contrary. This is the very method of argument of which he accuses More in his complaint about his opponent's conduct of the controversy.[172]

Any discussion of More's consistency has to concern itself with the intentions of his *Utopia*, which has been many things to many men. Some [173] have regarded the book as a blueprint for the secular and spiritual affairs of England, while others have seen it as more or less a literary *jeu d'esprit*.[174] Among those who favor the latter view, the tendency has been to compare the *Utopia* with *The Praise of Folly*, and to read both as exercises of humanist wit. But More himself does not seem to regard his friend's book in this light, for writing to a monk who wished to warn him against Erasmus' work, he says it contains little folly and much piety.[175]

If *The Praise of Folly* is a joke, it is a joke at the expense of the follies of the time, that is, a satire. Merely on the basis of this comparison, then, the *Utopia* must have had some serious aim, and both Erasmus and Budé agreed that it did.[176] Finally, More would scarcely have bothered to introduce his description of the island of Utopia with the careful analysis of England's condition contained in the first book if the entire work were intended merely as an exercise of wit. The first book shows England as it is; the second book contains what More found "easier . . . to wish for . . . than to have any hope of seeing realized,"[177] that is, what he has sense enough to realize England will never be, but which includes many criticisms of England as it is.

When More wrote the *Utopia* in 1515, one of the things he made the Utopians insist on was religious toleration, or rather, toleration of all religions which believed in a life after death and postmortem punishment and reward, for atheists and those who denied the immortality of the soul were considered dangerous from a political point of view. It is therefore probable that as these Utopians did to some extent represent what More would "wish for," one of the things to which he was not adverse was some form of religious toleration. This conclusion may be drawn in spite of the fact that the Utopians, unlike Englishmen, had no revealed religion, and that their religious toleration was premised on this lack, for, as has already been pointed out, the second book of *Utopia* was intended at least in part as a criticism of conditions in England. It is possible that in this case More's particular purpose was not so much to advocate religious toleration of heretics as to attack the narrow intolerance of some Catholics, as we find him doing in his letter to Dorp, which was written in the same year as the *Utopia,* or in his letter to a monk, written about three years later.[178]

If, on the other hand, More had in mind the religious toleration of non-Catholics, the following conditions have to be borne in mind. While in More's lifetime there had been isolated cases of heresy in England before 1515, the country then was in a relatively orthodox condition compared to what it became after 1520, when the influx of heretical books and ideas caused the Church to take the measures previously described. Consequently, More's tolerance at the time he wrote the *Utopia* was not a broad tolerance at all, in the modern sense that it would permit opposition from a large and powerful minority within the commonwealth, but was one based on the very small number of people who at that time dissented from the orthodox religion. When, during the next decade, the number of dissenters increased, even this narrow tolerance was abandoned, and More became the champion of religious conformity. The entire question of

More's consistency in his views on tolerance arises only if we anachronistically ascribe a twentieth-century concept of tolerance to a sixteenth-century work. Therefore a comparison between More's earlier and later views on this subject does not lay him open to the charge of inconsistency.

However he is inconsistent on a number of occasions in his controversy with Tyndale. For instance, More points out Luther's inconsistency by telling the messenger in the *Dialogue* that when Luther at first thought it would be easy to prove his case, he said he would submit it to the authority of the old Fathers, to the laws of the Church, and to the old Doctors' interpretation of Scripture, all of which he abandoned when he saw that they did not support his cause (*W*, p. 256). A little further on in the same work, More confronts Tyndale with the statement that "Luther hymselfe was neuer so shameless to say, that these holye fathers helde on hys syde" (*W*, p. 283), in which "these" refers not only to specific Fathers, but to patristic authority in general.

More complains about the fact that the Reformers, with unholy zeal to spread their pernicious doctrine, distribute heretical books gratuitously and leave them at people's doorsteps during the night (*W*, p. 727). Yet in reply to Tyndale's accusation of avarice, More has this to say: "yet see we wel ynough how gredely the pedelying knaues that here bring ouer theire bookes, grispe about an halfe-penny, and had almost as leue hange vp his euangelical brother as lese a peny by hym" (*W*, p. 639). And after railing against the evil living of the heretics, More says, "And as for their liuing, the good apparance whereof is the thyng that most blyndeth vs . . ." (*W*, p. 282).

While engaged in the task of refuting Tyndale, More became involved in controversies with a number of other Reformers. It is to some of these controversies that we now turn.

III

Robert Barnes

Barnes's Version
of History

The eighth book of More's *Confutacyon* consists of an attack on a section of Robert Barnes's 1531 *Supplicatyon . . . vnto . . . kinge henrye the eyght.*

Robert Barnes (1495–1540) was an Augustinian friar who became Doctor of Divinity at Cambridge shortly after 1523. On Christmas eve, 1525, he preached a sermon at Cambridge attacking what he considered to be ecclesiastical abuses. As a result of this sermon, he was charged with heresy, and in February of 1526 he was brought before Wolsey for examination. He was eventually persuaded to abjure, whereupon he was committed first to the Fleet and ultimately into the custody of his own order. After an imprisonment of more than two years, Barnes escaped to Antwerp in 1528 and from there proceeded to Germany.

At Wittenberg, in 1530, Barnes published *Sentenciae Ex Doctoribus Collectae* under the pseudonym of Antonius Anglus. The next year saw the publication at Antwerp of his *Supplicatyon* to

Henry[1], of which a considerably expanded and altered second edition, including an answer to More's attack, was published in 1534 in London.

Both Cargill Thompson and Clebsch[2] have demonstrated how Barnes modified—or discarded—many points he had made in his 1531 *Supplicatyon* by the time he came to write the 1534 *Supplicacion*. Barnes's 1531 attack against bishops was changed and extended in 1534 into an attack against the Pope. Whereas Barnes had previously taught that subjects owed obedience to the king only in temporal matters, in 1534 he taught that the king had jurisdiction in spiritual affairs as well, so long as he acted consonant with Scripture. Whereas Barnes taught in 1531 that faith justified to the exclusion of works, in 1534 he maintained that works had become an outward testimony of an inward faith. The 1531 articles against the veneration of saints and images, on the necessity of communion in both kinds for the laity, and the claim that human ordinances are not binding if they command a man to sin were suppressed. While it is conceivable that Barnes's convictions changed on all of these points, it is more likely that Barnes was accommodating his views to those of his royal master. Barnes's final contribution to the paper warfare of the Reformation is a polemical history of the papacy, entitled *Vitae Romanorum Pontificum*, published in Basel in 1535.

Late in 1531 Barnes returned to England under a safe-conduct from Henry, with the object of reconciling the King with the German Lutherans, whom Henry wanted to support his "divorce" from Catherine of Aragon. Barnes returned to the Continent early in 1532 but was back in London in 1534, and in the following year was employed by Henry in negotiations with the German Protestant princes. Barnes finally fell from favor along with Cromwell, whose protégé he had been, and was burned for heresy in 1540.

Much of Barnes's attack on the English clergy takes the form of the polemical use of secular and ecclesiastical history.

The bulk of Barnes's polemical references to secular history is contained in his 1534 *Supplicacion vnto the most gracyous prynce H. the viij.*, the title of which clearly indicates for whom the history lessons were principally intended. There is a possibility that these lessons were contracted for by a third party. The first edition of the

Supplicatyon contains only one of the numerous historical references of the later edition (sig. A5ʳ). It was in 1531 that Barnes was invited to return to England by Cromwell for purposes of negotiating with the German Lutherans and of assisting in the government's anti-clerical campaign;[3] it is therefore not unlikely that Barnes's considerable expansion of historical material in the second edition of his work was part of that campaign. The possibility that Cromwell influenced Barnes's polemical use of history is strengthened by the fact that Cromwell also attempted, without success, to secure the services of William Tyndale for the government's cause, and Barnes's additions to the 1534 *Supplycacion* seem to be patterned on Tyndale's polemical use of history in his 1530 *Practyse of Prelates*.[4] Either on his own initiative, then, or somewhat more probably at Cromwell's suggestion, Barnes took up a weapon of religious controversy fashioned by Tyndale.[5]

The purpose of Barnes's polemical use of secular history was to demonstrate that the clergy always had been and still were a subversive element in every realm, with particular emphasis on England. His strategy was to trace the development of temporal papal power with its increasing infringement on, and subsequent domination of, the authority of civil rulers. For evidence he turned to English and continental chronicles as well as to papal laws.

Skepticism as to the veracity of the chronicles was, as we have seen, an integral part of the technique of Tyndale, Barnes's forerunner in the polemical use of history.

Although in his 1535 *Vitae Romanorum Pontificum* Barnes also makes his professed attitude to his sources a definite part of his controversial technique (see pp. 000), he does not do so in his treatment of secular history for the 1534 *Supplycacion*. His later treatment of ecclesiastical history in the *Vitae* is, however, forecast in a threat he makes in the 1534 work, in which he promises the English bishops that if they challenge his assertion that the clergy have historically been subversive, "you shall see, what an heape of holy factes yᵗ I will bring you out of your own chronicles and bookes..." (*Ww*, p. 198).

The subversion by the English clergy, as the Protestant polemicists saw it, was a consequence of the growth of the temporal power of the papacy, and this growth Barnes traces in his *Vitae*, significantly also dedicated to Henry. In order to emphasize the initial relationship of power between Empire and papacy, Barnes points out that originally the election of a pope had to be confirmed by the Emperor.[6] As Barnes sees it, the beginning of papal interference in the affairs of European princes began with Pope Gregory III's deposition of Emperor Leo III for opposing the veneration of images, so that the Pope, who previously had to have his authority confirmed by the Emperor, now exercised that authority to deprive the latter of his throne.[7] To consolidate his position, continues Barnes, Gregory made an alliance with Charles Martel of France, and this French-papal alliance has been in force ever since, so that whenever the Pope quarrels with the Emperor or with another king, he uses the power of France to accomplish his ends (sigs. H4ᵛ-H5ʳ). Barnes here makes a double appeal to English nationalism, indicating not only that the papacy interferes in the internal policies of other nations but that its instrument has always been England's old enemy, France. The papal hold over France, he continues, was strengthened by Pope Zacharias I, who deposed the French King, Childeric III, and had him shut up in a monastery on the pretext that he had once been a monk, absolved the French people from their previous allegiance, and set on the French throne Pepin, who had requested the Pope's aid in gaining the crown (sig. H6ʳ). The growing ascendancy of papacy over Empire which had been demonstrated *de facto* by Gregory III's deposition of Leo III was elevated to *de jure* status by Martin II, who was the first pope to assume office without waiting for the Emperor's confirmation of his election, drawing the comment from Barnes that thus, gradually, the papacy was freeing itself from the jurisdiction of the Emperor, whom it was eventually to dominate completely (sig. M2ʳ). The evolutionary process was completed under Pope John XIII (Barnes's mistake for John XII) who forced Otto I to swear loyalty to the papacy before his coronation (sigs. N1ᵛ-N2ᵛ).

With the establishment of its ascendancy over the Empire, the papacy, according to Barnes, was in a position to manipulate the affairs of Europe for its own advantage. Turning to the history of his own country, Barnes traces for his King the following clerical *modus operandi:* If the King is weak enough, he is used by the clergy for the aggrandizement of their national and international power; if he proves recalcitrant, the clergy will oppose him; if the initial opposition does not make the King compliant to their wishes, the clergy will alienate his subjects, betray him to a foreign power, and, if necessary, finally depose him. As a last step, to frighten his successors into subservience, the clergy will vilify the deposed King's memory and canonize those who betrayed him.

To illustrate the clergy's control of power within England, Barnes says he will "recite some of their practises, both out of *Autenticke* crownycles, and out of their owne law" (*Ww*, p. 186). He tells Henry the story of the Bishop of Salisbury's servant in the reign of Richard II. A London baker, says Barnes, was carrying a loaf of bread when one of the Bishop's servants met him and took the loaf by force. When the baker asked why he did this, the Bishop's servant in answer hit the baker over the head. The baker cried out and a crowd assembled to "keepe the kinges peace" and the servant had to hide in a house nearby. But the people sent for the constable and the servant was imprisoned, only to be released shortly by the mayor and sheriffs. Nevertheless, the Bishop of Salisbury and the Archbishop of York were so angry at what had happened to the Bishop's servant, that they caused the King to remove both the mayor and the two sheriffs (*Ww*, p. 192). Barnes comments that if the clergy can do open violence, break the king's peace, rob men of their goods, "yea & that in the kynges chamber, and also in the kynges hygh strete, to the great disdayne of iustice, to the rebuke of the kyng, and to the great displeasure of his subiectes, and yet . . . can packe the matter so, that they bee white sonnes, and other men must suffer for it. I can beleue none otherwise, but that they haue witched the worlde, that men could neither heare nor see" (*Ww*, p. 192). Barnes's emphasis on breaking the king's peace in the king's highway—the part about robbing men of their goods in the "kynges chamber" seems to have been added merely for good measure—would not be lost on so autocratic a monarch as Henry.

When it comes to a king less compliant than Richard II, charges Barnes, clerical tactics are different. For instance, when Henry II ordered that no bishops should leave the realm without his permission and that the bishops should do nothing against the realm or the King, the English bishops got Pope Alexander III to declare the order heresy (*Ww*, p. 192). Barnes's historical reference does more than illustrate past clerical opposition to the Crown; it also indicates the probable attitude of contemporary bishops toward their oath of allegiance to Henry.[8] ". . . I dare say," Barnes comments on the clergy, "there was no rebellion in this Realme this v.C. yeares, if the kyng had displeased them, but they were at the begynnyng of it" (*Ww*, p. 192).

Another incident drawn from the reign of Henry II again has contemporary application. Barnes reminds the Henry currently reigning that the clergy denied his predecessor's claim to be supreme ruler over both clergy and laity within his own realm, adding that the clergy were especially opposed to Henry II's declaration that, in criminal cases, clerics should be tried in the King's rather than in the bishops' courts (*Ww*, pp. 201-202). The issue of separate clerical courts and of clerical jurisdiction over the laity in heresy cases was being sharply debated just at the time Barnes's 1534 *Supplicacion* was published, and Cromwell had engaged the services of the lawyer Christopher Saint-German to argue for the precedence of the King's courts against such apologists for the clerical side as Thomas More.[9]

When King John wanted a small sum of money to defend the realm, observes Barnes, the clergy refused to give him anything, but as much money as John had requested was gathered in one Lent to defend the Pope, and, Barnes continues, "I dare say of my conscience, that in fiue hundred yeares, there was not such a summe of money so lightly graunted, (were the cause neuer so great) vnto our right naturall, and lege Lord. Ye I doe beleeue, that if the kynges grace at this same day, should desire of ye spirituality, but half of this summe, I dare say they wold neuer graunt him with their good will . . ." (*Ww*, p. 194). This last comment by Barnes again serves to remind us that his history lectures to Henry were meant for contemporary application. The implication that the clergy had been parasites on the realm and historically had never paid their due share of national expenses was not intended to make more difficult Henry's expropriation of the monasteries, which began two years after Barnes's comment was published.

Furthermore, continues Barnes addressing the clergy, if you find it necessary you will depose a king, an emperor, or anyone else who stands in your way, just as Pope Zacharias deposed the King of France and set up Pepin in his stead. "And no doubt," adds Barnes to Henry, "but that the same or worse, will they attempt to doe vnto your grace, if you displease them . . ." (*Ww*, pp. 186-187). Now the clergy say that one of the reasons they deposed that king was that he was living in lechery, Barnes continues; if they think that a lawful reason to depose kings, why do they not preach this openly? Why do they permit any adulterer to be king (*Ww*, p. 187)? Considering that in the eyes of the Catholic Church the King to whom Barnes's words were addressed was just such an adulterer, it will be appreciated that these questions presented some unpleasant alternatives for the clergy: They had to admit that their previous deposition had been carried out on false grounds, or that they should now depose Henry VIII, or that Henry's marriage with Anne Boleyn was lawful.[10] And you will remember, Barnes says to the clergy, how obediently you drove King John from his throne, after you had excommunicated him, absolved his subjects from allegiance, and given England to the King of France. It took a lot of money for John to buy back his own kingdom, paid variously to the Pope, the papal legate, and the English bishops, charges Barnes (*Ww*, p. 189). Finally, he continues, as a warning to future kings who might oppose the clergy, you canonize your traitors and regicides. The monk who poisoned John was absolved of the deed before he did it and five masses have been founded for his soul forever, and this "for a willing traytor, and murtherer. . . . But there is no remedy, hee that dyes agaynst his king, and for the mayntayning of your treason must needes bee a saynt . . ." (*Ww*, pp. 189-190).

Besides using the events of the past as an oblique commentary on the contemporary situation and to prove his thesis that the clergy had always been a subversive element within the realm, Barnes comments directly on current political developments in order to demonstrate that the clergy's role had not changed in his day. His most extensive effort in this direction is his detailed and lengthy examination in the 1534 edition of the *Supplicacion* of the bishops' oath of allegiance to the Pope and a comparison of that oath with the bishops' oath of allegiance to the King. There is no discussion of the two oaths in the 1531 edition, and it is quite probable that in his treatment of the bishops' oaths Barnes was engaging in royal propaganda. For in 1532, on the occasion when he found that the clergy "be but half our subjects," Henry sent a copy of the two oaths to Parliament to be read and compared. However, for a number of reasons, Parliament was unable to act on the matter at that time,[11] and Barnes may have been encouraged to revive the subject in 1534. He cites the oath to the Pope in proof of his assertion that the English bishops were sworn to reveal state secrets (*Ww*, p. 195), referring specifically to the provision that if a bishop hears of any plans against the Pope or the Church, he shall inform the Pope. This provision was not in the original form of the oath, Barnes explains to his readers, and therefore the original form was changed "because that by it, the Bishops were not bounde to betray their Princes, nor to reuelate their counselles to the Pope" (*Ww*, p. 195). "But howe," Barnes asks the clergy, "standeth it with your othe toward your Prince, for to bee sworne to the Pope? which is not all onely an other Lorde: but also contrary," he points out, resurrecting the question of praemunire,[12] "yea and as the worlde now is the greatest mortall ennemy that our Prince hath," since he has excommunicated our King and is reported to have given his kingdom to another. "And this facte must you defende, for you are sworne to yᵉ Pope" (*Ww*, p. 198). And yet, marvels Barnes, at the same time you also swore in your oath to the King that you would renounce all clauses in your oath to the Pope which might be hurtful to the King—how can these two oaths agree? I cannot see, Barnes concludes, how you can avoid perjury in this matter (*Ww*, p. 198).

According to Barnes, the clergy have two related tactics intended to cover up their treasonable activities: suppression of a vernacular Bible, which would reveal to the people that God commands all subjects, both lay and clerical to obey the King, and accusations of treason against the Reformers, so that under the cloak of patriotism their own treason will go unobserved. The propagandistic value of the first charge lies in its promotion of the Reformers' theological objective of an open vernacular Bible by labeling opposition to such a Bible as motivated by fear of exposure; the point of the second accusation is that it characterizes opposition against the Reformers themselves as treasonous. Therefore Barnes keeps stressing the point that the Bible teaches loyalty. Did any of the biblical prophets, or Christ, or the Apostles ever encourage insurrection against princes, he asks, claiming it is evident that "those Bishops or rather Papistes, doe falsely accuse those true preachers and subiectes: which thyng woulde appeare in euery mans sight, if by their violence, the word of God were not kept vnder" (*Ww*, p. 185). The papists, Barnes tells Henry, accuse the preachers of disturbing the realm because "they would make your grace to mayntayne their maliciousnes. So that vnder the pretence of treason, they myghte execute the tyranny of their harts." For who would be a traitor against your grace, asks Barnes, since no man can be one without going contrary to God's commandment in the Scriptures, and so he who loves the Scriptures would least be a traitor (*Ww*, p. 184). "Is not this a subtile crafte of Antychrist," Barnes exclaims of the Pope, "to warne other men of heretykes and of traytours, and in the meane season, while men stand lokeing fhr [*sic*] traytours, commeth hee in and playeth the parte of an open traytour sauing onely hee coloureth his name, and calleth himselfe a true Byshop, & is ready to accuse other men of treason, that he might escape hymselfe . . ." (*Ww*, p. 186).

It was Barnes's intention to demonstrate not only the subversive nature of clerical power within the realm but also the tyranny with which that power was exercised. As an example of clerical tyranny, Barnes cities primarily his own case, although he also accuses the clergy of spiritual, legal, and economic tyranny over Englishmen generally.

Barnes's complaints about his personal treatment stem from the actions taken against him as a result of the sermon he preached at Cambridge in 1525. As Barnes tells the story, he was accused of preaching heresy and was brought before a tribunal of bishops and doctors.

One of his objectives in dealing with the trial is to justify himself by denouncing the doctrine and behavior of his clerical judges. He performs the first part of his task by listing the particulars of the heresy charge against him so that his readers might understand just what the clergy regarded as heresy. He records that he was charged with claiming that there were certain men who would accuse anyone of heresy who dared to say anything against them (*Ww*, p. 207).

Apart from the fact that the accusation obviously has nothing to do with heresy, his recording of the fact that for making such a statement he was accused of heresy proves the truth of his assertion. He was also charged with claiming that there was no scriptural authority for the clergy's great temporal possessions. To emphasize the ludicrousness of characterizing such a statement as heretical, Barnes speculates on how his opponents might justify their charge. "But they will say," he explains, "if they had not so great possessions, they could not kepe so many seruauntes, so many dogges, so many horses . . . & maintayne so great pompe, and pride, and liue so deliciously . . ." (*Ww*, p. 210). Barnes again scores a polemical point in anticipating a justification of the charge even more ridiculous than the charge itself.

Throughout his account Barnes emphasizes the cruelty and unfairness of his clerical judges. He records that when he was asked whether or not certain men were martyrs and he replied that he thought all those martyrs who died for the Word of God, the Bishop of Bath told him "hee woulde make . . . [him] to frye for this." "How thinke you by this holy prelate?" Barnes asks his readers; "was not this a charitable argument to refell myne aunswere with?" (*Ww*, p. 207).

When he asked who his accusers were, he was told, "wee proceede after an other forme of the lawe" (*Ww*, p. 223). The justice of permitting secret accusers in ecclesiastical courts was being debated between Thomas More and the Crown's spokesman, Christopher Saint-German, at the same time Barnes was dealing with this subject. Not only were the names of Barnes's accusers kept secret, but, according to his account, he was not even informed about the basis of the heresy charge, since the tribunal refused to tell him what they considered heretical about his alleged statements (*Ww*, pp. 223, 226). Barnes's description of the conduct of his trial is also intended to demonstrate that any ecclesiastical trial is a mockery and that the accused is already condemned by the mere fact of being accused, which is exactly the point the "official" pamphlets of Saint-German were making.[13] Barnes records that he was tricked into signing his alleged statements, in that he thought his signature meant merely that he was willing to discuss what he was accused of preaching, while in actuality it meant that he confessed to having preached what he sub-scribed (*Ww*, pp. 218-220). As soon as they had my signature, writes Barnes, illustrating clerical chicanery,

> than had they what they woulde, for I was nowe come in further daunger than I wist of, for now must I needes purge my selfe after their request, or else reuoke all thinges that they had laide against mee, as though they had beene myne, or els I must needes dye, after theyr lawe. The which thyng I than neyther knew, nor suspected. And thys hath beene the cause, that all maner of men, whatsoeuer they were that came afore them, were they neuer so good, nor innocent, must needes bee heretykes . . . (*Ww*, p. 223).

And so, on the mere basis of accusation, Barnes tells his King, he was given the choice of either doing open penance for preaching heresy or being burned as a stubborn heretic (*Ww*, pp. 224-226).

With regard to the clergy's oppression of Englishmen generally, Barnes tells Henry that the treatment he received in a clerical court is typical of the procedure used in all clerical courts in England; anyone appearing in such a court is automatically found guilty. Barnes asks, "Is it not a maruelous court that they haue? wherein there was neuer man accused of heresie, were he learned or not learned, but they found him gilty? Is not that a maruelous court y^t neuer hath innocentes? What court within your realme may say thys againe?" (*Ww*, p. 183). And what the clergy are so vigorously defending is not the gospel of Christ, Barnes tells his King, but their economic interests (*Ww*, pp. 184, 204).

In his campaign against the clergy, Barnes also used his knowledge of ecclesiastical history to trace the evolution of the ecclesiastical power of the papacy, to illustrate papal immorality, and to demon-strate the nonapostolic origin of many clerical customs. The ultimate purpose of Barnes's use of ecclesiastical history is the same as that of his use of secular history, to destroy the power of the clergy within England.

While a number of Barnes's discussions of ecclesiastical history are in his *Supplicacion,* the bulk are contained in his *Vitae Romanorum Pontificum* which, like the former work, was also dedicated to Henry. In his dedication, Barnes admonishes his King to act on the evidence with which he is going to be presented, to punish clerical wickedness and remove clerical tyranny over the English throne (sigs. A6ᵛ-A7ʳ); only when you have done this, says Barnes, will you truly deserve the title of Defender of the Faith (sig. A7ᵛ).

In his polemical use of ecclesiastical history, Barnes makes his professed attitude toward his sources a definite part of his technique. He explains that many fawning histories have been written, praising the popes' most evil acts as if they were noble accomplishments, but that he is going to follow only reputable authorities who, without any embellishment, set down the facts as they happened. Barnes emphasizes that had his authorities wished to do so, without in any way departing from the truth, they could easily have convinced everyone that many popes were no better than Nero (*Vitae*, sigs. A5ᵛ-A6ʳ). Thus Barnes tries to give the impression that he has actually followed authorities more favorable to the papacy than they might have been.[14] In the light of Barnes's claim, one is rather startled to find that one of his main authorities is Platina, whose *Vitae Pontificum* was written in revenge for the treatment its author had received at the hands of Pope Paul II,[15] and that as an authority for the life of Pope Gregory VII he cites Cardinal Benno, one of the Pope's bitterest enemies.[16] Not all of the authorities Barnes uses are antipapal,[17] but with the kind of selectivity which judged some authorities as reputable or not on the basis of their conformity to a preconceived picture of ecclesiastical history, Barnes had little difficulty in uncovering what he was looking for, although, as we shall see, he occasionally found it necessary to depart from the text of even his "reputable" authorities.

Barnes traces the evolution of papal power from the days when the Bishop of Rome was merely one important bishop among others, through the struggles between the Bishops of Rome and those of Constantinople and Ravenna, until Rome emerged preeminent (sigs. F1ᵛ, G1ʳ, D4ʳ, G7ʳ-G7ᵛ). His point is that the papacy, far from being a divinely created institution, is rather the tyranny of one bishop over his fellows: ". . . ita paulatim irrepit bestia Romana in suum primatum," as the marginal note comments on one passage (sig. G7ᵛ).

The character of these chief rulers of the Church is also investigated by Barnes. He tells his readers the legend of Pope Joan, for instance, the girl who came to Rome disguised as a man and was chosen pope, the secret of her sex not being detected until she gave birth to her chaplain's child in a public place.[18] He recounts the life of Pope Sergius III who, driven out of Rome, returned and desecrated its sepulchres,[19] and of Pope Boniface VII, who took his rival John XV prisoner, put out his eyes, and starved him to death in prison (sigs. N7^r-N7^v).

In Barnes's treatment of ecclesiastical custom, the institution of clerical celibacy receives by far the major share of attention. That clerical celibacy is not an apostolic or primitive institution Barnes seeks to establish by asserting that both Peter and Philip had wives (*Ww*, p. 325), as did many of the dignitaries of the early church (*Vitae*, sig. D5^v). As further evidence of the recent origin of clerical celibacy, Barnes supplies his readers with a list of popes who were the sons of priests (*Ww*, p. 326). In citing such a list, Barnes assumes that the popes in question were born in wedlock. That he made the assumption purely for the convenience of this particular argument is indicated by the fact that when it suited his purpose Barnes could draw the alternative conclusion, as he does in the case of John XI, on whom he comments, "Filius summi pontificis, sed natus tamen sine matre, quia pater uouerat celibatum" (*Vitae*, sig. M7^r). That clerical marriage was permitted in England until 1101 Barnes seeks to prove on the basis of the fact that in that year Anselm, Archbishop of Canterbury, made a decree against such marriages (*Ww*, p. 327). In order to leave no doubt as to just how and when compulsory clerical celibacy was introduced into the Western Church, Barnes traces the evolution of that institution. Nicholas I, about 860, tried to enforce clerical celibacy, says Barnes, but because of strong opposition he was unsuccessful (*Ww*, p. 328), as were Pelagius II, Siricius, and Gregory I, who repented his decree on clerical celibacy and revoked it. Innocent II's decree on the matter had no universal effect, says Barnes, and nothing further was done until Gregory VII—"a man of euill lyuyng, as the chronicles testifieth, and also a great nygromancer. . . . And as chronicles sayth, a man that had poysoned 4. or 5. popes before, that hee myght come the sooner to it"—in 1074 successfully began to enforce clerical celibacy (*Ww*, p. 331).

What have been the results of such an institution? asks Barnes. One of them was cited by Bishop Huldericus in a letter he wrote to

Nicholas I opposing the Pope's plans to enforce celibacy. Barnes cites the entire letter, in which the Bishop reminds Nicholas that Gregory I abandoned his enforcement after he had caught the heads of 5,000 illegitimate children in his net while fishing one day, the results of his decree on celibacy.[20] Lest his readers get the impression such things happened only in the past, Barnes says that he himself has "beene informed of credible persons" of a recent case of clerical child murder, and he tells his readers that he is sure they will all still remember the incident in which an honest man lost his daughter because she was killed by a priest who tried to hide the fact that he made her pregnant (*Ww*, p. 329). Even if his readers remembered no such thing, such confident assertion on the basis of personal knowledge or "credible" information—a commonplace of Tudor religious polemics —would have its effect. And in the fashion later to be made famous in the Marprelate tracts, Barnes promises the possibility of even more dire revelations:

> I coulde recite a great many of abhominable, and detestable factes, if I were not more ashamed to tell them, then priestes hath beene to doe them. . . . But this I promyse them, if any of these protectours of this fylthy chastitie doth take in hand to defende it agaynst mee, I will not bee ashamed to write, that they haue not been ashamed to doe. Nor I will not keepe secrete how certayne byshops of England . . . doth let whores to ferme vnto priests (*Ww*, p. 329).

As a warning of what the English prelates might expect, Barnes momentarily manages to overcome his shame: "Yet heare will I tell you one pretty tale," he says to his readers. There is a bishop now living in Germany—"I could tell his name if I would," adds Barnes— who found that he needed a large sum of money and asked one of his friends how he might obtain it. The friend advised him to command all the priests in his diocese to get rid of their whores and after that secretly to inform each priest that for a certain sum of money his whore could be retained. The advice was followed, Barnes recounts, and the bishop gathered a fortune (*Ww*, pp. 329-330).

Finally, Barnes prejudices the idea of celibacy from a political point of view. Suppose, he says, that someone were to preach that marriage was carnal and were to exhort all Englishmen to abstain; I would like to know if such a man could be the King's friend. The fact that no Catholic preacher was preaching such a doctrine and that his analogy has no relevance to the question of clerical celibacy does not deter Barnes. "... I am sure," he says, "there could not bee a greater traytour to the kinges grace the*n* hee is. For if hee might bring to passe that hee intendeth by his doctrine. Fyrst he should destroy ye kyngs succession. Secondarily, hee should within this seuen yeres, make ye king a Lorde of a fewe subiectes, or none, and fynally of none indeede" (*Ww*, p. 339). The point about "ye kyngs succession" would not be lost on a monarch who, to secure that succession, had gone to such great lengths as Henry had.

Turning to consider Barnes's historical veracity, we find that he is far more accurate than Tyndale in the polemical use of history. Often his specific references to chronicles are correct and the passages referred to say exactly what Barnes claims. But while Barnes manipulates his sources to a lesser degree than some others, he does so on a number of occasions. Such manipulation can be broken down into unwarranted multiplication of authorities in order to make a greater impression on the reader, the biased interpretation of evidence contained in the chronicles, and misstatement of fact about the content of the chronicles.

In support of his assertion that Pope Agapetus I was the son of a priest, for instance, Barnes cites both Platina and Volaterranus (*Vitae*, sig. F4^r); however, only the former records this.[21] Again, Barnes writes that after Pope John XIII (i.e., John XII) had made a pact in Rome with the Emperor Otto I, the Pope made another pact against the Emperor with Albertus Berangarius, citing Nauclerus, Pius II, and Antoninus (*Vitae*, sigs. N2^v-N3^r), whereas only Nauclerus records the second pact.[22]

An example of unwarranted interpretation of the chronicles is Barnes's claim that in the reign of Henry III priests could lawfully marry wives, based on Fabyan's statement that Anselm, Archbishop of Canterbury, made a decree against clerical marriage. All Fabyan records is the decree, and his account does not necessarily imply that clerical marriage was regarded as lawful prior to the decree.[23] A different type of unwarranted treatment of authorities occurs during Barnes's account of the deposition of Childeric III, King of France, by Pope Zacharias I. Barnes says that the Pope deposed the King ostensibly because he was unfit to govern but really because of an agreement with Pepin, and that on the pretext that he previously had been a monk called Samuel, Zacharias had Childeric shut up in a monastery and made Pepin king in his place (*Ww*, pp. 186-187; *Vitae*, sig. H6ʳ). Among the authorities Barnes cites are Platina, Nauclerus, and Sabellicus. By citing his authorities in a string at the end of the passage Barnes gives the reader the impression that his account is supported by these three authorities; however Platina does not even mention that Childeric became a monk, Nauclerus says that Childeric was feebleminded and therefore was deposed and shut up in a monastery, and Sabellicus writes that Childeric became a monk of his own volition. None of the three says that the Pope pretended the French King had at one time been a monk called Samuel.[24] Another kind of manipulation occurs when Barnes cites Platina as his authority for the story of Pope Joan (*Vitae*, sigs. K5ᵛ-K6ʳ). Barnes fails to inform his readers that Platina wrote that the entire story was a rumor without the support of reliable authority, which he has included in his history only so that he would not be accused of omitting anything.[25] In the same category is Barnes's citing of Antoninus for the assertion that on his deathbed Gregory VII admitted he had been a wicked man (*Vitae*, sigs. R6ᵛ-R7ʳ). Barnes omits the fact that his authority disclaims belief in the story.[26]

A number of Barnes's statements are directly contrary to the evidence of the "Autenticke crownycles" he claims to be following. For instance, the sweeping assertion that the clergy have been responsible for all depositions of kings (*Ww*, p. 186) is contradicted by the evidence of the chronicles concerning Harold and Richard II.[27] Barnes's claim about Childeric that "the crownicles geue . . . witnesse, how yᵗ he was a very good man" (*Ww*, p. 186) is not supported at all by the authorities he himself cites.[28] In the same category comes the statement that after Pope Urban VI had stirred up Edward III to war with France and had achieved his objectives from the war, ". . . our chronicle saith, that Pope Urban would haue made peace betwene the French king, and ours at the last," which allegation Barnes uses to illustrate how kings are manipulated by the Pope (*Ww*, p. 193). Froissart, whom Barnes gives as his authority, mentions no papal part in the peace negotiations which were, in fact, not for but against the

Pope's interest.[29] Barnes's statement that Gregory VII was "a man of euill lyuyng, as the chronicles testifieth" (*Ww*, p. 331) is contradicted by himself in dealing with that Pope in his *Vitae*, where he complains that Gregory has been immoderately praised by historians who were biased in his favor because he defended the Church. "Verba ac facta illius testes sunt, Hildebrandum alium fuisse quam scriptores dicunt," says Barnes, in promising his readers a true account (sig. P8r). Nor do the authorities he cites support Barnes's claim that the election of Rudolphus to replace the Emperor Henry IV was arranged by Gregory VII (*Vitae*, sig. R3v). On the contrary, Platina, for instance, specifically says that Gregory refused to take sides between Henry and Rudolphus, and that it was the German princes who determined to give the imperial crown to the latter.[30]

Barnes's polemical use of history influenced contemporary events both directly and indirectly. He was used as a source, for instance, by both John Bale and Thomas Becon in their polemical accounts of the papacy.[31] He was particularly important to Bale, who blandly passed off Barnes's biased account as one of the sources friendly to the papacy which he had promised to use.[32] Indirectly, Barnes helped to create a climate in which the anticlerical legislation of the Reformation Parliament and the subsequent expropriation of the monasteries appeared to be historically justified. His emphasis on the abuses prevalent in clerical heresy trials, along with the writings of Tyndale and Saint-German on the same subject, prepared the way for legislation which strictly defined heresy[33] and brought heresy trials under the procedures of the common law (35 Henry VIII, c. 5). His tracing of the evolutionary process by which a "subversive" element within England owing allegiance to a foreign potentate had achieved power, and his demonstration of the abuse of that power at the expense of the English people, helped condition them to acquiesce in Henry's decision to take into his own hands the spiritual as well as the temporal reins of the realm.

Barnes's Techniques
of Argumentation

Let us now examine other elements in Barnes's polemical technique, namely, the manner in which he attempts to establish a favorable image of his own position as contrasted to that of his opponents, as well as some of his methods of argumentation.

Barnes attempts to impress his readers with his correctness in two ways: by identifying his theological beliefs with those of the accepted heroes of the Christian faith and by creating for himself a *persona* to embody all the Christian virtues. For instance, he rebuts the charge that he and his fellow Reformers are treasonous by claiming that, as followers of the biblical prophets, of Christ and his Apostles, and of the Doctors of the Church, the Reformers could not possibly be disloyal, since these founders of their faith never advocated insurrection against princes (*Ww*, p. 184). Apart from the incorrectness of the first part of the analogy—on occasion Barnes has no difficulty in remembering the names of those who opposed princes[34]—the process of identification involves begging the question, for whether or not the Reformers were following the example of Christ, the Apostles, and the Church Fathers was one of the principal points in dispute. Often the technique of identification with the good takes the form of what might be called the "substitution-of-opponent" tactic, as when Barnes asks of the bishops how they hope to defend themselves not against him but against Christ and his Apostles. "Aunswere you to them," he tells the bishops, "aunswere not to me. If I hold my peace, they will speake" (*Ww*, p. 187). Barnes uses the same technique when he seeks to rebut his opponents' reasoning by demanding whether "all these things, that they haue reckened, can ouercome Christ, and his holy worde, or set the holy ghost to schole?" (*Ww*, p. 226).

Barnes attempts to project a favorable personal image chiefly by seeking to impress his readers with how reluctant he is to enter into controversy or to say an unkind word about anyone. In the manner popularized by late Tudor satirists, Barnes claims that he has criticized no individuals but only evil institutions (*Ww*, p. 318) and defends his having recorded incidents of clerical immorality by saying to the clergy: "You will recken that this is a shame for me to write, but it is more shame for you to doe it. And if you did not these shamefull deedes, I shoulde haue none occasion to make this shame full writyng. Take you away ye cause and I will take away ye writyng" (*Ww*, p. 265). He claims that Christian charity has caused him actually to extenuate clerical wickedness: "Beleeue me," he says to his opponents, "if I were your mortall enemy (as you reken me to bee, and as you haue wel deserued, that I should bee) I could so set out this matter, that all mèn should spytte at you: but I will vse my selfe charitable toward you . . ." (*Ww*, p. 192). One of the most effective examples of Barnes's "charitable" attitude toward his opponents occurs during his dispute with More on the nature of the church. Writing at the time More was in the Tower before his execution, Barnes says:

> But I will not at this tyme greatly dispute with *M. More*. But, and if hee were as hee hath beene, I would say some thyng more to hym, then I will doe at this tyme. . . . But now, that it hath pleased God (without any helpe, or knowledge of me) to bryng hym vnto this fall, I will praye to God for hym, to geue hym grace, that hee may reuoke all such false doctrine, as hee hath brought into the worlde. . . . But truely, as God shall iudge me, I am sory for hys trouble, if I could helpe hym with any lawfull meanes, I would doe my best, so euill will beare I him (*Ww*, p. 253).

Barnes's magnanimity stands out in greater contrast when compared with what More said about him.[35] His display of graciousness also affords him the luxury of praying publicly for his opponent's conversion and of implying that More's imprisonment was God's punishment for his evil actions—a shrewd blow at More, who had cited the death of Zwingli as evidence of God's displeasure with that Reformer.[36]

Complementary to establishing a favorable image of one's own side is the creation of an unflattering picture of the opposition. This task Barnes seeks to accomplish by identifying his opponents with recognized "evil" characters, by providing them with a self-condemnatory mock creed, and by giving an account of his trial for heresy which is intended to impugn the doctrine and conduct of his clerical persecutors.

The established "evil" characters with whom Barnes seeks to identify his opponents are the Jews, the Turks, the Pharisees, Judas, and the Devil himself (*Ww*, pp. 203, 211, 285). The last identification is made in a passage in which Barnes imagines himself conversing with the Devil in bishop's clothing (*Ww*, pp. 192-193).

One of Barnes's most effective techniques for establishing the character of his opponents is the claim that they are stifling their own consciences for the sake of worldly advantage. Turning to deal with an argument of Bishop Fisher's, Barnes says:

> But my Lord, say to me of your conscience, how doe you recken to auoyde the vengeaunce of God. . . ?
>
> I doe thinke verely, that your owne conscience doth sore accuse you, for thus blasphemyng the holy worde of God. Wherefore my Lord, for Christes sake remember, that you bee aged, and shall not long tary here . . . (*Ww*, p. 237).

The assertion that one's opponent secretly admits his error is a preliminary to having him actually condemn himself, and this is another technique Barnes uses to create an unflattering picture of his adversaries. It is always a more convincing tactic to have an opponent condemn himself than for the polemicist to condemn him, on the assumption that it will be the substance of the "self-condemnation" and its alleged, rather than its actual, authorship which will linger in the reader's memory. One of the methods by which an opponent may be made to condemn himself is by the formulation of a mock creed for him.[37] The mock creed technique shares many of the attributes of the polemical dialogue, in which the author assigns weak arguments and self-incriminating speeches to his opponents, and of polemical drama, in which the playwright makes his enemies condemn themselves by their own words and actions.[38] It is in this tradition that Barnes concludes that since the Pope is not chosen in accordance with Christ's law, there must be some other prescription the Roman clergy use for his election, such as the following:

> In primis, Hee that shall bee able to be Pope, must bee a vengeable tyraunt, neuer keepeing peace, but all wayes warryng for the defence (as yee call it) of S. Peters patrimonye. To suffer no Prince to dwell in rest by hym but to snatch his possessions, to the vnholy Church of Rome. To set princes together by the eares, tyll they bee both weary, and then to take ye matter in his hande, and neuer to make an ende, tyll both partyes hath geuen some possessions to his holy fatherhed. . . . Moreouer, he y^t keepeth fewest women, and hath most of them, that you

wote of,[39] hee is holyest, & apte to bee head of your church. . . .

Furthermore, hee that is a whores sonne . . . and can finde the meanes, that *.12.* men will forswere them selfe, that hee is lawfully borne. . . .[40] This is a fitte father, for such children. Finally, he y^t can geue most mony, and bye ye greatest part of cardinales of hys side, hee is best worthy to bee called Pope, & to sit on Peters stoole (*Ww*, p. 199).

The picture of the cardinals at a papal election following instructions such as the above is not calculated to enhance either their own reputation or that of their ultimate choice.

Barnes also uses the "rumor" technique, so popular in Tudor polemics, to persuade his readers that the clergy's crimes are so flagrant as to be public knowledge, and to promote prejudice against the clergy by the method of claiming that the prejudice already exists. For instance, Barnes points out that the English bishops have sworn one oath to the King and a contrary oath to the Pope; that they consider only the latter binding "all the worlde knoweth," he claims (*Ww*, p. 197). According to Barnes, "all the worlde knoweth" too that the clergy make fortunes from selling salvation (*Ww*, p. 212).

In building up his own case, Barnes usually resorts to the rather pedestrian allegation of scriptural and patristic authority. One technique, however, deserves comment, and that is his use of what I shall call "polemical *exemplum*." Polemical *exemplum* is a device which attacks the opposition under cover of illustrating and clarifying the point in discussion. For instance, to illustrate his point that even the best works a man is able to do cannot justify him before God, Barnes provides his episcopal opponents with the following example:

> I put this case my Lordes . . . that our noble prince would call you all before him, and say. My Lordes, so it is, that it hath pleased vs to cal you vnto the spiritual dignitie of Byshops. . . . Now wold we know of you which of you all hath deserued it. . .? What will you say to this? What will you aunswere to the Kynges grace? Is there one amonge you all, that dare be so bolde as to say to the kinges grace, that he hath not geuen it vnto hym freely, but that hee hath done the king so faythfull seruice that he was bound to geue it vnto him? . . . If there were one that were so proude, as to say this, thinke you that ye kings grace

woulde not laye to his charge, how that hee had not done halfe
his dutie, but were rather bound, to doe ten tymes as much more,
and yet the Kinges grace were not bou*n*d to geue hym a bys-
shopricke . . . (*Ww*, p. 234).

Barnes's "illustration" displays great economy of technique: It is of
such a nature that the bishops dare not deny its truth or validity; it
emphasizes the King's authority over the clergy by reminding the
bishops that they depend on the King and not on the Pope for their
bishoprics;[41] it flatters Henry; and it uses the previously discussed
substitution-of-opponent device, in that it leaves the bishops to argue
with their King and with God rather than with Barnes, who ends the
passage by saying, "When you haue aunswered to this, before the
kinges grace, then come and dispute with God, the iustification of
your workes. . . ."[42]

More's Answer to Barnes

The particular section of Barnes's 1531 *Supplicatyon* More attacked dealt with Barnes's view of the church. Barnes maintains,
with Tyndale, that the church consists of all true believers in Christ
who, while they may err on nonessentials, cannot sin unto damnation
so long as they follow the Word of God. Such a view of the church,
of course, denies the special character of an earthly priesthood,
against which, as we have seen, Barnes inveighs vehemently.

In opposing Barnes, More maintains essentially that no such sinless
church as Barnes describes exists on earth and that only in heaven will
the church be spotless. Therefore, argues More, Barnes is in error
when he denies the Catholic Church, admittedly containing both
sinners and nonsinners, to be the true church of Christ on earth.

When More attacked Barnes's doctrine of the church, he followed
the established convention of Tudor polemics and did his best to
belittle his opponent's ability. Some writers, concentrating only on
More's extensive attack on Barnes's competence, have concluded that
More had less respect for Barnes than for some of his other opponents,[43] but since it was More's constant practice to denigrate the
prowess of any adversary with whom he happened to be disputing,

his action implies no special attitude toward Barnes. In fact, Barnes's supposed learning in divinity was used by More as a weapon against Frith,[44] and the learning of both Frith and Tyndale is ridiculed by More when he disputes with them, just as is Barnes's learning in the controversy now under consideration.

However, More's assault on his opponent's abilities is so extensive that it lends itself to classification into various kinds. First, there is the method of invidious comparison. In line with his usual policy of characterizing any opponent as the strongest in heresy and the weakest in argument he has ever encountered, More says that Barnes in relation to Tyndale "doth . . . as farre outrunne him in rayling, as he draggeth behinde him in reasoning, wherin with Tyndall Barns can holde no foote, as down right as Tindall halteth therin" (*W*, p. 735). In fact, claims More, Barnes derives his main argument on the nature of the church from Tyndale, except that he does not have "so much witte" as to understand Tyndale and so presents Tyndale's weak reasoning in even weaker form (*W*, p. 750). It is not unlikely that such comparisons between Reformers represent an attempt by More to create between them on a personal level a split he claimed already existed in doctrinal matters. More further seeks to establish Barnes's inadequacy by telling his readers that Barnes was so soundly beaten in an oral disputation on his doctrine "that all hys euangelicall bretherne [*sic*] . . . would haue ben ashamed to se it."[45] Another method employed by More to disparage his opponent's abilities is to set up a reported dialogue between Barnes and two unlearned women —who defeat him in disputation (*W*, pp. 760-770). Barnes's alleged ineptness is further emphasized by More's charge that while Barnes argues sophistically and distorts the texts he cites to make them appear to support his views, his very sophisms and distortions are so badly managed that they prove the exact opposite of what he wants to prove (*W*, pp. 796, 803). Finally, as was Tyndale, Barnes is accused by More of making mistakes in English. More charges that Barnes is unable "to speake reason nor true englishe neither," because he once used "learn" instead of "teach." Although there are some "vnlearned," comments More in wordplay, who confuse "learn" and "teach" in certain situations, not even they misuse the two words in the manner Barnes has done (*W*, p. 742).

It is therefore not surprising that with such a professed view of his opponent's competence, More will engage in ridicule of Barnes's arguments. For this purpose he uses a variety of techniques, one of which is ridicule by distorted paraphrase, as when he claims that while Barnes has inveighed against clerical pomp and immorality, it is not that which troubles him most. Barnes's real charge against the clergy, asserts More, is his complaint that they believe the Fathers, that they desire good order in the Church, that they vow chastity, that they persecute heretics, and that they themselves are not persecuted (*W*, p. 735). Barnes's accusations are cast into a purposely ridiculous form in order to discredit them; obviously there is nothing wrong per se with any of the things More mentions, but his list is a distorted summary of what Barnes has actually said (see *Ww*, pp. 242-252). Another method of ridicule is that of misplaced emphasis, noted previously.[46] For instance, in trying to limit his subject, Barnes said that there are various meanings of the word "church," one of them being "the whole congregacion both of good and badde . . . . baudes and harlottes," and that this is not the meaning of the word he is going to discuss (*W*, p. 736). Although all Barnes is doing is trying to define the term to be discussed, More pounces on the purely illustrative words "baudes and harlottes" and launches into a tirade against him, as though Barnes were giving a disquisition on prostitution. What could Barnes possibly have against "baudes and harlottes," demands More, to want to exclude them from his church, since "the archeheretikes of all theyr sectes, are the chiefe whore maysters . . . and haue whole townes open baudes vnto theyr beastly lecherye" (*W*, p. 737). More purposely misunderstands his opponent's point, a common polemical device of the period.[47]

Intentional misunderstanding is again used to ridicule Barnes's claim that the true church is so spotless that "it shall not be lawful for saynt Peter to fynde any faulte in her." Barnes is again defining the qualities of the church (see *Ww*, p. 244), but, to permit himself to ridicule the definition, More pretends to misunderstand Barnes's meaning. It seems, comments More, that Barnes agrees with me that while she is on earth the church has spots, but that he is going to forbid Peter to tell her so. He is trying to "make saint Peter afearde to call her spottes spottes, or her wrincles wrincles. But," says More, "it will not be Barns, it will not be," for when Peter was a member of the church here on earth he had faults and could be frightened, as when he denied Christ, but now that he is a member of the glorified church in heaven, "he is now so farre out of al feare of reproofe, that yᵉ thunder of your great woorde cannot let him to say true, for anye feare of youre gargyle face, yᵗ ye came disguised with, at your last resorting hither" (*W*, p. 751). This passage, again based on an intentional misunderstanding of Barnes, is a good example of More's economy of technique, for it presents the reader with a delightful vision of Barnes trying to frighten Peter into agreeing with him, indicates that Barnes and Peter disagree, and uses the experience of Peter himself to prove More's point that the church on earth consists of both sinners and nonsinners and that only the church glorified is spotless. In addition, it makes an *ad hominem* reference to Barnes's assuming a disguise while visiting England,[48] for purposes of implying that there is something disreputable about him and his doctrine, neither of which can stand the light.[49] More also achieves ridicule of his opponent's position by another favorite device of his when, in a reported dialogue set up between Barnes and Saint Gregory, More assigns Barnes a self-deriding speech. Barnes is made to claim that he, Luther, and Tyndale, "with Luthers wife yᵉ nunne be the whole church" (*W*, p. 781). While the picture of "the whole church" consisting of three Reformers is improbable enough, the addition of Luther's wife to tip the scales to farce is a masterstroke.

The above is one of the very few occasions when More's reference to Luther's marriage is brought off with some polemical acumen rather than being merely offensive. Usually, as part of his attempt to discredit Barnes, More belabors him with Luther's marriage with such monotonous regularity that this device, as much as More's reiterated claim of infallibility for the Church, deserves to be called his *deus ex machina*.[50] But More does not restrict himself to confuting Barnes with extracts from the life of Luther. Barnes's own activities are also pressed into service to create prejudice against his doctrine. More reminds his readers that when they read Barnes they are reading the work of a man who once abjured the very heresies he is now again proclaiming and who, by the act of proclaiming them, has perjured himself (*W*, p. 735). And this is not the only time Barnes has broken his vow, notes More, answering one of his opponent's references to Augustine, and he promises to make Barnes "as wearye of saynte Austynes woordes, as euer hee was weary of saynte Austines workes, for wearynesse whereof he runne out of saynte Austines rule" (*W*, p. 771). Barnes, the renegade friar, is again the point of More's ironic request that readers excuse Barnes's incompetent arguments because sometimes his head becomes so hot that he does not know what he is saying—a hotheadedness caused by the hair he has allowed to overgrow his tonsure (*W*, p. 778). More also employs what might be called "reverse" *ad hominem* argument when he uses Barnes's reputation for learning against him.[51] More has one of his characters in a reported dialogue say, "Howe be it synce, I se nowe that you father Barnes that were ones a doctour can saye no better for it, by our Layde I begynne . . . to mystrust all the matter . . ." (*W*, p. 769). That More is capable of attacking Barnes with his own divinity degree, while continually portraying him as unlearned and incompetent, is in line with More's using that same degree of the allegedly unlearned Barnes to refute Frith. It is but another example of the preference of Tudor polemicists for immediate effect over consistency.

More's exposé of Barnes's technique is proportionate in extent to his denigration of Barnes's abilities and results in a campaign of greater concentration than that carried out against any other opponent. Often the denigration and exposé are associated, as in the passage already noted in which More accuses Barnes of merely copying Tyndale on a certain subject, without understanding what Tyndale said. But More wants to have it both ways, and so, after deriding Barnes at some length for his stupidity, More concludes that in fact Barnes probably did not misunderstand Tyndale at all but, noting the difficulties Tyndale got into by his precise treatment of the subject, decided to avoid these difficulties and to "walke so much more in the darke then Tindall doth . . ." (*W*, p. 750). Denigration and exposé are again associated in the passage, also noted above, in which More charges Barnes with trying his best to obscure the issue, but doing it so incompetently "that the more blinde he goeth about to make the reader, yᵉ more he stumbleth vnware [*sic*] vppon yᵉ trouth . . ." (*W*, p. 796).

Another method by which Barnes tries to divert the reader's attention from the incompetence of his argument, claims More, is by scoffing and railing. More promises that if the reader will only ignore such diversionary tactics, he will not be able to avoid seeing in Barnes's book "such foly and such falshed, and such repugnance and contradiccion in itselfe, that he [Barnes] shoulde neuer after nede any man elles to aunswer him but himself" (*W*, p. 749). More, himself a master of rhetoric, further charges Barnes with using rhetorical devices in an attempt to influence his readers.[52] What is the point, demands More, parodying Barnes, of all "that thys fonde frere fiddeleth forth here by letters, after the rude rimelesse runninge of a scottishe ieste . . . . but to shew hys rial rethorike, and to contende with Tyndall in witlesse eloquence. . . ."[53] Usually, however, More sees in Barnes's use of rhetoric the more sinister aim of "pleasaunt scoffing" at the clergy and the "goodly garnishing" of a bad matter (*W*, p. 750), although, he allows, there are also occasions when Barnes gets so carried away by his own technique, "is so sore beside aboute his rethorike, that it is no meruaile though he can not entende to speake reason . . ." (*W*, p. 742). Nor does More, practitioner par excellence of polemical humor, care for Barnes's use of the same weapon, which he does his best to denigrate by ridiculing its user and questioning the morality of its admirers. More tells his readers that after Barnes has scoffed at the clergy, "the*n* he lyketh much hys mery mockes, and fareth as he wer fro*m* a frere waxen a fideler, and would at a tauerne goe gete hym a peny for a fitte of myrth." But, continues More, I shall not discuss his "mockes, his mowes, his iesting, and his railing," since those who like such a method of disputation "be not of so great honesti that I greatly long to content them . . ." (*W*, p. 735). The reason for More's animus against Barnes's use of humor is that Barnes used humor for the same purpose as More himself occasionally did, namely, to divert the reader's attention. More is no happier to have turned against him the weapon of humor he uses himself than was Luther to be attacked with the device of *praemunitio* he used constantly. And so More accuses Barnes of playing "Tindalles parte . . . in flitting from the point . . . and after in lyke maner of rayling." And, More continues, although one might suppose "that Tindall were in suche fond scoffing perelesse: yet doth frere

Barns . . . outrunne him in rayling . . ." (*W*, p. 735). Finally, More accuses Barnes of mistranslation, of distorting the sources from which he quotes, and of purposely giving faulty references to prevent his sources from being checked.[54]

As he did in other polemics, so in his controversy with Barnes, More dramatizes his opponent's weakness and promulgates his own views through the medium of the dialogue form. He sets up three reported dialogues, the first between Barnes and a simple woman, the second between Barnes and the even more simple hostess of the inn at which he was staying, and the third between Barnes and Saint Gregory. Each of the three in turn is made to debate Barnes on the nature of the church, and each, not too surprisingly, confutes him.

More's use of two simple characters as Catholic spokesmen is noteworthy, for, as we have seen, the simple character was usually a Protestant.[55] More already satirized this development by the unfavorable delineation of the simple Protestant interlocutor in his *Dialogue*, but now he reverses the stock situation and has a Protestant Doctor of Divinity bested in argument by two simple Catholics. To enhance the effect of Barnes's defeat, More goes out of his way to emphasize the simplicity of the two women. The first is described as a simple soul, perplexed by the great variety of religious views, "a wise woman y^t could no more but reade englyshe," but who, nevertheless, overcomes Barnes (*W*, pp. 763, 766). The second woman, who is illiterate, confesses that whether Catholics or Protestants "declare the scripture truely . . . passeth my capacity to perceiue," but she, too, defeats Barnes (*W*, pp. 769-770). To heighten the effect, More makes both women inclined to give Barnes a more than sympathetic hearing at the outset—they wish to be instructed by the learned doctor—but the more they listen to what Barnes has to say, the more disenchanted with his doctrine they become (*W*, pp. 760, 766, 769). Thus More places Barnes in the position of being defeated not by militant Catholics, but by two simple souls who have begun to doubt the truth of Catholicism and who are genuinely perplexed—but who have the truth of their original faith confirmed, because Barnes unwittingly demonstrates to them the ludicrous nature of his own doctrine for which he urged them to abandon the Catholic faith. The import of More's dialogues is not only Barnes's defeat, but also that an unlearned yet unprejudiced person will inevitably choose the orthodox faith and not, as was the implication of the Protestant "simple-soul" propaganda, the Reformed one. Thus in his two characters More manages to have the best of both worlds: They are at one and the same time represented as not committed to Catholicism—indeed Barnes's hostess inclines toward heresy at the beginning—and yet serve as More's spokesmen for the Catholic position.

That they are really More's spokesmen is quite clear. After one of the "simple" souls has established the basic Catholic position that the ultimate source of correct doctrine is the Church and not the Scriptures, she ends her disquisition by rebuking Barnes for failing to make clear in his treatise how the true church of which he talks so much might be known (*W*, p. 763), a point at which More has been hammering away throughout his polemic. Barnes's hostess is even more critical, expressing the opinion, after hearing him propound his doctrine, "that she had alwaye taken hym for wiser, and wold haue went he could haue taught better" (*W*, p. 769). For she has perceived the true relationship of Scripture to Church, and she tells Barnes that "you do not so much as knowe which it [Scripture] is but by the meane of her" (*W*, p. 769). I can see also, Barnes's illiterate hostess is made to continue, that you were once with the Church and have left her out of anger, that you slander her, that many saints were brought up in her—whereas your church cannot boast of a single saint, that our Church has miracles and yours has none, and that you have invented a church that cannot be known on earth only because each of your many churches claims to be the only true church and yet "eche of you seeth hys owne part so feable and so farre vnable to be defended in that point, that sith no one church of al yours may be match to our church . . . ye be faine for this cause to sende vs to an vnknowen churche" (*W*, p. 770). *Aut Morus aut nullus.*

More's technique in using Saint Gregory as interlocutor to Barnes in the third reported dialogue is essentially the same as in the "simple-soul" dialogues, except that the implications of character are reversed. While in the former two dialogues More drew on the ostensible simplicity of his characters, in his use of Gregory he naturally relies on the saint's reputation for sanctity and learning. Another reason for the selection of Gregory to debate Barnes is provided by More himself, namely, that Gregory lived before the time Barnes claimed the

Church fell into error (*W*, p. 780). Thus More brings against Barnes a disputant whose reputation Barnes cannot ignore. Of course, the very act of pitting Gregory against Barnes also implies that the saint agrees with More and that he disagrees with Barnes. And once again Barnes's opponent is made into More's private spokesman, so much so that Gregory-More can demand of Barnes and Luther, who claim to follow only Scripture, why they have "runne both out of religion, and the tone wedded a nunne, and both broken theyre holy sacred uowes," when the breaking of vows is condemned in Scripture (*W*, p. 783). One of the most amusing uses of this Gregory-More character occurs when More pictures the saint wishing to be shown Barnes's church. Gregory asks an attendant to count the members of this church and have a crier call out their names, whereupon the count is taken and the crier calls out: "frere Luther one, Cate his nunne twayne, Tyndall three, frere Barns foure. . . ." To this More's spokesman responds in astonishment:

> what here be but foure of you . . . & you be al knowen, & your false faith & abhominable beastely sectes by your owne beastly profession, altogither knowen, & therfore you cannot be yᵉ church of true good men vnknowen. . . . he that by hys open euill and abhominable dedes doing, & open profession of false abhominable heresies sheweth himself naught, cannot be for yᵉ time secretly a good man (*W*, p. 785).

There is no attempt here to use any of Gregory's actual words; he is merely a prestigious vehicle for More's own opinions, prejudices—and faulty logic, for in this passage as elsewhere More assumes that his opponents are evil because they are heretics and that they are heretics because they are evil.

We come now to a consideration of portions of More's polemic in which he seems to be trying to frighten Barnes out of England. That More did try to frighten Barnes into leaving the country and that it was on account of More that he left is indicated by the testimony of Frith (*Ww*, p. 155). If the interpretation is correct that one of the means More used to intimidate Barnes was to include in his polemic certain passages about Barnes, to be discussed presently, then this work—or at least certain portions of it—although published as the eighth book of *The second parte of the confutacion of Tyndals answere* in 1533, must have been written before Barnes left England early in 1532. That More's references to him in the preface to the first part of the *Confutacion*, published in 1532, were written while Barnes was still in England is quite clear from the language More uses. He refers to Barnes as "at thys daye comen to the realme" (*W*, p. 342) and says he "shall . . . haue leaue to departe" (*W*, p. 343). It seems probable, then, that More wrote these allusions to Barnes in the preface and in the parts of his book against Barnes at the same time, for, as we shall see, some of the references in the eighth book of the *Confutacion* are, like all of the references in the preface, to someone still present in England. There remains the question why More did not excise these passages from his 1533 publication, since in 1533 Barnes was no longer in the realm—and More had been out of power since May, 1532—so that there was no longer any point in More's trying to frighten him into leaving. The most likely answer is that More was too busy to change what he had written previously, since 1533 was a year of peak polemical production for him, and he merely used the material as it stood. It is just possible that he also retained these passages in the hope that Barnes would be frightened from ever returning to England, no matter who was Chancellor.

Seemingly to frighten Barnes, then, whether into fleeing England in early 1532 or possibly to keep him from returning thereafter, More inserted in his work passages which were intended to reveal to his opponent how closely he was being watched and how well the most minute details of his movements and associations were known. More tells Barnes, for instance, that "when he came laste into the lande by the kynges licence,"[56] when he realized that "he coulde no better aunswere for his heresies, and that hys false folishe hope had fayled him" he shaved off his beard and went about disguised as a merchant of eel skins (*W*, pp. 741-742, 751), specifically, in "a marchauntes gowne with a redde Myllayn bonet" (*W*, p. 756). Considering the fact that, as More tells us elsewhere (*W*, p. 761), Barnes did not really disguise himself because "he coulde not better aunswere for his heresies," but rather to escape detection and apprehension by More, who was claiming that Barnes's safe-conduct was invalid and that he could lawfully be burned,[57] the information that his disguise was so ineffective would not tend to calm Barnes's fears. Uneasiness would doubtless again be created by the information that More also knew the exact location of Barnes's hiding place, namely, "the house of hys secrete hostes at the signe of the bottell at Botolfes wharfe" (*W*, p. 756). And More keeps up the pressure. Again and again he slips into his polemic references to Barnes's disguise, lodgings, and acquaintances. In one of the reported dialogues More has Barnes confess to his interlocutor that he,

> sauing for the kinges safe conduct, should haue standen in peryl to be burned. . . . Whyche safe conducte, because it was graunted but for vi. weekes, nowe more then almost passed, for which cause he chaunged his . . . apparell . . . and shoue his beard, and went like a marchaunt, that he myghte be the lesse marked in taryinge after the saufe conduct. . . . Wherefore sythe he may not safelye tarye here, but must except he would be burned, go get hym ouer [the sea] againe . . ." (*W*, p. 761).

The setting of the dialogue is the eve of Barnes's departure from England, and so one could argue that the words "nowe more then almost passed" are merely part of More's dramatization of his character and were written after Barnes had left. However, there would be little point to such dramatization—especially the time reference to the safe-conduct—were Barnes not present in England. It appears more likely, therefore, that the passage was written while he was still in England. That its purpose is to frighten Barnes is fairly clear, whatever may have been the reason for publishing it so long after his departure. Again, More makes Barnes's second interlocutor "hys owne secrete hostesse the good wyfe of the bottell of Botolphs warfe," about whom More knows a wealth of detail. He knows, for instance, that she has a limp, a fact to which he refers frequently (*W*, pp. 766, 767, 768, 770), and that "she is not tounge tyed," for he himself has heard her talk (*W*, p. 766). He also remembers examining her as Lord Chancellor on a charge of harboring renegade members of the religious orders.[58] In other words, More gives Barnes's hostess plain warning that he remembers she has already been apprehended once for exactly the same thing she is doing now in sheltering Barnes. That his intention is to frighten her, as well as Barnes, is further emphasized by the fact that More puts into her mouth the resolution to have nothing more to do with harboring heretics and to attend only to her business—a rather plain hint as to what her future course of action should be (*W*, p. 769).

IV

Simon Fish

Among the number of works which the Church judged to be heretical coming into England from the Continent, there appeared in 1528 a book entitled *A Supplycacion for the Beggars*,[1] written by Simon Fish (?–1531). Fish had been a law student at Gray's Inn, where he had acted in an anti-Wolsey interlude and thereby had incurred the wrath of that prelate. Fish fled to the Netherlands where he met Tyndale and his associate Roy, and from them he imbibed the Reformed theology. His *Supplycacion*, which was dedicated to Henry VIII, was printed in Antwerp and from there smuggled into England. Fish himself, shortly after publication of his treatise, risked a visit to London for the purpose of aiding in the distribution of Tyndale's New Testament. He was apprehended and charged with heresy, but before he could be tried by an ecclesiastical court, he died of the plague in 1531.[2] According to More, Fish returned to the Church before his death (*W*, p. 881).

Fish's work is ostensibly aimed at improving the lot of the English

152

poor, especially that of the beggars. In order to enhance its effect, Fish puts his purported appeal on behalf of the beggars into the mouths of the beggars themselves, who address Henry VIII directly:

> To the King Ovre souereygne lorde. Most lamentably compley-neth theyre wofull mysery vnto your highnes, youre poore daily bedemen, the wretched hidous monstres (on whome scarcely for horror any yie dare loke,) the foule, vnhappy sorte of lepres, and other sore people, nedy impotent, blinde, lame, and sike, that live onely by almesse, how that theyre nombre is daily so sore encreased, that all the almesse of all the weldisposed people of this youre realme is not halfe ynough for to susteine theim, but that for verey constreint they die for hunger (p. 1).

Fish contends that while the clergy constitute but a small part of England's population, they control one-half of its wealth, and he charges that the monasteries, instead of caring for the destitute, increase the number of beggars in the land through excessive taxation (pp. 1-2).

He seeks to support his arguments with an array of statistics, by means of which he hopes to impress his readers with the veracity of his statements. He claims that the clergy own one-third of the realm, one-tenth of all farm produce and livestock, and that they receive a tenth part of all servants' wages (pp. 1-2). He computes that from the 52,000 parish churches which, he states, are in England, and assigning only ten householders to every parish, the five orders of mendicant friars alone get £43,333 6s. 8d. per annum (pp. 2-3). In sum, he claims that the clergy own almost half the wealth of the kingdom, while their number is only one hundredth of the male population, or one four-hundredth, counting women and children (p. 4).[3]

Fish's real aim in writing the *Supplycacion* was to have the English clergy expropriated and their power reduced. Since much of that power derived from the wealth accumulated as a consequence of the doctrine of purgatory, in that people paid the clergy to pray for the souls of departed relatives and friends, Fish questions the existence of such a place.

He does so not by revealing his own opinion but rather by report-

ing that there are many learned and pious men who refuse to believe
in purgatory. His short treatment of the subject is studded with
expressions such as "there be many men [who] . . . declare," "They
sey," and "Lyke wyse saie they" (pp. 10-11). Thus Fish uses the
reportorial technique with which Skelton had protected himself in
his anti-Wolsey poems and under cover of which Christopher Saint-
German was to launch his attack on the clergy a few years later.[4]
Fish's caution probably stems from his desire not to lose acceptance
of his economic allegations by committing himself on a subject in
which he obviously had no competence; he had no reputation as a
theologian. More important, he did not want to have his pamphlet
discredited as being the work of an openly heretical author;[5] he
himself points out that the men whose opinions he cites are called
heretics for holding these opinions (p. 11).

Fish also charges that the clergy are, and always have been, a
subversive element within the realm. Just at the time when his friend
and associate William Tyndale was formulating his own peculiar
interpretations of secular and ecclesiastical history and was using
them as a weapon against the Church (see fn. 6), Fish was advancing
charges of a long record of clerical subversion very similar to those
made by his more famous contemporary. Like Tyndale and Barnes,
he regarded the past and present activities of the English clergy as
one huge conspiracy.

Long ago, Fish's beggars tell Henry, the clergy crept into the kingdom with the intention of eventually taking it over, and this they
accomplished by setting up their own clerical state within a state,
which in time grew to be more powerful than the secular kingdom in
which it flourished (p. 1). In spite of the fact that your ancestors
made laws to curb the power of the clergy, Fish's spokesmen continue to Henry, the clergy always managed to evade these laws and
retain their power (p. 9). The intention of such an historical reference—as is, indeed, the intention of all of Fish's references to
history—is to remind the tradition-conscious Henry and his Parliament of historical precedent for anticlerical legislation, and that such
previous legislation failed because it was not enforced stringently
enough and did not go far enough. Fish's history lessons evidently
found willing pupils, for the so-called Reformation Parliament,

which met soon after the publication of his pamphlet, passed very effective anticlerical legislation indeed.

Fish has the beggars warn Henry that if he will not carry out all the clergy's wishes, they will stir up his people to rebel against him as they stirred up the subjects of his predecessor, King John.[6] Playing on the King's pride in his Welsh ancestry, the beggars remind Henry that the ancient kings of the Britons were supreme in their own dominions; they did not suffer their subjects to be taxed by the emissaries of a foreign power such as the papacy (p. 3). Broadly hinting that the clergy are the cause of all of Henry's foreign difficulties—a theme we have seen expanded by Tyndale[7]—Fish's spokesmen assert that neither the Danes nor the Saxons could ever have conquered Britain, nor could Arthur have withstood the Romans, had they had so many clerical parasites among them as now infest the realm of England (p. 3). The mention of Arthur was again an appeal to Henry's family pride, for he claimed descent from the British hero, and his elder brother had been named Arthur.[8]

Fish sees the problems of his own time as a product both of past clerical conspiracies and of a continuing process of clerical treason paralyzing the realm. He points out to Henry that a people impoverished by the rapacity of the clergy will be unable to pay him taxes when he needs them for national defense, because all their money is in the hands of the clergy (p. 3). In his treatment of the subject, Barnes wrote that the clergy always refused to provide the King with money when he needed it (*Ww*, p. 194), but uncharacteristically failed to ascribe a motive more sinister than greed to the clergy's reluctance to aid the King with taxes. For once Fish goes beyond Barnes and Tyndale, claiming that helping the King with money is furthest from the clergy's thoughts because they want all the money they can obtain to build up their power against him (p. 4). Fish is prepared to provide details of this clerical "treason fund" in operation. It is used, for instance, he claims, to reward those who have opposed the Crown or its adherents, as it was used to reward Dr. Horsey for murdering Hunne.[9]

To extort his money and that of his subjects, Fish's spokesmen tell Henry, the clergy have a very convenient and efficient tool: the charge of heresy. Anyone who refuses to give the clergy all the money they demand is immediately branded as a heretic (p. 2). The same tactic is used against anyone who attempts to expose the clergy's machinations, continues Fish, and as proof of his contention again cites the case of Richard Hunne (p. 9). He charges further that it is to prevent their being exposed as traitors to their King that the clergy resist a vernacular Bible for the laity, for they do not want the people to know that the Bible teaches that all men, including the clergy, should be subject to their temporal rulers (p. 11). The point of these accusations is to turn against the clergy the very weapon Fish claims they have been using, namely, the blanket charge that anyone who criticizes them must be a heretic. Fish turns the weapon around, aims it at the clergy, and fires off the assertion that any cleric who tries to counter criticism by charging his critic with heresy must be trying to cover up treason. Fish's final count in his general charge of treason is that the clergy of England have placed themselves above the law of the realm. A few years before the great controversy was to take place between More and Christopher Saint-German over whether members of the clergy should be tried in secular courts,[10] Fish points out to Henry that the existence of clerical courts is another pillar in the structure of clerical treason which needs to be pulled down if the King is to be master of his own house (p. 12).

The clergy, Fish warns Henry, plan to take over the entire kingdom. They have

> of one kyngdome made tweyne: the spirituall kyngdome (as they call it), for they wyll be named first, And your temporall kingdome. And whiche of these .ij. kingdomes (suppose ye) is like to ouergrowe the other? ye [yea] to put the other clere out of memory? Truely the kingdome of the bloudsuppers; for to theym is giuen daily out of your kingdome (pp. 9–10).

Was not that the reason, asks Fish, that they murdered Hunne, because Hunne claimed that the King's law was above theirs? And, continues Fish, this is the reason why the chief of the royal council, the most important law-making body in the land, is always a cleric, to ensure that the King's law never will be above the spiritual, for he

> hath euer such an inordinate loue vnto his owne kingdome, that he will maynteyn that, though all the temporall kingdoms and

commo*n*welth of the worlde shulde therfore vtterly be vndone
(p. 13).

To remedy England's economic and political ills, Fish makes two
proposals. He urges that effective laws be passed to curb the clergy's
power, but warns that this will be a very difficult thing to do, since
in the King's Parliament the clergy are stronger than the King himself, and anyone who has in the past dared to criticize their actions
has been declared a heretic (pp. 8-9). His other suggestion is that the
idle monks be turned out of their monasteries and made to work:

> Then shall, aswell the nombre of oure forsaid monstruous sort,
> as of the baudes, hores, theues, and idell people, decreace. Then
> shall these great yerely exaccions cease. Then shall not youre
> swerde, power, crowne, dignite, and obedience of your people,
> be translated from you. Then shall you haue full obedience of
> your people. Then shall the idell people be set to worke. Then
> shall matrimony be moche better kept. Then shal the generation
> of your people be encreased. Then shall your comons encrease
> in richesse. Then shall the gospell be preached. Then shall none
> begge oure almesse from vs. Then shal we haue ynough, and more
> then shall suffice vs; whiche shall be the best hospitall that euer
> was founded for vs. Then shall we daily pray to god for your
> most noble estate long to endure (pp. 14–15).

How true are the claims which Fish makes? His statement that
the Church owned one-third of all the land in England is generally
concurred in by modern scholars,[11] but it seems that his figure of
£43,333 6s. 8d. for the annual income which the five mendicant
orders derived from just the one source of quarterly taxation is highly
exaggerated, since my computations, based on what data are available,
suggest that the total annual income of the English friaries was actually only a small fraction of that sum.[12] Fish's statement that the
clergy constituted only one four-hundredth of the population is incorrect,[13] while his assertion that before the clergy gained power in
England there were no thieves and vagabonds richly deserved More's
answer that there had been thieves and vagabonds since before the
Flood (*W*, p. 311). It is interesting to note that the evil conditions
which Fish describes did not disappear; for after the monks had been
turned out of their monasteries, their lay successors continued exactly

the same practices of which Fish had complained, so that in the years 1542 and 1546 there appeared two works[14] just like Fish's *Supplycacyon*, the only difference being that this time the complaints of poverty, high rents, and lack of hospitals were made against the lords who had succeeded to the monastic lands, instead of against the monks who had previously owned them.

More's Defense

More answered Fish's work in the same year it reached England (1529) by publishing *The supplicacion of soules*, the aim of which was to defend the position of the clergy and to uphold the doctrine of purgatory.

More's work is divided into two books; the first is taken up with a confutation of Fish's statistics and a general defense of the English clergy; the second and longer book deals with the question of purgatory, which was really one of Fish's minor concerns. In a fashion reminiscent of Fisher's works against Luther,[15] More sets out to prove the existence of purgatory from reason, the Fathers, and Scripture but, unlike Fisher, he takes into consideration his opponent's prejudice against using the first two as authorities and concentrates on the last.

Not only does More pattern the title of his book on that of his adversary, but he also adopts Fish's technique of making his appeal come from the mouths of those people most immediately concerned. As More sees it, a discontinuance of the belief in purgatory would most affect those already there, who depend for deliverance on the prayers of friends still on earth. Whereas Fish's beggars appealed for relief from their earthly misery, More dramatizes the reality of purgatory by reporting the pleas of the tormented souls who suffer there. That More consciously adopts his opponent's form and makes it part of his own technique is further illustrated by the fact that his opening exactly parallels that of the *Supplycacyon for the Beggars*, already cited:

> To all good christen people.
> In moste pieteous wise continuallye calleth & cryeth vpon your

deuoute charitie & most te*n*der pitie, for help, cou*m*forte, & reliefe, your late acquaintance, kindred, spouses, co*m*panions, play felowes, & frendes, & now your hu*m*ble & vnacquaynted, and half forgotten supplyantes, pore priesoners of god, yᵉ sely soules in purgatory . . . (*W*, p. 288).

More immediately establishes the souls as rivals to the earthly beggars by having the former declare that no one on earth can possibly be in greater need than they are, nor anyone else so sick and impotent (*W*, pp. 291-292). He pictures the souls as very grieved that anyone should doubt the existence of purgatory, which has been an article of belief for 1500 years, or question the reality of the torments which they are even now suffering (*W*, p. 314). At the beginning and end of the work, More records the complaints of the souls and their physical agony, in order to emphasize to his readers the actuality of this state intermediate between heaven and hell through which they, too, will one day have to pass.

By the device of having the souls speak from purgatory itself, More is able to make his appeal for a belief in the existence of this place a very immediate and personal one. The souls wonder how anyone could be so hardhearted as to let relatives burn in the fire before his eyes, and More makes them petition the alms and prayers of friends:

For if your father, your mother, your child, your brother, your sister, your husband, your wife, or a very stranger too, laye in your syght some where in fyre, & that your meanes might help him: what hert were so hard, what stomacke were so stony, that could sit in rest at supper, or slepe in rest a bedde, and let a ma*n* lye and burne? (*W*, p. 334).

The souls regret that, instead of sending it to purgatory before them, they left so much money behind on earth where it is not being used on their behalf to buy priests' prayers for their release (*W*, p. 335). More carries personification to such lengths that in one place he has the bodiless souls complain that they are so poor that they do not even have cloaks to put on their backs (*W*, p. 337). However, at the end of the book, the souls explain that they were forced to speak in human terms to make themselves understood; otherwise it would have been impossible for living men to perceive their pain (*W*, p. 338).

What More does, in fact, is to create a persona for himself.[16] Just as in his *Dialogue concernynge heresyes* he had created the persona of the character "More" as a gentle, wise, and considerate disputant who was eminently fair to his "Protestant" interlocutor, so in the *Supplicacion* he creates the persona of the souls. This device serves him not only to make the highly emotional appeal for a belief in purgatory just discussed but also provides him with a number of other polemical advantages. For instance, through the persona of the souls who are, after all, beyond all human passions, More manages to endow his attack on Fish with an aura of otherworldly graciousness and impartiality. More's spokesmen are very solicitous of Fish's temporal and spiritual welfare. They feel comforted that, since his book is anonymous, their exposing his malicious and heretical intent in writing it will cause him no earthly harm, and they pray to God to remit his punishment in the hereafter (*W*, p. 289). An attack made in such a spirit can gain only credibility for the charges made—and admiration on our part for the skillful technique of its author. More evidently appreciated the value of his spiritual spokesmen, for through them he tries to convince his readers—among whom, it should always be remembered, was Henry—that far from being prejudiced against a speedy and effective solution to the problems of the poor, no one could be more concerned than he himself and the clergy he is defending. Indeed, for himself More could make this claim with some truth, for he had discoursed on the subject in his *Utopia*, but in the *Supplicacion* his solutions are of a different order from those offered in 1516. Now More has his souls declare that, far from envying Fish's beggars as rivals for alms, they pray that people will be generous in extending charity to their earthly brethren, for these alms are begged in the name of the Lord they all serve, and earthly devotion is a comfort to the souls in purgatory (*W*, p. 292). Thus More tries to establish his work as being not only impartial, but actually much more concerned about the plight of the beggars than Fish's book.

Another advantage More derives from his persona is that his spokesmen are not merely merciful and impartial but are also endowed with more than human knowledge. After all, Thomas More may err, but the souls already in purgatory are peculiarly well situated to know whether or not there is such a place (*W*, p. 289). In fact, their knowledge extends much further. They can assure More's readers, for instance, on the basis of their superior information gathered from sources in heaven and hell, as well as from purgatory, that every anticlerical allegation Fish makes is false (*W*, p. 298).

Finally, More uses his persona to ridicule both Fish's style and content. His souls recount how Fish's rhetorical cannonade of charges against the clergy thundered all the way to purgatory, where it made the inhabitants start up in terror at the fearful noise, but noise is all it turned out to be (*W*, pp. 294-295). And More unforgettably characterizes the quality of one of Fish's arguments when he has the tormented souls in purgatory declare that it "is so mery and so madde, that it were able to make one laugh that lieth in the fire . . ." (*W*, pp. 306-307).

To "make one laugh" at his opponent, that is, the polemical use of humor, is, as we have seen, characteristic of More's technique of controversy, but because many of the arguments Fish presents are weak, More seems to feel no necessity for using humor as a means of escaping from difficult situations, for which purpose he had sometimes used humor when answering Tyndale. Also, More's *Supplicacion* contains no passages of theological exposition equal in length to those found in the *Dialogue concernynge heresyes* or in the *Confutacyon of Tyndales answere*. Consequently, the *Supplicacion* contains few "merry tales," the specific medium of humor More favors for diversionary purposes and to relieve tedium. What is more in evidence is a series of dry observations on some of Fish's less accurate statements. For instance, More wonders how it could be possible, if the clergy constitute so small a percentage of the population as Fish asserts, that the clergy's celibacy could depopulate the land, as the *Supplycacyon for the Beggars* claims. Also, continues More, considering that the clergy have been celibate for centuries, it is surprising that there are any people left at all in England (*W*, p. 305).

More makes short work of quite a number of Fish's assertions. He says that if all the beggars were dying of hunger, they should be found lying dead in the streets, but he has not noticed any (*W*, p.

293). He points out that if the monks should be cast out of their monasteries, as Fish proposes, the number of beggars, instead of being reduced, would be considerably increased, since all the ousted monks would swell the ranks of the unemployed (*W*, p. 302). More also reminds his readers that from the clerical income which Fish mentions a goodly number of laymen employed by the clergy get their wages (*W*, p. 300), while he merely ridicules Fish's estimate of the proportion of the clergy to the laity as only one hundredth part of the male population (*W*, p. 300).

But his most devastating assault is on Fish's claim that he is really concerned about the condition of England's poor and that the expropriation of the clergy is a means toward alleviating the plight of the beggars, rather than an end in itself. If Fish were really concerned with the fate of the beggars, argues More, parodying the form of one of Fish's passages,[17] one would think that he would have suggested some provision for them:

> But nowe to yᵉ pore beggers. What remedy fyndeth theyr proctour for them? to make hospitals? Nai ware of yᵗ, therof he wyll none in no wyse. For therof he sayth the mo yᵉ worse, because thei be profitable to priestes. What remedye than? Giue the*m* any money? Naye naye not a grote. What other thynge then? Nothing in yᵉ world will serue but this that if the kinges grace will build a sure hospitall yᵗ neuer shal fayle to reliue al the syck beggers for euer, let hym giue nothing to the*m*, but looke what the clergye hath & take all that from the*m* (*W*, pp. 301–302).

As a matter of fact, there is very little humor in More's *Supplicacion,* and what there is consists of the biting kind just cited. Another good example of this heavy-handed and bitter wit is to be found in More's satirical examination of Fish's statistics with the object of disproving the assertion that there are 52,000 parish churches in the realm, yielding an annual income for the mendicant orders of £43,333 6s. 8d. Let us examine Fish's figures, says More, because they are very instructive for anyone who wants to learn arithmetic. Fish tells us that there are 52,000 parishes with ten householders each, which he calculates makes a total of 520,000 householders. Now every order of the five orders of friars, says Fish, gets a penny a quarter from each householder. From every house then, continues

More, each of the five orders gets 5d., and here is the first point Fish teaches us, More comments, namely, that five times one makes five. Then Fish shows us that the five orders get 20d. from each household every year, from which we may learn that five fours make twenty. So, expounds More, the total comes to 520,000 quarters of angels, according to Fish. Now, continues More, just because the realm has no coin called a quarter angel, we must not be confused, for it is evident that Fish invented this coin to teach us a point in calculation, namely, that 20d. is the fourth part of 6s. 8d., at which rate he values the angel. Then Fish continues his computation to show us that 520,000 quarter angels make 260,000 half angels, after which he demonstrates further that 260,000 half angels amount exactly to 130,000 angels, whereby, concludes More, all may learn that half of sixty is thirty and the half of two is one (*W*, p. 294). This is not exactly hilarious. Probably for the reasons previously noted, *The supplicacion of soules* fails to attain the heights of humor which mark many of More's other controversial works. The best More seems capable of here is to jeer at, by constant repetition, the phrase "the great broade botomles occean sea of euilles" (*W*, pp. 295, 301, 305), which Fish uses to describe the iniquities of the clergy.

More concludes that Fish's book is "a booke in dede nothynge lesse intending" than its professed purpose (*W*, p. 289). Therefore he undertakes to provide his readers with an exposé of Fish's true intention, as well as of his tactics and strategy. The mere demonstration that in the discussion of religious truth an opponent used any tactics at all was calculated to prejudice readers against that opponent. According to More, not only was Fish much less interested in the plight of the beggars than in attacking the clergy, but his ultimate intention was even more dastardly: It was nothing less than the extirpation of the Christian faith and the substitution of Luther's heresy (*W*, p. 314). Thus More tries to demonstrate that Fish's attack on the clergy is motivated purely by his heresy, hoping that such a demonstration will "minish & berieue him his credence" for the charges he makes (*W*, p. 314). Fish's technique, in order to carry out his purpose, reveals More, consists of deception and sophistry, "falshed vnder pretext of playnnesse, crueltie vnder the cloke of pietie: sedicion vnder the colour of counsayl . . ." (*W*, p. 290). As More sees it, Fish's attack on the English clergy is the spearhead of a revised Protestant strategy. At first, More explains to his readers, the Reformers openly attacked the faith of Christ in such books as Tyndale's New Testament, *Obedience*, and *Mammon*, and Barlowe's *Rede me and be nott wrothe*.[18] But when they saw that such direct attacks alienated people instead of converting them to Lutheranism, they decided on a different plan. They would write one book specifically attacking the clergy, which would not include any open heresies that might be offensive to the masses. Then, if this book proved successful, the entire Protestant attack would adopt the new line of attacking only the clergy rather than Catholic doctrine. With the defenders of the Catholic faith discredited, it would then be easier to attack and wipe out that faith itself (*W*, p. 310).

More is not content with charging merely that his opponent intends to subvert the established ecclesiastical order. To demonstrate that Fish is far more dangerous to the commonwealth than the clergy he accuses of subversion, More charges him with "communism": This man, warns More, "vnder pretext of reformacion (bearing euery man that ought hath, in hand that he hath to much) shall assay to make newe diuision of euery mannes land and substance . . ." (*W*, p. 313). More goes on to reveal to his readers his opponent's devilish machinations and tells them that Fish's plan is first to attack the clergy and deprive them of their goods, after which he will attempt to do the same with the merchants, then with the nobles, and, finally, with the King himself (*W*, p. 304). And soon, cautions More, he will write another treatise, in which he will find reason to take away the lands of all the people by force and distribute them among the beggars (*W*, p. 305). To add weight to his dire prophecy, More turns to recent history for illustration:

> We be content that ye beleue vs not, but if it haue so proued all redy by those vplandishe Lutherans that rose vp in Almayne. Which beyng once raysed by suche sedicious bookes as is thys beggers supplicacion . . . set firste vppon spirituall prelates. But shortly thereupon . . . stretched vnto the temporall prynces . . . (*W*, p. 305).

This reference to the Peasants' Revolt by no means exhausts More's use of history in his polemic against Fish. More's extensive references to the English chronicles were made mandatory by the fact that so many of his opponent's charges were based on what was alleged to be the historical record. Therefore More, in his turn, calls the chronicles to witness that Fish's allegations have no basis in fact (*W*, p. 296). For instance, he denies all of Fish's assertions about King John and his reign. It is not true, maintains More, that the Pope forced John to make England tributary to Rome by the grant of a thousand marks. Nor is it true, More continues, that Stephen Langton, the Pope's appointee to the see of Canterbury, was ever a traitor to John, as Fish maintains. More also brands as a lie Fish's allegation that there was anything irregular about the Archbishop's election, maintaining that he was lawfully elected by the monks of Canterbury, "in whom as the king well knew and denied it not," the election of the Archbishop belonged. Equally false, according to More, is the contention that John opposed Langton's election because Langton was a traitor. John was "discontented" because he had recommended another for the post, whom the monks rejected. "And," concludes More, "that thys is as we tel you . . . Ye shal nowe perceiue . . . by diuers cronicles . . ." (*W*, p. 296).[19]

To Fish's charge that the existence of clerical courts detracts from the authority of the King's courts, More answers that in times past the king and the nobility have always permitted such courts, "and the people too, haue by plain parliamentes confirmed them," so that, in fact, the matter has not been in dispute at all (*W*, p. 296). Turning to more recent events, More challenges the veracity of one of the major premises on which Fish had based his pamphlet: It is simply not true, maintains More, that lately the number of beggars has increased in England (*W*, p. 292). As we have already noted in More's reference to the Peasants' Revolt, not all of his appeals to history and current events are defensive. Sometimes he turns to the chronicles for ammunition with which to attack his opponent. An example occurs during More's attempt to impugn Fish's motives in criticizing the wealth of the clergy. It is because the clergy punish heresy that Fish demands their expropriation, More tells his readers. And, he continues, such a tactic on the part of heretics is nothing new; it is their standard defence against exposure and punishment. As an illustration, More points out that in the reign of Henry IV when a certain heretic was burned, immediately a bill was introduced into the next Parliament to expropriate the clergy. However, when it became clear that the supporters of the bill were favorers of heresy —their only reason for introducing the bill—the bill was "sette aside for nought." A little later, continues More, in the reign of Henry V, some other heretics were burned, and antiheresy laws were passed in Parliament. Immediately, the supporters of the heretics reintroduced the bill to expropriate the clergy, which "eft sones considered for such as it was & cumming of such maliciouse purpose as it came: was againe reiected, & set aside for nought." Finally, a long time later, records More, yet another heretic was burned, as a result of which a mob of heretics rose up in the town of Abingdon, determined not to "leese any more labour by putting vp of billes in the parlyamentes," but to kill all the clergy and "to make an open insurreccion & subuerte all the realme . . ." (*W*, p. 302). The last incident, of course, provides More with another potent illustration to support his contention that opposition to the clergy culminates in opposition to the King.

By far the largest section of More's work dealing with history concerns itself with a rebuttal of Fish's charges about the case of Richard Hunne. That More expended so much time on this case, after just having treated it at considerable length in his *Dialogue concernynge heresyes*, shows how important he considered it to be, as indeed it was. The case stemmed from 1514, when an affluent Londoner, Richard Hunne, refused to pay a mortuary (a kind of burial fee) to his parish priest for the burial of his child. When the priest sued him in an ecclesiastical court, Hunne countered with a suit of praemunire, claiming that the ecclesiastical court encroached on a cause pertaining to the common law. After he had brought the action, Hunne was arrested on a charge of heresy and remanded by the clerical authorities to the Bishop of London's prison where, after two days, he was found hanged. The clergy claimed that Hunne had committed suicide, but a coroner's inquest returned a verdict of willful murder against Dr. Horsey, the chancellor of the Bishop of London. However, the Bishop appealed to Wolsey, who managed to obtain a royal pardon for the accused cleric.[20] More supports the clerical position on the Hunne case in its entirety. He labels as lies

Fish's assertions that Hunne was accused of heresy only because he sued a cleric and that Hunne was murdered by the clergy (*W*, pp. 290-291). More claims Hunne was "detected of heresye" long before he brought his suit against the priest, that he brought the suit only to stop the heresy proceedings against him, and that when his suit was thrown out of the King's court, Hunne hanged himself in despair. It is also untrue, charges More, that Dr. Horsey paid the King £600 to buy his pardon and that the clergy reimbursed him in benefices. Dr. Horsey never sued for pardon, insists More, but Henry saw that he was "fautelesse, & testified hym himself for an innoce*n*t" (*W*, p. 299). By the introduction of specific details such as these, More evidently hoped to impress his readers with his veracity and command of the facts in a case which was still stirring up heated controversy in 1529, fifteen years after Hunne's death.

We should not be surprised to find that More's version of historical events is not always in accord with that of the chronicles he claims to be following, or if his claims for contemporary events sometimes cannot be reconciled with the facts. As did other polemicists on both sides of the religious dispute, More sees the record of past events through his preconvictions. Most of More's assertions about the reign of King John are contradicted by the very chronicles to which he appeals. John was indeed forced to make England tributary to Rome by the grant of a thousand marks. John did object to Langton's appointment to the see of Canterbury because he regarded Langton as a traitor, and John did not confess, as More claims he did, that the Archbishop was lawfully elected. Rather, John contended that no such election was valid without his consent, and so, at first, did the monks of Canterbury.[21] Nor does More's claim that the issue of clerical courts usurping the power of the King's courts had never been in contention accord with the facts. The matter was hotly debated as an aftermath of the Hunne case in the Parliament of 1515 and was at issue about the very time More was writing, as witnessed by the debates in the Parliament of 1529 and More's controversy with Saint-German on this very subject.[22] More's claim is obviously an attempt to quiet criticism of clerical courts by the device of saying that no such criticism exists. And if in 1529 More thought it untrue that the number of beggars in the kingdom had recently increased, then con-

ditions must have improved in England since 1516 (there is no indication that they had), for in that year he voiced a similar opinion to
the one Fish was now expressing.[23] As for More's assertions about
previous attempts to expropriate the clergy, they derive from his
view of heresy rather than from the chronicles. For while Fabyan,
the chronicler who gives the most detailed account of the incidents
to which More refers, mentions that in 1409 a heretic was burned and
then also mentions that in the Parliament of the same year a bill was
introduced to expropriate the clergy, it is More, not his source, who
says that one event was the consequence of the other. The chronicler
does not record that the supporters of the bill were heretics or that
the bill was "sette aside for nought." All he writes is that Henry IV
said he would think the matter over.[24] Nor is More's account of the
reintroduction of the bill in accordance with the record. He says the
bill was again rejected because it was apparent to Parliament that it
was introduced by heretics. This is not the reason for its rejection
given in Fabyan, and More is very careful not to mention what the
chronicle in fact does say. For what Fabyan records is that, "according to some authorities," the clergy were so afraid the King would
have the bill passed that they diverted his attention from it by inciting
him to war with France, offering him a huge sum of money to equip
his army.[25] Neither is there any indication in Fabyan that the burning
of a heretic in London in 1430 had anything to do with an insurrection of heretics in the town of Abingdon near Oxford in 1431, as
More claims, and certainly no indication that the insurrection had
anything to do with the failure of the 1412 bill to expropriate the
clergy.[26] As for More's assertions about the Hunne case, most of them
have been proved incorrect by Arthur Ogle's *The Tragedy of
the Lollard's Tower.* Ogle demonstrates that Hunne was indeed
murdered, an opinion also expressed by A. F. Pollard *(Wolsey)*
and J. D. Mackie *(The Earlier Tudors).* That Hunne was not "detected of heresye" before he sued his parish priest, Ogle shows to be
almost certain (pp. 24, 49-51), as well as the fact that Hunne could
not possibly have brought an action of praemunire against the priest
to stop heresy proceedings against himself, as More claims he did,
since "no temporal writ of praemunire or any other could hamper the
Church's absolute jurisdiction in cases of heresy" (p. 30). Ogle does
not mention the fact that More's statement that Henry found Horsey

"fautelesse, & testified hym himself for an inno*n*cent" may also be open to question. Foxe gives the text of Henry VIII's letter commanding Horsey to pay restitution to Hunne's wife and children:

> And whereas you were indicted by our laws, of and for the death of the said Richard Hunne, and the said murder cruelly committed by you . . . nevertheless we of our special grace, certain science, and mere motion, pardoned you upon certain consideration us moving. . . .[27]

One technique More uses consistently to bolster his historical assertions is the "common knowledge" device—that is, the declaration that what he is saying is so true as to be common knowledge. The purpose of the device is twofold: Firstly, it may serve as a substitute for proof, and, secondly, it invites the reader to climb onto an ostensible bandwagon of opinion. Thus it manufactures the very opinion it claims already exists. And so More tells his readers that it is "well knowen" that Hunne was suspected of being a heretic long before he brought his suit of praemunire against his priest (*W*, p. 297), and he rejects as preposterous Fish's charge that Horsey and his accomplices murdered Hunne in prison, "for therof is the co*n*trary well knowen" (*W*, p. 298). In fact, according to More, every single allegation of Fish's concerning the Hunne case is false: "of all that this man so boldely affirmeth, the contrary is well and clerely knowen" (*W*, p. 298). Now if anything at all can be said about the Hunne case, it is that More's version of it was not "well knowen"; the evidence is overwhelming that, whatever the merits of the case itself, most people were convinced that Hunne had been declared a heretic and murdered solely because he dared to bring suit against a cleric in a temporal court.[28] More uses the same formula to counter another of Fish's charges, claiming that it was "well knowen" how the facts really stood and that "all that knowe the matter" would perceive that Fish was either lying or was ignorant of the truth (*W*, p. 297). A slight variation of the "common knowledge" technique occurs during More's exposé of Protestant strategy; he claims the Reformers had to substitute an indirect for a direct assault on the Catholic faith because they perceived that "good people abhorred their abhominable bokes . . ." (*W*, p. 310).

One of the most interesting facets of More's *Supplicacion* is its

attempt to discredit Fish by the repeated charge that his book is full
of rhetoric. For while at the time More wrote it was customary to
accuse an opponent of being ignorant of logic or of using sophistry,[29]
so far as this writer has been able to ascertain, it was not customary to
accuse him of being too rhetorical. The sixteenth century's veneration for rhetoric is attested to by the large number of handbooks on
the subject published during the period.[30] One might think that in
his criticism of Fish's ornate rhetoric More is anticipating Bishop
Jewel's famous *Oratio contra Rhetoricam* (1548). Yet, as might be
expected, More's own polemical works are full of rhetorical devices,
such as his use of *prosopopeia* in the present book, in having the souls
in purgatory speak for him. Actually, all of More's accusations about
Fish's rhetoric stem from the contention which he expresses in the
following highly rhetorical passage, characterizing his opponent's
work as

> florishing without fruite, sutteltie without substance, rethorike
> without reason, bold babling without learning, & wylines with-
> out wit. And finally for the foundacion & ground of al his proues
> ye shall find in his boke not halfe so many leaues as lyes, but
> almost as manye lyes as lynes (*W*, p. 291).

That is, it is only rhetoric, to the exclusion of matter.[31] And so More
accuses Fish of using "rayling rethorique" (*W*, p. 295), of "rolling in
hys rethorike from figure to figure" (*W*, p. 295), of striving to find
out "comely figures of retoryque" (*W*, p. 299), and of demonstrating
to all "that he can so rolle in hys rethorike, that he wotteth not what
hys own wordes meane" (*W*, p. 306). More, who in good humanistic
fashion made it policy to attack opponents' use of language,[32] here
presents his readers with the picture of a man whom language has so
intoxicated that he writes utter nonsense.

Turning to More's second book, we find that, because the Reformers will admit of no other authority, More mainly cites the
Scriptures as support for the existence of purgatory. As he believes
that there always has been a purgatory and that the ancient Israelites
were aware of such a place (*W*, p. 315), he feels no qualms about
drawing many of his supporting texts from the Old Testament. This
sometimes leads to interesting results. For instance, as a proof of
purgatory More cites I Samuel ii.6, which he translates as "our Lord

bryngeth folk down into hel and bringeth them thence agayn." To More it seems clear that the word "hel" must here mean "purgatory," for, as he says, God would not bring anyone out of hell (*W*, p. 317). However, as another opponent was to point out to him,[33] the word here used in the Hebrew text is "sheol," which should have been translated as "grave" or "pit," not "hell," and therefore the text says nothing at all about purgatory.

While More's main reference to authority consists of citations of Scripture, he also supports his claims with his usual appeal to custom and the number of those who share his opinion. Of the scriptural texts which he cites, More says that for the last thousand years they have been understood by all the old Doctors to refer to purgatory (*W*, p. 322), while a little further on in his work he considers it a sufficient proof for the existence of purgatory that the Catholic Church believes that there is such a place (*W*, p. 324).

More's *Supplicacion* has its share of blanket assertions and extralogical devices of controversy. An example of the former is his claim concerning Acts ii.24, which speaks of Christ loosing the pains of hell, that "certain is it & very sure, y^t Christ descended not into al these low places, nor into euery place of hel, but only into *limbus patrum* & purgatory" (*W*, p. 320). As purgatory was the very institution which was being questioned, the truth of More's statements could hardly have been self-evident. After giving one interpretation of a Pauline text, More cautions his readers against those who will try to deceive them by saying that on this portion of Scripture various Doctors have different interpretations; More admits that this is so, but adds "yet letteth that nothing these wordes to be properly by saint Poule spoke of purgatory" (*W*, p. 322). Again, after citing a number of texts in support of purgatory, More comes to the conclusion that

> surely if these folk wer reasonable & indifferent as it is not wel possible for them to be, after y^t thei refuse once to belieue ye catholike churche . . . thei should sone se their heresy reproued & purgatory surely confirmed . . . (*W*, p. 317).

That is, if the Reformers would only grant that the Church is correct in everything she says, then More would have no difficulty in proving to them that there is a purgatory.

In spite of its many wild exaggerations, or rather, just because of them, Fish's pamphlet posed an extremely dangerous threat to the clergy and to the Catholic faith, as More realized. He saw in it an insidious attempt to open England to Lutheranism by means of appealing to the greed of Henry and his nobles for monastic property. Apparently because he thought such an appeal could be highly effective, More went to considerable pains to try to discredit Fish's proposals. But he was not successful, and his fears proved to be well founded, for one year after More's death, Henry VIII began the very expropriation of the monasteries Fish had advocated.

V

John Frith

Background to the
Frith–More Controversy

More's *Supplicacion* was not left unanswered. In 1531 there appeared a work by John Frith entitled *A disputacion of purgatorye*. Frith (1503–1533) attended Cambridge as well as Oxford, where he was made one of the junior canons of Cardinal College through the influence of Wolsey who was attracted by Frith's great abilities. When Frith's preaching of the Reformed doctrine came to the attention of the Oxford authorities, he was imprisoned in the fish cellar of his college in 1528, but released at Wolsey's request on the condition that he remain within ten miles of Oxford. However, Frith fled to join Tyndale on the Continent, where he wrote the abovementioned work.[1] This really consists of three different books directed, respectively, against the writings on purgatory of Fisher, More, and John Rastell, More's brother-in-law.[2]

Frith's book confines itself to denying the existence of purgatory and rebutting the arguments which his opponents advanced in favor of that belief. Although More intended to answer the *Disputacion* (*W*, p. 342), he never did.

However he did write against one of Frith's works. When Frith returned to England in 1532, he was arrested on a charge of heresy and imprisoned in the Tower. While there, he was asked by a supposed friend to set down his opinions on the Eucharist, and the resulting book, which Frith had not meant for publication, was then given to More.[3] During the same year (1532) the latter answered Frith in a long letter which he took care Frith should not see,[4] perhaps to prevent him from becoming aware of the fact that he was being "pumped" for self-incriminating information. However, Frith did manage to secure a copy of More's work, which he, in turn, answered in *A boke . . . answeringe vnto M. mores lettur* (1533).

Frith's treatise on the Eucharist, *A christen sentence and true iudgement of the moste honorable Sacrament of Christes body & bloude* (*STC* 5190), not published until about 1545, states that the doctrine of the Real Presence is no article of faith necessary to be believed on pain of damnation, that Christ's natural body cannot be in two places at once, and that when speaking of the Eucharist the Scriptures use figurative language. It also declares how the Eucharist ought to be received.

Frith's later *Boke* contains a defense of his views on the Eucharist and an attack on the practice of image worship.

Frith's Use of Rhetoric and Logic

When we examine Frith's polemical technique, we find that in his works the figures of rhetoric and the processes of logic and sophistry play major roles. He evidently did not share his coreligionists' professed dislike of "worldly" learning. For while such Protestant polemicists as Tyndale and John Bale actually made considerable use of various rhetorical and logical devices,[5] they were at pains to point out to their readers that their hope for victory lay in the unadorned presentation of God's Word rather than in rhetorical or dialectical skill. Their use of rhetoric and logic was occasional and, especially in the case of Tyndale, rather reluctant. And while Catholic apologists such as More shared none of the Reformers' distrust of earthly wisdom, no early Tudor controversialist on either side made rhetoric and logic such important elements in his controversial technique as did Frith. Although for him, as for his fellow Reformers, the final authority on church doctrine and practice was the Scriptures, his penchant for the very apparatus of controversy itself is so apparent in all his works that it provoked the accusation of intellectual pride from all who disputed with him.[6]

That Frith's use of rhetoric for polemical purposes was a conscious and deliberate one is made clear by a passage in his dispute with John Rastell. When Rastell complains about his practice of replying to his own questions, Frith justifies the procedure and condescendingly explains its nature to his opponent: ". . . because you seeme ignoraunt in the matter," he tells Rastell, "I shall declare it vnto you, and how it standeth, [*sic*] It is a coulour of Rhetorike, and is called *Auantopodosis*, that is to saye, An aunswere to an obiection that a man might haue here made . . ." (*Ww*, p. 64). On another occasion Frith draws attention to his opponent's use of *commoratio*, claiming that Rastell makes as many accusations as possible "to leaue nothing behinde which should seeme to make for him, like a noble orator. . . ."[7]

A "coulour of Rhetorike" which plays an important part in Frith's controversial technique is the popular figure of *praemunitio*,[8] the orator's preparation of the audience for some succeeding portion of his speech. In common with Luther, Henry, and More, Frith uses this device to prejudice his readers either against his opponent's entire work prior to dealing with it, or to prejudice them against a particular passage he is about to cite from that work. For instance, before Frith begins to deal individually with the apologies for purgatory written by Rastell, More, and Fisher, he does his best to convince his readers that More and Fisher really do not require an answer, since by their mutual inconsistencies they answer each other. For More, Frith tells his readers, says there is no water in purgatory while Fisher says there is; More says the administrators of punishment in purgatory are devils while Fisher says they are angels; and More says the grace and charity of the sufferers are increased, while Fisher says they are not (*Ww*, p. 5).

Again, when Rastell complains that in his books Frith often substitutes "raylyng and iesting" for argument, Frith retorts:

> I cannot inough meruell that my brother *Rastell* would vse such maner of reasoning with me as to improue my doctrine because of my rayling and iesting.
>
> For therwith he hath made a foule hole in his kinsmans best coate for euery man perceiueth that *M. More* his bookes are so full of rayling, gestyng and baudye tales, that if the furious *Momus* & *Venus* had take out theyr partes there should be very little left for *Vulcanus* (*Ww*, p. 68).

It is in Frith's attack on Fisher's apology for purgatory that we have what is probably his most effective strategic use of *praemunitio*. The bulk of Fisher's proof depends on patristic citations. Before tackling Fisher's arguments, Frith puts all the patristic citations out of court by reminding Fisher that he himself had said that no man was bound to believe the Doctors unless they could be proved correct by Scripture. Therefore, reasons Frith, let us ignore the Doctors and examine only the Scriptures (*Ww*, p. 54). With the true economy of a master craftsman, Frith here prejudices his opponent's own declaration.

Even more than their disunity, the alleged stupidity of his opponents is emphasized by Frith in his use of *praemunitio*. He is constantly prejudicing the issue with introductory comments such as "Now let vs see his second argument which . . . is surely fond, how beit [*sic*] his solution is yet more foolishe," directed against the arguments and responses of Rastell's dialogue (*Ww*, p. 16). Passages from More's works are given similar derogatory introductions: "I say it is a shame for our prelates," Frith exclaims, "that they haue gotten such an ignorant procture to defend them. And I am sure that they them selues could haue sayd much better . . ." (*Ww*, p. 144). That the foregoing is meant to impugn the ability of More rather than to extoll the ability of the clergy is made clear by the fact that Bishop Fisher's arguments are prefaced in a similar manner. When Fisher cites the parable of the rich man and Lazarus (Luke, chapter 16) in support of purgatory, Frith ironically begins his rejoinder by saying: "I am sure that my Lord is not so ignoraunt as to say that a parable proueth any thyng." Having thus sought to prejudice the authority of the cited text, Frith, with a characteristic show of "generosity" to his opponent, condescends to take up Fisher's weak argument and demonstrate that even if parables were authoritative for doctrine, the one cited by Fisher still would not prove purgatory.[9]

Frith's most characteristic polemical device consists of elaborations on, and variations of, Quintilian's recommendation that occasionally the orator should demonstrate that the opposition's arguments are really favorable to his own cause (*Institutio Oratoria*, V.xiii.17).[10] Beating an adversary with his own stick seems to have afforded particular satisfaction to Frith who, whenever possible, claimed that it was just the very point or text proposed by his opponent which most effectively destroyed his opponent's case. For instance, when Rastell attempts to confute an argument by use of analogy, Frith claims that Rastell's analogy is false. "But," continues Frith, "if he will imagine that it be lyke, then doth he not confute it but maketh it stronger . . . . then hath he made a rod for his own arse" (*Ww*, pp. 14-15). Frith usually combines this *a fortiori* approach with the practice of turning the opponent's own argument against him in order to emphasize the completely untenable nature of the latter's position (*Ww*, p. 25). It is in the game of the allegation and counterallegation of texts that Frith most often has recourse to the highly effective formula prescribed by Quintilian. The very text his opponent cites is always the one which Frith claims most weakens his adversary's case. Rastell's citation of Ephesians ii.8, for instance, according to Frith, "bryngeth in that thyng which cleane confuteth his opinion . . ." (*Ww*, p. 76).

Sarcasm is another rhetorical figure which plays an important role in Frith's controversial technique.[11] The main targets of Frith's sarcasm are the alleged disunity and venality prevailing among his opponents. Frith's emphasis on his opponents' lack of unity is no doubt partly a response to such Catholic apologists as More, who made invidious comparisons between what they claimed was a united Catholicism and an internally divided Protestantism.[12] And so Frith begins his *Booke of Purgatory* by declaring that after he had read More's and Fisher's apologies for purgatory he realized the truth of the saying that it is much better for a man to be sharply rebuked by his enemy than slenderly praised by his friend.[13] For, says Frith, if even a man's friends can praise him only slenderly, that is proof that the man must have great faults. Thus when I read what these defenders of purgatory had to say, and saw how they could not even agree among themselves on the nature of the place they claimed did exist, he concludes, I was all the more convinced that there is no such place (*Ww*, p. 5). However, says Frith later in his book, "in one poynt they agree full well, that is, both of them say vntruly . . ." (*Ww*, p. 56). That the clergy supported purgatory from pecuniary rather than spiritual motives was the classic line of Protestant attack on that institution, and it is in this tradition that Frith trains his sarcasm on clerical venality. More talks about the hot fires of purgatory, comments Frith; certainly

> among all his other Poetrie it is reason that we graunt hym this. Yea and that our fire is but water in comparison to it. For I ensure you that it hath alone melted more gold and siluer for our spiritualties profite out of poore mens purses, then all the gold smithes fires within England. . . . it melteth castels, harde stones, landes and tenementes innumerable. . . . And so must we graunt hym that this fire is very hote (*Ww*, p. 50).

Irony[14] is an effective weapon of controversy, as has already been demonstrated, and it is as a weapon that Frith uses it. Clerical venality is again a target. Concerning Judas Maccabeus' gathering of money as a sacrifice for the dead (II Maccabees xii.43), used by More to prove the existence of purgatory, Frith tells his readers: ". . . you may not consider that they haue taken this text of .xij. thousand drachmas for an Epistle in soule masses, for then peraduenture you might fall into some shrewd suspicion, that they should do it of couetousness, which faulte can not be espyed in our spiritualtie, as you know well inough" (*Ww*, p. 39). No one familiar with the Convocation sermon of John Colet, the diatribes of Skelton, or the contemporary pamphlets of Christopher Saint-German could have missed the irony.[15] Again, emphasizing his opponent's alleged ineptitude, Frith pretends to have great difficulty in ascertaining on whose side More is disputing; perhaps he is secretly on my side, speculates Frith: "Verily," he exclaims, "I haue not heard of a patrone that so vnprofitably defendeth hys clyent, nor yet of any man that geueth himselfe such proper trippes to cast himselfe, except he went about to betray and vtterly destroy the part which he would seeme to fauour . . ." (*Ww*, p. 45). What might be called ironic *interpretatio*[16] is used by Frith when Rastell objects to Frith's having called him a liar: "Here I would desire my brother Rastell to pardon me of a little ignoraunce," says Frith humbly, "for surely I thought it had bene no more offence to call a lye, a lye, then to call a sheepe a sheepe: notwithstanding sith he recounteth it to be rayling, gesting, and scolding, I will here-after temper my selfe, and chaunge my words, and will say that when he lyeth (that by hys leaue) he maketh a fitten."[17]

Significatio or innuendo is another rhetorical figure used as a weapon by Tudor controversialists, Frith among them.[18] For in-stance, Rastell's dialogue, which attempts to prove the existence of purgatory by natural reason, contains a discussion of repentance conducted by a Turk. This is ridiculed by Frith, who insists that it is impossible to discuss repentance apart from the death of Christ; Frith reminds his readers, "you must first consider that neither he [Rastell] nor his Turke *Gingemin* know any thyng of Christ" (*Ww*, p. 12). The innuendo derives from the amphiboly contained in the word "know": On the one hand, Frith means that Rastell cannot have a Turk refer to Christian repentance in a discussion limited to the use of natural reason, but, on the other hand, Frith means that anyone who would seek to support dogma by the use of natural reason rather than by the Scriptures does not "know any thyng of Christ," that is, is not a Christian. More's allegedly venal reasons for undertaking to defend the clergy also are a target for innuendo, the aim of which is to weaken More's position by hinting that he has been induced by money to argue a case in which he himself does not really believe (*Ww*, pp. 42, 48, 107). But whatever the motivation of More's zeal for the clergy, comments Frith, that zeal has carried him so far that in spite of the fact that the Reformer Robert Barnes had the King's safe-conduct to return from exile to England, More dares to say in print that he could lawfully burn Barnes, "which thyng whether it be treason or not let other men define" (*Ww*, p. 156).

The innuendo of the "let-other-men-define" technique borders on *praeteritio*, mention by declaration of intent not to mention, another figure of rhetoric used as a weapon by Tudor controversialists.[19] The device is combined with the "some say" or rumor technique[20] when Frith says that More undertook "to bee Proctour for Purgatory (I will not say that he was hyred therto of our spiritualtie although many men dare sweare it([*sic*] . . ." (*Ww*, p. 6). After Rastell has discussed repentance, Frith declares, "I would be loth to moue the man and ask hym what repentaunce is" (*Ww*, p. 13), while the same technique is again employed as part of Frith's campaign to impugn his opponents' ability when he tells his readers that "if it were lawfull to require wisedome in a man so wise as *M.More* is counted, here would I wish him a litle more wit . . ." (*Ww*, p. 33).

Praeteritio is only one of the elements in Frith's use of *illusio*, his continual attempt to denigrate his opponents.[21] His opponents' alleged ignorance is a constant object of Frith's ridicule, disguised in the following passage as pretended pity: Rastell's "reasons and solutions are so childish and vnsauery, so vnlearned and baren, so full of faultes and phantasies," says Frith, "that I rather pitie the mans deepe ignoraunce and blindnesse . . . then I feare that he by his vaine probations should allure any man to consent vnto hym" (*Ww*, p. 6). And Frith plays his opponents off against each other not only to emphasize their disunity, as previously noted, but also to demonstrate their incompetence; whichever opponent he happens to be dealing with is compared unfavorably with his fellows. Thus Rastell is told that while he "coueteth to counterfayte his kinsman [More] . . . his braines be nothyng so radiaunt nor his conveyance so commendable in the eyes of the wise" (*Ww*, p. 7), and More, in turn, is informed that he "hath in a maner nothyng but that he tooke out of my Lord of *Rochester* [Fisher] . . ." (*Ww*, p. 32).

Further to emphasize their ignorance, Frith gives his adversaries lessons in logic, the use and abuse of which discipline forms an important part of his controversial technique, and it is to a consideration of this aspect of Frith's works that we now turn. That a Tudor controversialist would make some polemical use of logic is to be expected, since the university curriculum stressed the polemical function of logic.[22] However, as previously noted, the Reformers as a body were opposed to anything which smacked of "worldly learning." Yet the fact that Frith, unlike his fellow Reformers, and in spite of some rather weak disclaimers, took great delight in his dialectical skill is made evident by even a cursory reading of his works.

Frequently, for instance, he makes ostentatious use of the formal syllogism, as he does in the following passage in order to prove that for Christians there can be no purgatory: ". . . because you are somewhat slow in perceauing the matter," he patronizingly tells Rastell,

> I shall reduce it into a Sillogismus on this manner: There is no damnation vnto them that be in Christ Iesu if they liue not after the flesh, but after the spirite. Euery hell is damnation. *Ergo*, there is no hell to them that be in Christ Iesu if they liue not after the flesh but after the spirite. This is in the first figure made by *Relarent* [*sic*]. not by any profite that I thinke that the poore commons can take by such babblyng but onely to satisfie your mynde and pleasure (*Ww*, p. 71).

But Frith uses "such babblyng" so often that it appears he does it for the benefit of his own "mynde and pleasure" rather than that of his opponent.

An important element in Frith's attempt to refute and ridicule his opponents' arguments is his use of *reductio ad absurdum*. When, for instance, More asserts that on being told of his impending death it was for fear of purgatory King Hezekiah wept (Isa. xxxviii.3), Frith reminds More that Christ also wept before his death and concludes More must mean Christ was also afraid of purgatory (*Ww*, p. 34). The same approach is used against More's citation of Acts ii.24 ("whom God raised up, having loosed the pangs of death") as referring to purgatory. If More believes this text refers to purgatory, says Frith, he must also believe that a sinless Christ was purged in purgatory, since Christ is the subject of the text in question (*Ww*, p. 43).

Presenting his opponent with a dilemma is another tactic to which Frith frequently resorts, the classic example of which occurs during his debate with More on the fallibility of the clergy. The clergy say, comments Frith, "yᵗ they be the Church, and can not erre: And this is the grounde of all their doctrine. But the truth of this article is nowe sufficiently knowen. For if Queene *Katherine* be kyng *Henries* wife, then they do erre, and if she be not, then they haue erred, to speake no more cruelly. . . ."[23]

Included in this discussion of Frith's polemical use of logic must be some consideration of his exposé of his opponents' fallacies.[24] A frequent charge Frith makes is that his opponent's conclusion is a non sequitur. One such charge is particularly interesting because it contains within it a number of rhetorical, as well as dialectical, devices and illustrates the effective combination of rhetoric and logic for polemical purposes. Rastell, Frith begins, says that my expositions of Scripture give people freedom to sin because I say there is no hell or purgatory—"thereto Rastell by his leaue (maketh a fitten) I dare not say hee maketh a lye," ironically comments Frith, "for that he would call rayling for I neuer denyed hell." But as for the claim that denial of purgatory gives license to sin, continues Frith, "you shall see how wisely the ma*n* co*n*cludeth, for he thinketh that *ab inferiori ad suu*m *superius confuse distribue*, men shall thinke it a good consequent as if I should say," says Frith, illustrating the non sequitur by *reductio,* "that we lacke fire in priso*n*, then would he co*n*clude that there lacked fire in all Middlesex. Or if I wold say," he continues, adding polemical *exemplum* to the *reductio,* "their were no wit in Rastels head then would hee conclude that there were no witte in no ma*n*s head, but he hath so long studyed Philosophy, that hee hath cleane forgotten his principals of Sophistry, notwithstandyng we will forgeue him this faute for the man is somewhat aged . . ." (*Ww*, pp. 68-69), concludes Frith, sarcastically alluding both to Rastell's attempt to prove the existence of purgatory by the use of philosophy and to his indignation that so young a man as Frith dared to contradict the opinions of three older men such as More, Fisher, and himself (*Ww*, p. 63). Finally, the entire passage serves as *praemunitio* to Frith's point, which he now makes, that a belief in purgatory is no restraint for sin (*Ww*, pp. 68-69), after which he again comments that "though Rastel appeare to hymselfe to conclude lyke a sage Philosopher, yet I answer you he co*n*cludeth lyke an ignorante Sophyster as all me*n* may see, for it foloweth not . . ." (*Ww*, p. 72). Frith also charges his opponents with using false analogies to support their contentions.[25] Finally, he accuses his opponents of intentionally using ambiguous terminology.[26] When More claims that apparitions have shown themselves to men and that this proves the existence of purgatory, adding that even Luther had admitted that many of these apparitions are true, Frith replies: "Here playeth master More the suttle sophister, and would deceiue men wyth a fallace, which lyeth in thys woorde, true, so that when he sayeth that such apparitions be true, thys sentence may be taken two maner of wayes. One, that it is true that such phantasticall apparitions do appeare. . . . But to suppose this true that they are the soules of Purgatory which so appeare, is very fonde false . . .' (*Ww*, p. 46).

That Frith himself frequently attempted to "deceiue men wyth a fallace" is another interesting aspect of his use, or rather abuse, of logic as a polemical weapon. For instance, he builds up a very effective diatribe against the clergy on the basis of a false premise arrived at by a device which, for lack of a better term, will be called "polemical metathesis." He tells his readers that the clergy "keepe the scripture and word of God from you, and beare you in hand that it is heresie" (*Ww*, p. 97). It is highly unlikely that a man of Frith's education was under the impression that the Church had declared the Bible itself rather than its unauthorized English translation to be heresy,[27] but this is exactly the impression he attempts to convey to his readers by transposing the application of the term "heresie" from the translation to the text. From this false premise there is, of course, no limit to the amount of anticlerical abuse and ridicule to be derived, and Frith takes full advantage of the situation he has created for himself. "Are you so mad," he asks his readers,

> that this blessed worde which made the euill good, will make the good euyll? thynke you that thys holsome medicine which healeth all infirmities, is now chaunged into such a nature that it will poyson you? Are ye so simple and childishe to surmise that this godly doctrine which discloseth all hipocrisie, and confoundeth all heresies, should make you to erre and fall into heresies? (*Ww*, p. 97).

Akin to the false premise is the assumed premise (*petitio principii*), and this Frith uses along with the deliberate-misunderstanding device to ridicule Rastell for having written on purgatory. You claim, Frith says to Rastell, that you wrote your book because so many people pervert the Scriptures. But what good will your book do these people, asks Frith of his opponent who, of course, had not said that

he wrote to help the perverters of Scripture but so that others could
detect the perversion:

> . . . if they be so obstinate that they will not receaue the verye
> Scripture but expounde it after their own willes & wrest it after
> the same, then wil they much lesse receaue your booke which is
> so playne agaynst scripture. . . . So that I can espye no maner of
> profite that ca*n* come of your booke if you can alledge no better
> causes then you yet shew, but that it had bene a great deale
> better vnwritten (*Ww*, p. 63).

Frith's premise, that Rastell's book is contrary to Scripture, is, of
course, the very point in dispute. Again, while Frith attacks More for
deliberately using ambiguous terminology in his arguments, he himself does the same thing in one of the instances in which he corrects
More's logic; ironically, the word used ambiguously by Frith is
"true"—the same word he charged More with using ambiguously.
When More attempts to support the belief in purgatory by alleging
that even the heathen believes in such a place, Frith responds by
saying there is "no wiseman that will graunt this to be a good argu-
me*n*t, ye Turkes . . . beleue it to be true, *Ergo*, we must beleue that
it is true. . . ." Then Frith characteristically offers to correct More's
argument: "But if *M.More* will haue his reaso*n* hold, he must argue
on this maner: The miscreauntes and infidels before named beleue
that there is a Purgatory & their belefe is true, therefore we must
beleue that there is a Purgatory. Now foloweth this argument somewhat more formally."[28] It should be noted that Frith's minor premise
refers the word "true" to the object of the belief, that is, the heathen's
belief in purgatory is "true" in the sense of "correct": purgatory does
exist. Then Frith contends that the argument he has corrected for his
opponent is now formally correct but still factually wrong, in that
the heathen's belief "is not true as co*n*cernyng Purgatory . . . . that is
false, for neither Turkes, Saracenes Paynimes nor Iewes whiche
beleue not in Christ haue or euer shall enter into any Purgatory . . ."
(*Ww*, pp. 33-34). It is clear that here Frith refers the word "true"
to the quality of the belief, that is, the heathen's belief in purgatory
is not "true" in the sense of not "justified": they will never go to
purgatory.

Let us now turn to a consideration of some broader aspects of Frith's polemical technique. He goes to considerable lengths to demonstrate that since his opponents are attempting to defend an indefensible position, they have to resort to unfair polemical tactics. Exposé of his opponents' controversial technique is an important element in Frith's own technique.[29] He charges that his adversaries distort the meaning of scriptural texts and intentionally mistranslate them, and that they pervert his statements and those of his friends for purposes of easy refutation. He generalizes from his previously noted citations of More's logical fallacies to claim that More habitually employs both rhetoric and logic sophistically. More distorts the meaning of Isaiah xxxviii.3 to make it appear that King Hezekiah was afraid to die for fear of purgatory, alleges Frith, and when More cites Matthew xii.36 for his purpose, which says that for every idle word they have spoken, men will have to give a reckoning on the day of judgment, the last three words "leaueth he out full craftely" to make it appear this reckoning is to be given in purgatory.[30] More mistranslates Acts ii.24 and writes "dissolving the pains of hell" instead of "of death," charges Frith, in order to make that text appear to refer to purgatory. The fact that the Latin reads *infernus*, which in Scripture may mean "death," "grave," or "hell" is no reason arbitrarily to choose the last, maintains Frith. For, he continues, while the word *infernus* has no specific connotation in Latin, the word "hell" has a very specific meaning in English. First More arbitrarily translates *infernus* as "hell," complains Frith, and then further insists that "hell" here means purgatory (*Ww*, p. 42). The force of this argument is considerably increased by the fact that Frith's readers must have realized he was once again paying his opponents in their own coin: More's chief objection to Tyndale's translation of the Greek New Testament was that Tyndale took words which had no special connotation in the Latin of the Vulgate and translated them into an English which robbed the clergy of their authority (*W*, pp. 220-221, 424).

What his opponents do to the text of Scripture, charges Frith, they also do to his own words. In replying to his work on purgatory, asserts Frith, Rastell misquotes him, for he "hath cut out all that shoulde make for me, so that he hath geuen it cleane an other shape

then euer I entended . . ." (*Ww*, p. 63). More, also, is accused of
purposely taking Frith's statements in a sense obviously never intended (*Ww*, pp. 137, 144). Not only do they pretend I said what I
never did say, charges Frith, but the entire position of the Reformers
on purgatory is misrepresented in Rastell's dialogue on that subject,
in which his interlocutor does not really represent the Reformers, as
is claimed, but advances weak arguments for Rastell to demolish.[31]
Frith also accuses More of making sophistical use of rhetoric and
logic to deceive his readers, telling them that "M. More wyth hys
painted Poetrie and craftye conueyance doe cast a miste before your
eyes" and that his opponent's endeavor has always been to answer
Frith's arguments "with some sophisticall cauillation, which by hys
painted poetrie he might so haue coulered, that at the lest he might
make yᵉ ignoraunt some appearance of trouth . . ." (*Ww*, pp. 84, 108).

Most prominent among Frith's techniques directed specifically
against More is his use of *ad hominem* argument and personal accusations. Frith uses *ad hominem* argument in both the orthodox and a
less common manner, for he attempts to overthrow More's arguments
by reference to his virtues as well as to his alleged vices. In the latter
conventional category is Frith's allegation that More tried to prevent
his seeing a copy of the *Letter* attacking Frith's arguments because
More was probably secretly ashamed of having written it (*Ww*, p.
108). Frith thus uses a supposed action of More's to give the impression that even More does not really believe the case he is arguing and,
consequently, to throw doubt on the validity of everything he says.
Some of Frith's many references to More's "poetry" have already
been quoted. This labeling of More's argument is intended to remind
Frith's readers that his opponent is the author of that eminently
fictional and imaginative work *Utopia*, and that thus, as a poet in the
habit of writing "poetry," which the sixteenth century often equated
with "lies,"[32] More is likely to have carried this practice over into his
works of religious controversy. But much more interesting to the
student of polemical technique is Frith's use of "reverse" *ad hominem*
argument based on his opponent's ability. That More does not really
have a case to defend, Frith tells his readers, is obvious from the inad-
equate defense he makes. "You may well know that if hys matter had
ben any thing lykely, he would haue coloured it of an other fashion.

But sith such a patrone so greatly commended for his conueyance & wisedome handleth this matter so slenderly, you may well mistrust hys cause" (*Ww*, p. 45). The fact that More has been unable to confute my treatise on the sacrament, says Frith, again turning More's reputation against him, "is a great argument y^t it is very true: For els hys pregnant wit could not haue passed it so cleane ouer . . ." (*Ww*, p. 108). In his use of this unconventional *ad hominem* argument Frith is making a double point: He assumes that his readers agree More's arguments are weak and explains that if so learned a man presents weak arguments he must have a poor case.[33]

The most serious accusation Frith makes against More is that of treason, on the basis of his alleged statement that he might lawfully have burned the Reformer Robert Barnes in spite of the King's safe-conduct. It is fortunate Henry removed you from the chancellorship, Frith tells More,

> For els it is to be feared, that you would further haue proceded agaynst his graces prerogatiue which thyng whether it be treason or not let other men define. But this I dare say, that it is Printed and published to our Princes great dishonour: For what learned man may in tyme to come, trust to hys graces safeconduite, or come at his graces instaunce or request, sith not onely the spiritually (whiche of their profession resiste hys prerogatiue) but also a laye man promoted to such preheminence by hys graces goodnes, dare presume so to depresse hys prerogatiue, and not onely to say, but also to publishe it in Print: that notwithstanding his graces safe conduite, they might lawfully haue burnt hym (*Ww*, p. 156).

The fact that More said no such thing, but claimed that Barnes had forfeited the terms of his safe-conduct (*W*, p. 343), did not alter the gravity of such a charge during the reign of such a monarch as Henry VIII.[34]

More's Letter
against Frith

That Frith's polemical technique was eminently successful is attested to by one of his opponents who characterizes Frith as "the moste subtill, craftie, and wilie solititour of his masters cause, that euer traueled in this matter," laments that Frith "hath drawen . . . many disciples after hym," and deplores the fact that "suche a number wolde folowe him as there hath done, and take him for so plaine, beying so deceitfull: Take him so simple, being so craftie. . . . And of that numbre, so many welthie . . ." (Gwynneth, *Detection*, B4ʳ, A4ᵛ, N4ʳ).

It is not surprising therefore that More decided to answer such an influential propagandist for the Reformed faith. The particular point on which he chose to attack Frith was the question of the Eucharist. In his *A letter . . . impugnynge the erronyouse wrytynge of Iohn Fryth* (1532), More rebuts the views expressed in Frith's treatise on this subject, maintaining that the bread and wine are changed into the actual body and blood of Christ.

More's answer to Frith's treatise takes the form of a letter addressed not to Frith but to the friend who sent More the first copy of Frith's work. Although in his answer More does not resort to his usual practice of quoting at length from his opponent and then appending commentary—he paraphrases Frith—his work is again much longer than the one he is answering. We know from what More says in his *Apologye*, written about the same time as the letter against Frith, that he was becoming troubled about the length of his works,[35] and in the present polemic he expresses the same concern, especially when contrasting the length of his own works to the "many shorte treatyses" his opponents were writing.[36] Unfortunately for More's effectiveness as a polemicist, he never got beyond merely recognizing the problem to doing very much about it, so that at the end of the letter he has to confess to his friend that "in stede of a letter haue you almost a boke, longer than I truste good Chrysten folke shall nede . . ." (*Correspondence*, p. 462). To this admission More adds the yet more revealing information that once he had begun, Frith's book "drew . . . [him] forth ferther and ferther, and scant coulde suffer . . . [him] now to make an end," and that he had wanted to cover at length another subject, which he omitted only because he intended to include it in a treatise against Barnes (ibid., p. 462). Such lack of control over his material as More here confesses certainly did not increase the impact of his polemics.[37]

The most remarkable feature of More's letter against Frith is its mildness of tone, a feature which, as has been demonstrated, is not characteristic of More's polemics against other opponents. It has been thought that More's gentleness was caused by his respect for his opponent's learning or by consideration for his youth,[38] factors which evidently influenced many contemporaries, including Henry;[39] but More's tone in this polemic is, as we shall see, also a major weapon of his controversial technique. Whatever More may have thought privately of Frith, he makes it quite clear what he wishes his readers to think. He calls Frith the greatest heretic he has ever had to deal with; he is worse than Luther and worse than Tyndale (*Correspondence*, pp. 441-442). More enlarges on his portrait of Frith by associating him with the Arian heresy (ibid., pp. 445-446) and by claiming that he is the disciple of Wycliffe, Zwingli, Oecolampadius, and Tyndale—and what kind of people they are, adds More, alluding to Zwingli's death in battle, everyone knows, and God has "in parte with his open vengeaunce declared" (ibid., p. 444).

Therefore More professes himself very grieved to see his youthful adversary "begyled by certain olde lymmes of the deuyll," and he prays that God will call Frith back to the truth before it is too late (ibid., p. 444). Praying in print for an opponent's salvation is a device which affords the suppliant certain advantages: He thereby demonstrates his absolute conviction in the righteousness of his own cause—no small matter when controversialists characteristically accused each other of insincerity—and at the same time enhances his "image" in the eyes of his readers as a generous antagonist. And as in his other works, More in the letter against Frith gives his readers no chance to forget just how generous a controversialist he is. He will, for instance, go out of his way to meet his opponent in argument, as he does when he tells Frith that although the rules of disputation do not require it of him, he nevertheless will undertake to debate Frith on a peripheral point and prove that he is wrong on that, too, as well as in his main argument (ibid., p. 456). Such eagerness to oblige confirms again the image of More as supremely confident of his position, an image which, whatever may have been his private doubts and fears, he always strenuously tried to uphold in his defense of the Church. That his gentleness and declared sympathy for Frith are not without guile is further indicated by More's profession of sorrowful bewilderment that his opponent should hold the views he does or that he should think his arguments in their defense are of any value (ibid., pp. 450-451).

Associated with More's air of gentleness is his fatherly or—depending on the point of view—patronizing attitude to Frith, whom he consistently addresses as "young man." More is sorry that "thys yonge man" sees fit to disagree with a doctrine which the entire Catholic Church has held for 1500 years and hopes that "thys yonge man" will come to his senses, for against the doctrine "of thys yonge brother" stands the testimony of the "olde holy Fathers" (ibid., pp. 444, 458). More feels sure that if his readers note the contents of "thys yonge mannes" book, they will perceive its errors, for "thys yong man" has fallen into all the old fallacies of the Arian heresy (ibid., pp. 441, 445-446), although, adds More, "thys yonge man" thinks he can "se forther with his yonge syghte, than I can see wyth myn olde eyen and my spectacles. . . ."[40] In sum, More is "sory to se thys yong man presume so farre vpon his wytte, so soone ere it be full rype" (*Correspondence*, p. 457). It is fairly obvious that however kindly More may have felt toward him, he is also rather broadly implying that Frith is too young to know whereof he speaks or, as Rupp puts it, using "the argument by seniority."[41]

As did Frith himself, More delighted in playing his opponents off against each other, and in his letter against Frith he does this in a particularly effective fashion. He manages to combine a thrust at his youth with the fact that not all Reformers agreed with Frith's particular view of the Eucharist, by reminding his readers that Robert Barnes " beynge a man of more age, and more rype dyscressyon . . . than thys yonge man is," holds a different view (*Correspondence*, p. 461). That the purpose of this remark is solely to embarrass Frith and not at all to commend Barnes's "rype dyscressyon" is made clear by the fact that, as we have seen, when More wrote against Barnes, he ridiculed his competence more than that of any other Reformer.

More's ostensible kindness to Frith extends to helping him correct his arguments, one of More's favorite devices and one which Frith may have copied from him (see *Ww*, pp. 12, 137). In one instance More plays schoolmaster in logic to Frith, claiming that he used faulty reasoning to arrive at a conclusion, in that he used "should" in the major premise, which he changed to "can" in the minor premise and the conclusion. Then More shows Frith how his argument should be recast to achieve more valid logical form. Of course, comments More, even after I have corrected the form of Frith's premises, his entire syllogism is still invalid, since its premises do not produce the conclusion (ibid., pp. 455-456). Probably because Frith's works lean so heavily on formal logic, More spends considerable time criticizing the formal validity of his opponent's arguments. As did some of Frith's other opponents, More accuses him of sophistry (ibid., pp. 445, 462), which does not prevent More himself from engaging in quibbles and using hypothetical arguments to prove a point (ibid., pp. 450, 452).

Perhaps also in reaction to his opponent's obvious delight in rhetoric, More's letter to Frith contains a somewhat heavier concentration of rhetorical devices than do most of his other polemics. He uses *repetitio*,[42] for instance, to hammer into his readers' minds the alleged weaknesses of Frith's position: "For he denyeth nat nor can nat say nay. . . . He denyeth nat also. . . . The yong man denyeth nat nor can deny . . ." (*Correspondence*, pp. 442-443). He engages in wordplay[43] to emphasize the ostensibly ridiculous nature of Frith's doctrine, calling it a "yong mannes vayne childysh folosophy" (*Correspondence*, p. 462) and, using the popular device of *praeteritio*, says of his opponent that he will not "for courtesye" claim that he is mad, but will content himself with the observation that he is very "yonge" (ibid., p. 459). To rebut Frith's objection to the Real Presence, that Christ's body cannot be in two places at once, More uses sarcasm; he declares that Frith is a "yonge man [who] hath yet in hys youth gone to lytell whyle to scole" to know what God can and cannot do (ibid., p. 456). More also trains his favorite weapon of irony on Frith. If, says More, Frith graciously allows us without peril of damnation to believe about the Eucharist as we please, then he will no doubt with equal grace grant us that we may without peril of damnation believe that he lies when he tells us that the consecrated bread and wine are not changed into the body and blood of Christ (ibid., p. 458).

More never had the opportunity to deal with Frith's book on purgatory, as he had intended, for while he was defending the orthodox view of the Eucharist against Frith, the Church and its clergy were being attacked from another quarter, and More found himself embroiled in yet another controversy.

VI

Christopher Saint-German

Background and Summary of the
Saint-German–More Controversy

The rival claims of canon and common law had been a vexed question in England at least since the time of Thomas Becket. But to what had once been a simple struggle for power between the King and Church there was added during the early sixteenth century a combination of two factors which considerably increased the complexity and the importance of this question, namely, the Protestant Revolt and Henry's desire to obtain an annulment of his marriage to Catherine of Aragon.

The spread of the Reformed doctrine throughout England influenced the issue in two ways: On the one hand, it added to a body of opinion which was bitterly critical of the Church generally—and consequently of the privileges it enjoyed—while, on the other hand, it caused the Church to attempt to eliminate this dissenting opinion by means of clerical law applied in ecclesiastical courts. Neither of these was a new development; there had always been heretics, and the Church had always fought heresy. But what was new was the relatively great number of people who were involved, both in the spreading of heresy and in its suppression.

The Pope's refusal to grant Henry an annulment led the latter to abolish papal jurisdiction over the Church in England and to reexamine the advisability of having within his realm a body of people who would not be governed by the laws administered in the King's courts. By declaring himself Head of the Church of England, Henry brought the ecclesiastical courts under his own jurisdiction, for by the Act in Restraint of Appeals (1533) all cases which previously had been appealed to the Pope were now to be appealed to Henry's appointee to the see of Canterbury.[1]

Henry obtained his ends by working through Parliament. What was subsequently to be known as the Reformation Parliament held its first session on November 3, 1529, and before the year was out the Commons had drawn up an impressive list of grievances against the English clergy, complaining that the latter oppressed the laity with probates of wills and with mortuaries, that abbots and priors were engaged in the cloth and wool trade, and that clerics who were stewards and officers to bishops occupied farms.[2]

During the third session of Parliament, on March 18, 1532, the Commons presented to the King a supplication against the ordinaries which had probably been drafted by Thomas Cromwell, a recent addition to the Privy Council.[3] The document stated that because of the dread of heresy and the excessive severity of the ordinaries in punishing that heresy, much discord had of late arisen between the spirituality and the temporality. The document went on to charge that the clergy made laws without the consent of either the laity or the King and conducted ex officio[4] heresy trials in which revenge for criticism of their lax manner of living was often the motivating factor, rather than any heresy on the part of the accused. Under such a system, it was added, poor people were put to considerable expense, for which they were never reimbursed even if the court absolved them.[5]

In April, Convocation gave Henry its reply, which denied that there was any discord between the laity and the clergy and proposed a compromise by which clerical laws would not become operative without a royal license. However, Henry rejected the document. On

May 15, 1532, Convocation surrendered its right to make legislation without royal approval, and the next day More resigned his office as Lord Chancellor of England.

It was against this background that there appeared in 1532 an anonymous book, *A Treatise concernynge the diuision . . . betwene the spirytualtie and temporaltie*,[6] which was later identified by John Bale as the work of Christopher Saint-German.[7]

Saint-German was a prominent London lawyer whose services were occasionally employed by Henry VIII and Cromwell, but his desire for anonymity—he never signed any of his works—has blotted out much of his public career. In 1523 he published a Latin work entitled *Dialogus de fundamentis de legum et de conscientia*, a treatise on equity in the form of a dialogue between a doctor of divinity and a student of law. In 1530 he completed the *Dyaloge in Englysshe*, which he followed in 1531 with a translation of his first dialogue and certain "Additions." The translation and the additions together were known as *Doctor and Student*, a work which became a standard text for law students.

The *Diuision's* two main points are that strife exists between the laity and the clergy, and that this strife is owing to the pride and avarice of the latter. An interesting feature of the work, for which it was first drawn to More's attention (*Apologye*, p. 57), is that these contentions are made in what appears to be a very mild and impartial spirit. There is no vehement denunciation in Saint-German; instead he reports the misdeeds of the clergy with an air of infinite regret and maintains throughout his criticism that what he most desires is to see the clergy regain the laity's respect and love which they have momentarily lost through their impolitic behavior (*Diuision*, p. 250).

Saint-German also discusses the problem of heresy, toward which he displays a rather ambiguous attitude. He says that there should be laws against heresy and that heretics should be punished (ibid., p. 223), but he adds that a man is not guilty of heresy if he utters heresy out of ignorance; he is guilty only if he speaks in the full knowledge of what he is saying (ibid., p. 225). In a later work he maintains that he does not know of a single heretic in the entire realm, because the proof offered to support charges of heresy has never satisfied him,[8] while in still another work he concludes that there is really no difference except one of terminology between the Reformers' doctrine of justification by faith and the Catholics' insistence on good works.[9]

Finally, Saint-German questions the Church's sincerity in prosecuting heresy and suggests that in many cases people have been haled before ecclesiastical courts not so much for their doctrine as for their daring to criticize clerical morality.

The apologye of syr Thomas More knyght, which More published in 1533, was intended as a general defense of himself and his conduct of the religious controversy, as well as of the Church and its clergy. But as matters turned out, although More did devote some space to these subjects, thirty-nine of the book's fifty chapters were taken up in answering the *Diuision.*[10] The work is really a huge digression on Saint-German.[11]

In the *Apologye* More denies that there is any serious ill feeling between the clergy and the laity or that the clergy prosecute heretics merely because they criticize clerical conduct. He defends the substance and jurisdiction of the canon law, in particular the laws against heresy, as well as the practice of conducting heresy trials ex officio, claiming that no one, either at his own hands or at those of others, has ever suffered wrong on a matter of heresy because of the existing judicial system.

What is of most interest in the personal section of the *Apologye* is More's discussion of his controversial works which, to judge by the manner in which More defends them, had come in for a good deal of criticism. Others evidently noticed More's reluctance to admit error,[12] for he commences the *Apologye* by denying any claim to infallibility and admitting that he, too, can make mistakes (*Apologye,* p. 1), but he still seems unable to bring himself to mention any which he has actually made.

More lists a number of the objections which had been made about his polemics, among them that he treated his opponents in an unseemly manner. To this he answers that he always dealt with his adversaries as he would wish them to deal with him, that he concentrated on their serious errors while overlooking their trivial faults, that he quoted Tyndale fairly, while Tyndale left out his most important points, and that, far from misrepresenting the Reformers' position, he has actually been in the habit of making his opponents' side stronger than it really is (ibid., pp. 1-5). More detracts somewhat from the effect of this self-portrait by stubbornly defending his vituperation with the excuse that his opponents used abusive language against the clergy and that, therefore, he has to requite them in kind. But he modestly yields to his antagonists the mastery in this art (ibid., p. 49). As Luther had done, he even finds texts in Scripture with which to defend his invective, citing the occasion when Paul applied the terms "whited walls" and "dogs" to his opponents, and when Jesus called the Pharisees hypocrites (*W*, p. 939).

Another criticism made of More's polemics was that they were too long and that, consequently, few people read them. After all the labor he had expended on his works, this must have been particularly galling to More, and the writing of the *Apologye* marks a conscious attempt to achieve brevity. He defends the length of his previous books by saying that he had to quote extensively because the Reformers purposely wrote in an obscure fashion, and that from short quotations it would have been impossible for his readers to determine the meaning of the cited passages (*Apologye*, p. 7). It is easier, continues More, to write heresies than to answer them; one page of heresy may require forty pages of refutation. He adds that he is repetitious for the convenience of his readers, in order not to have to refer them to other works (ibid.). Perhaps as an incentive to others, More mentions that some men have read his *Confutacyon of Tyndales answere* (505 folio pages) three times (ibid.).

In the same year (1533) Saint-German answered More's criticisms of the *Diuision* in a work entitled *A dialogue betwixte . . . Salem and . . . Bizance*,[13] most of which is devoted to rather technical legal points. The main contention of the work is that the common law should be strictly adhered to and that those parts of the canon law which are contrary to the common law should be repealed.

Still within the same year, More attacked Saint-German's second book by publishing *The debellacyon of Salem and Bizance* which, he tells us, he wrote in a few days (*W*, p. 931). More's work is divided into two parts, the first of which is an answer to his opponent's criticism of the *Apologye*, while the second defends the existing canon law and the manner in which the Church was conducting heresy trials.[14]

In 1534 Saint-German published *The addicions of Salem and Byzance*,[15] a curious work which, while elaborating on many of the points made in the author's previous books, never once mentions More's name or makes any reference to him whatsoever. This treatise contains another extensive list of alleged clerical abuses and maintains the thesis that the ecclesiastical courts exist in England not by the law of God but merely by the sufferance of the King.

Saint-German's Techniques of "Some Say" and "Objectivity"

The most outstanding controversial device employed by Saint-German is his use of the reportorial "some say," by which he himself makes no accusations but only records what "some say" are the facts. In a way this device is similar to that of the dialogue, since both pretend merely to report what other people are saying, while completely disclaiming any responsibility for the matter they contain. Actually, the "some-say" or rumor technique is a less emphatic version of the "common-knowledge" device More used against Fish. Both of these techniques have as their object the creation of opinion, but the former has the added advantage of protecting the polemicist who uses it from being identified with the view he is in fact advocating.

For the method he adopts Saint-German has a brilliant model in the satires of Skelton, as well as in some aspects of Fish's diatribe. The butt of Skelton's ridicule is the mighty Wolsey, and, among other means, Skelton protects himself by the device of reporting what other people are saying about the Cardinal. This Skelton does most notably in *Colyn Cloute*, a poem in which the speaker wanders about the countryside listening to people's conversation:

> Thus I, Colyn Cloute,
> As I go aboute,
> And wandrynge as I walke,
> I here the people talke. (ll. 287–290)

Colyn does not know why people speak as they do; he merely reports what they say:

> I wot neuer how they warke,
> But thus the people barke;
> And surely thus they say. . . .   (ll. 119–121)

> Take me as I intende,
> For lothe I am to offende
> In this that I haue pende:
> I tell you as men say. . . .   (ll. 186–189)[16]

Saint-German begins his *Diuision* with a whole barrage of "some says." After asserting that there is friction between the spirituality and the temporality, he wonders why the laity hate the clergy as they do. He supplies the answer by reporting that some men give various reasons, one of which is that the clergy serve God only to magnify themselves.[17] It is for this reason, continues Saint-German, that some men think that the Church should have no earthly possessions. And because the Church receives so much money from people to pray for souls in purgatory, says Saint-German in a manner reminiscent of that used by Fish, some men have affirmed that there is no purgatory and that there is no need for pilgrimages (ibid., p. 207).

Some people say further, reports the *Diuision*, that the clergy should not be allowed so lightly to arrest people on suspicion of heresy (ibid., p. 226), and that a layman can never win against a cleric in a spiritual court (ibid., p. 227). There are also many people, continues Saint-German, who think that the Church has made laws that it has no power to make (ibid., p. 240), while some take offence at the clergy's manner of living (ibid., p. 244). The book claims that there are many other grievances abroad among the people similar to the ones already mentioned, more than there is time to set down (ibid., p. 208).

With an air of injured innocence, Saint-German complains in *Salem and Bizance* that while More criticized his method of "some say," More used it himself in the *Apologye:*

> Master More in his apologie speketh many times ageynst a
> certayn maner of spekinge, that I vsed in dyuers places of the
> saide treatise, which is this: when I recited what opinions I haue
> herde sey, there were amonge the people, I seyd, that some seye,
> or they seye this or that, or that many say so, and suche other

lyke sayenges, withoute affyrmynge that I knew it of myn owne knowlege, that it was so: for in some thynges I dyd not in dede. At this maner of speking mayster Moore findeth a defaute, in suche a straunge gesting maner, that I merueile greatly at it. And I merueylle the more, bycause he vseth the same termes hym selfe in dyuers places of his apologie . . . (*SB*, fol. 62ᵛ).

What happened was that More adopted the phrase in mockery of Saint-German's use of it, which must have been quite obvious to the latter who, nevertheless, seems to have been determined to squeeze the utmost tactical advantage possible out of the expression.

Then Saint-German goes on to defend his method of argumentation, claiming that it makes for the greatest truth and accuracy (*SB*, fol. 63ʳ). He keeps up the device right through his *Addicions*, where he employs variations of the usual phrase by telling his readers that "many men thynke" that the great number of ecclesiastical laws on clerical irregularity were made by the higher clergy to get money rather than to increase virtue (*Addicions*, fol. 5ᵛ). It is in the *Addicions*, too, that Saint-German advances a further defense of his method of recording other people's criticisms of the Church, by observing that "the common prouerbe is trewe, that there is neuer smoke without somme fyre . . ." (ibid., fol. 17ᵛ).

Next in importance to the reportorial device just discussed is the air of objectivity and impartiality with which Saint-German endows his accusations against the Church. It was for this quality that his works were brought to the attention of More, who was urged to adopt Saint-German's mildness in his own writings (*Apologye*, p. 45). While it would be incorrect to argue that all of Saint-German's restraint and objectivity is simulated, it is, as we shall see, so often accompanied by innuendo that it must be considered as part of his controversial technique.

For instance, at the very beginning of the *Diuision*, after he records that the laity hate the clergy, Saint-German states his conviction that if the clergy would only become a little meeker instead of being so proud, all the strife would cease and the people would once again obey their superiors as they should (*Diuision*, p. 209). He reminds his readers that there are many good members of the clergy, but adds that because the wicked few are suffered to continue unpunished, all the clergy are in disrepute (ibid., p. 231), and he ends with a prayer for reformation, whereupon the laity will once again respect and obey the clergy (ibid., p. 250).

He continues to belabor the clergy with left-handed compliments in the *Addicions,* in which he repeats that he criticizes the spirituality only because a reformed clergy is needed to produce a righteous laity (*Addicions,* fols. 33ʳ-33ᵛ), adding that he wants the former to receive all the honor due them by the law of God—with which, if they would only be content, they would have much more honor than they now enjoy (ibid., fols. 29ᵛ-30ᵛ). After demonstrating at considerable length that Thomas Becket was wrong on every point in his dispute with Henry II, Saint-German adds that he does not mean to say that Becket was not a saint, for he acted according to his own conscience which—and here Saint-German seems to be afraid he has not made his point—was a misguided one (ibid., fols. 53ᵛ-58ᵛ).

Even more than Tyndale was, Saint-German is intent on exposing More's controversial technique. In *Salem and Bizance* he complains that More falsely summarized the content of the *Diuision,* and that it is More's custom to turn his opponent's meaning to another effect "than can be reasonably taken to folowe of it . . ." (*SB,* fol. 2ᵛ). Saint-German also complains that More pretended the *Diuision* said that the life of the priest is more perfect than that of the monk. After spending some time explaining that this was not what he said, Saint-German comments:

> And if maister Moore wold charitably, and to the beste so haue taken it, he shulde not haue neded to haue taken so moche peyn as he hath done in the making of the saide exception, ne yet to haue caused me to haue taken so moch peyn in the answeryng (*SB,* fol. 23ʳ).

Saint-German goes on to caution the reader always to ask himself whether or not More's objections lead to reformation. In this way, says Saint-German, the reader will know whether a particular objection is meant sincerely or whether it is merely part of More's controversial technique (*SB,* fol. 25ʳ).

Saint-German also makes a point of indicating the passages More has failed to answer (e.g., *SB,* fol. 70ʳ), and at the end of *Salem and*

Bizance he lists all the chapters to which More did not reply (*SB*, fol. 91ᵛ). As some of the issues Saint-German notes are very important and certainly demand response, the assertion that More has left them unanswered gives Saint-German a strong finish to his book. Whether More was really trying to evade these points or whether he merely omitted them from the *Apologye* for the sake of brevity, it is impossible to say. In any case, he realized the tactical advantage his omission had given to Saint-German, for he took up most of the neglected chapters in his *Debellacyon*.

Similarly, Saint-German is quick to point out what he considers to be inconsistencies in More's works. He says that while More at first denied that there was any division between the clergy and the laity, he later referred to the "late sprongen diuision" (*SB*, fol. 5ᵛ). Saint-German also finds difficulty in reconciling More's professed love for the gospel with his defense of prelates who do not give their wealth to the poor, lest heretics should accuse them of hypocrisy.[18]

In addition, Saint-German accuses More of distorting facts and of tampering with the meaning as well as with the actual text of his books. He maintains, in effect, that More lied in saying that there was no dissension within the clergy itself; Saint-German points out that there was variance between curates and chantry priests over the statute which subordinated the latter to the former and that priests were in habit of suing each other over tithes and benefices (*SB*, fol. 22ᵛ). He complains that More misquoted the statement that men "as of a policie" were attacking the doctrine of purgatory to deprive the Church of income, to make it appear that he approved their action and said that the men doing this were "politic" men.[19] Saint-German also claims that More incorrectly quoted the *Diuision* as saying that it was unlawful for anyone to have many possessions; what the work said was that it was unlawful for the clergy to have many possessions (*SB*, fol. 16ᵛ).

Saint-German uses the dialogue form in both *Salem. and Bizance* and in *The addicions*—as indeed he does in his "noncontroversial" *Doctor and Student*—but he never makes it an important part of his technique as More does. These works are dialogues only in the formal sense of the term, and neither Salem nor Bizance really represents opposing points of view nor contends with the other. Very often even the form of the dialogue is abandoned for passages in which Saint-German directly combats the views of his opponent.

More's
Rebuttal

One of the main tasks More sets himself in opposing Saint-German is to tear down the latter's façade of impartiality. He wants to demonstrate that behind his opponent's apparent mildness lies a ruthless desire to destroy the prerogatives of the Church and to discredit its clergy. As More is an expert at finding dangerous implications in even the most innocent passages,[20] and as most of Saint-German's passages are far from innocent, he is able to present a convincing case which pictures his adversary as one who really wants to create dissension rather than to heal it.

More begins his discussion of the *Diuision* by saying that he does not agree with those who regard this book as a model of fairness; he thinks that it is no milder nor any more impartial than his own publications (*Apologye*, pp. 57-58), an opinion which he supports by pointing out the extent to which Saint-German blamed the clergy for the disorder within the kingdom, while of the laity he said little or nothing at all (ibid., p. 60).

Saint-German, More tells his readers, acts like a man who finds two men standing innocently together, rushes between them on the pretense that they are about to fight, pushes one man back, slaps the face of the other, and then leaves, saying that he has prevented a fight and reconciled two enemies (ibid., p. 63).

Or, says More, Saint-German's behavior could be compared to that of a man who finds a husband angry with his wife and attempts to make peace between them in the following manner: He brings the husband and wife together before all their neighbors so that, to begin with, everyone will know that they have had a quarrel. Then he tells them what a pity it is that while once they were at peace they have now fallen out, and that many neighbors, he hears, wonder how their dispute arose. Therefore, to restore their former love for each other, he will tell them what some people say are the causes of their quarrel. After this, continues More, the man will tell the husband everything which anybody has ever said against his wife, among the accusations perhaps even some which are true but which the husband has never suspected. And then he will turn to the wife and say that he does not know if these charges against her are true, but this is what he has heard people say, and that he cannot understand why she does not change her way of living. Then, More continues, to show his impartiality the man turns on the husband and scolds him for spoiling his wife, for he has heard that the wife has been allowed to be much too idle, has been given excessive time to gossip with her friends, and has had too many good clothes. Furthermore, continues this peacemaker, I hear that you call her a shrew, and some people have told me that behind your back she calls you a cuckold. So that he will not be held responsible for any of these accusations, he reports them all "vnder *th*e fayre figure of some say." However, concludes More, so far as Saint-German is concerned, "all hys Some sayes be of his owne sayenge" (ibid., pp. 63-65).

More concludes that a man who can write a book such as the *Diuision* has no great care for the furtherance of the Catholic faith (ibid., p. 67), and he attributes to *Salem and Bizance* the same malicious intent as that of the *Diuision*, namely, to make the ordinaries afraid to arrest heretics for fear of slander (*W*, p. 930). He is not deceived, writes More, by the claim that this book does not attack the clergy but is really supposed to help them, for that claim is like telling someone that the fact you are praying he will gain some wit is no indication that you think him witless. Let such a book be made against any other body in this realm, says More, and we shall soon see whether or not that body will think it is being attacked (*W*, p. 958). More sums up his opinion of Saint-German's impartiality when he says that those who accuse him of not writing like Saint-German are quite correct: "How be yt euery man hath not lyke wytte nor lyke inuencyon in wrytynge. For he fyndeth many proper wayes of vtterynge euyll mater in good wordes, whyche I neuer thought vppon, but am a simple playn body . . ." (*Apologye*, p. 45).

More realized the potency of Saint-German's "some say," and occasionally he adopted it satirically. To show how impartial he was, Saint-German listed all the clergy's faults he had omitted, but of which "some men" held them guilty. To this More answers: "But now to these excuses, some other men answere agayne, that the leuying out of felonye, sacrylege, & murder, is rather a token of wylynes the*n* any forbering or fauour." And, continues More, some men say also that since Saint-German realized that the entire clergy could not possibly be accused of such sins, he mentions only such faults as could be ascribed to the Church as a whole (ibid., p. 62). Again, when he compares Saint-German's method of stopping a fight between two men by slapping one while merely restraining the other, More concludes that "some men wolde say agayne (as I suppose) that he had as lyue hys enmy [*sic*] were let alone with hym . . . as haue such a frend steppe in betwene to parte theym" (ibid., p. 63). Other instances of this kind of satire are numerous, as when More says, "Now of a very trouth thys pacyfyer, as some saye, goth yet wurse to wurke i*n* his boke of dyuisyon, then this Some say, that we put for a sample bytwene the man & hys wyfe" (ibid., p. 66); or, "And yet bysyde all the fawtes that he bryngeth in vnder some saye and they say/some that him selfe sayeth without any some say, be such as some saye that he can neuer proue, and some they say be playne and open false."[21]

Besides ironic adoption of the "some-say" device, More invents two ironic epithets for his adversary. Indicating his mistrust of Saint-German's intentions, More often refers to him as either "the Pacifier" or "this good man" (*W*, pp. 989-992).

Sometimes More counters Saint-German's arguments with ridicule. He contends that if Saint-German's proposals on the handling of heretics were adopted, all a heretic would have to claim in order to be absolved would be that he did not mean what he said in a heretical sense. Then, concludes More, we could do the same with thieves; if the thief said that he did not commit the crime, we would have to let him go (*W*, p. 961).

Not only does he ridicule what Saint-German said, but, for good measure, he sometimes also ridicules what Saint-German did not say, but what More "understands" him to have said. One example of this technique, already touched on, occurs when More understands Saint-German to say that the men who "as of a policie" attack purgatory are "politic" men. More goes on to say that if a tinker were caught stealing, he might very well excuse himself by saying that he was merely doing it "of a policie" in the sense that he was a "politic" man to do it, in which there is no harm.[22] Taken in context, Saint-German's phrase bears no such interpretation, for his description of the men who "as of a policie" attacked purgatory is in no way commendatory but is merely meant to indicate that there are some men who hate the clergy to such an extent that they will attack anything which yields revenue to the Church.

Another occasion on which More misreports Saint-German is during a discussion on the impartiality of clerical judges. On this Saint-German says the following:

> ... therfore if any lay man report any euyll of a preest, though it be openly knowen, that it is as he saythe, yet they wyll be more diligente to cause the laye man to ceasse of that sayeng, than to do that in them is to refourme that is a mysse in the preeste, that it is spoken of, takynge as hit were occasion to doo the lesse in suche reformations/bycause laye men speke so moche agaynste them: (*Diuision*, p. 224).

When he originally quotes the portion of the chapter in which the above appears, More renders the passage in question accurately, but when he subsequently comes to deal with it in detail, he summarizes Saint-German's carefully chosen language about the clerical judge with a blunt "That he is through suche pride farre fro such indifference and equitie, as ought and must be in . . . iudges . . ." (*W*, p. 1008). While this might be a possible inference to draw from Saint-German's text, it would be only an inference, and the fact remains that Saint-German does not say what More claims he does.

Yet another example of misinterpretation is More's reply to Saint-German's complaint that in all of More's answers to the charges against the clergy, he is not really coming to grips with the existing situation of clerical abuse. Saint-German's words are these:

> ... and he goeth very moche aboute also to perswade, that some of the thinges that be aleid in the said treatise for part of the causes of the said diuision, be no causes of diuision. And somtyme he saith by general wordes, that there is no sufficient cause of diuision aleyed, takynge that as it were a good answere to the said tretise. But surely it is not so, for seinge that he hath con-

fessed a diuision hym selfe, it foloweth that al though he coude auoyde all the considerations that be aleyed for causes of the sayde diuisyon, as he doeth not ne can not do: yet had he littel done to helpe the diuision . . . (*SB*, fols. 5ᵛ–6ʳ).

The gist of what Saint-German is saying here seems reasonably clear, but it is not so to More, who answers:

> Now here he saith that I kepe secrete such abusyons and pre-tences as be yᵉ principall causes of the deuision, whereof himselfe hath he saieth shewed some: either he meaneth that those which I kept secrete, be those that himselfe hath written, or other beside theym. If he meane other: then either hymselfe knoweth them or not. If he know theym not: how knoweth he that I know them, or that there be any such at all? If hymself know them and shew them not: then he hydeth them and kepeth them secrete himself as well as I. Nowe if he meane but those that himselfe hath wrytten: how can I kepe those secrete that he hath written? (*W*, p. 1025)

By these dazzling verbal gymnastics, More avoids answering Saint-German's main point, which is that More himself has never admitted that the clergy are in any way to blame for the split between them and the laity; and by the device of pretending to be puzzled about his opponent's possible meaning, instead of taking it in the most obvi-ous sense, More manages to give his readers the impression that somehow Saint-German's charge is absurd.

While More occasionally takes such liberties with his opponent's words and their meaning, he, in his turn, charges that the latter frequently distorts the text and the meaning of the *Apologye*. More continues by saying that after he has criticized one of his passages, Saint-German will change the passage and omit some of his own words to make it appear that the criticism was unjust (*W*, p. 931).

To the above charge More adds that of prevarication. He writes that Saint-German not only describes causes of grievance between the clergy and the laity previously unknown to either party, but that he also adduces as causes of the split other matters which are untrue (*Apologye*, p. 62). Some things, says More, he alleges under the cover of "some say," and "yet ouer thys wythout hys masker of

Some say/he saith open faced some of the wurste hym selfe, and that in some thynges *that* are as some trewe men saye not trewe" (ibid.). As an example of one of these untruths, More cites Saint-German's charge that the clergy accuse anyone who criticizes them of wanting to destroy the Church (ibid., p. 121).

Among the less serious accusations More makes against Saint-German are that his grammar is incorrect, his rhetoric unclear, and his writing generally lacking in lucidity. These charges More makes in a portion of the *Apologye* in which he submits eleven of Saint-German's lines, containing no anticlerical accusations whatever, to almost two folio columns of microscopic examination. Besides yielding the above conclusions, the investigation also establishes that what appeared as an innocent passage really has a subtly hidden malevolent intent, and that Saint-German is wrong on a number of factual points, such as his distinction between "monks" and "priests," when actually some monks are members of the priesthood (ibid., pp. 69-70).

More also thinks it necessary to inform his readers that the title *Salem and Bizance* is not very descriptive, as only 15 of the 106 leaves deal with either character, and also that although the book has been advertised as a dialogue, in reality it is not a dialogue at all (*W*, pp. 932-933).

Sometimes, intentionally or otherwise, More takes liberties with logic in order to counter one of Saint-German's points. He defends ex officio trials, for instance, in which the accuser remains secret, by claiming that the accuser might be afraid to make himself known, as happens very often in civil cases where a poor person is afraid to complain openly of an injustice suffered at the hands of some powerful person lest even worse should follow (*W*, p. 907). This is a case of false analogy, for while it was quite possible that a poor man who had suffered an injury from a powerful man might have been afraid to lodge a complaint against him, no man had any need to be afraid in a matter of heresy as, by More's own testimony, there was seldom if ever a case where "any great man whome folke neded to feare, was condempned in this realme for heresye" (*W*, p. 978).

More also implies of the whole what is true only of the individual parts. Saint-German complained that the clergy with their chantries,

trentals, pardons, and pilgrimages placed too heavy a financial burden on the laity. More answers by saying that "some of these thynges
be suche that they make not the prestes so very ryche, that all the
clergye shold for the great lucre so sore bend vnto the settynge forth
therof" (*Apologye*, p. 81). More's answer is correct so far as it goes,
namely, that "some" of these taxes when considered individually did
not bring in very much money, but Saint-German's point was that
their sum total did, in fact, yield a very great deal of money for the
clergy. More, by restricting his claim to the parts rather than applying it to the whole, manages to cast doubt on Saint-German's
assertion.

More provides us with a good example of the non sequitur when
he concludes that Saint-German himself does not really believe the
truth of one of his own charges because he has put it in the form of
"some say" instead of making it in his own person:

> And wheras for the farther mayntenaunce of hys matter, he
> sayth, that if I make search therin to know the trouth, I shall fynd
> that much people take it so, that many which haue been punished
> for heresy, the spiritualtie haue done it of no loue but of will. . . .
>
> And surely that their saying is false & nought in his owne
> secrete iudgement: you may see good readers by this that he
> laboureth so sore to put it from himself, and would be so loth to
> haue it taken for his owne. And therefore while hymselfe
> thought their saying so false, he shoulde not haue told it after
> them (*W*, p. 954).

The last part is a truly wonderful conclusion based on a remarkable
assumption. This novel kind of reasoning, if universally applied,
would brand as false in More's opinion all that he himself ever alleges
on the same authority, for instance, much of his *Richard the thirde*—
and everything not spoken in his own person in any of his dialogues,
such as all of his *Dialoge of comfort*.

Since he has heard that because of their length his books are not
finding many readers,[23] More deals with this problem in the *Apologye*. He defends the length of his previous books, claiming that if he
had added all his opponents' minor faults to the major errors he
mentioned, his works would be even twice as long (ibid., pp. 2-3).

He reveals a time-saving method for reading the *Confutacyon*. In order to make things easier for his readers, More informs them that each chapter of this book has been written to contain within itself a complete refutation of the entire Reformed position, so that they need read only one chapter selected at random.[24]

More now probably lacked the time to be brief, and shortly after the above discussion, he quotes twice within a few pages the text of a sermon he wants to refute (*Apologye*, pp. 15-18, 25-40). However, he evidently realized what he had done, for after commenting on the text at length, he draws himself up, remembers that he has been told that his works are too long, and decides to leave the matter. Yet he is reluctant to accord the subject such brief treatment and refers his readers to one of his other works, for which he supplies specific references (ibid., p. 40). Had More only adopted this course sooner, or had he even followed it consistently after he did adopt it, he would have shortened the length of his controversial works by hundreds of folio pages.

Complaining of the fact that the Reformers refuse to read his *Confutacyon* not only because they think it is too long but also because they are so sure of their own position that they disdain, as they say, to waste their time on the book, More meets his critics more than halfway by marking for them certain portions which he thinks summarize his arguments (ibid., pp. 41-42). This indicates again that he was not writing merely to save the English public from the doctrines of the Reformers but that he actually hoped that his works would convert some of these Reformers themselves.

It is, perhaps, also partly for the sake of brevity that in the *Apologye* More contents himself with answering only three of Saint-German's sixteen chapters. In previous controversies More occasionally disregarded passages in his opponents' books, but he was never quite so selective as this. However, this procedure led Saint-German to imply that what More left out he was unable to answer (*SB*, fols. 91^r-92^r); therefore, in his *Debellacyon*, More abandons this method and takes up most of *Salem and Bizance*. At the same time, while writing the *Debellacyon*, he got into the habit of referring his readers to the *Apologye*, instead of starting another discussion of a subject already treated at length in the earlier work.

Both controversialists were occasionally guilty of inaccuracies. Saint-German is in error when he accuses More of misquoting him and denies having ever said that the clergy punish many persons because they think that anyone who finds fault with them hates priests (*SB*, fol. 36^v). He plainly said of the clergy that "they take hit, that they that fynde defaute at suche abusions and disordre, loue no prestes. . . . And therefore haue they punysshed many persons . . ." (*Diuision*, pp. 208-209). Another misrepresentation on Saint-German's part occurs over the question of the impartiality of clerical judges. Saint-German claims that in the *Diuision* he said, "it wyll be harde to fynde any one spiritual man that is not infecte with the sayd desyre and affection, to haue the worldly honour of pristis exalted"; he insists that at this point his discussion of the subject ended, and that in quoting him More maliciously added the clause: "That he is through such pride ferre fro such indifference and equitie, as ought and must be in tho iuges" (*SB*, fol. 66^r). Saint-German's accusation is unfounded, for while More did summarize Saint-German's words with the clause in question, he never pretended that it was a verbatim quotation; furthermore, Saint-German's sentence does not end where he says it does.[25] More is inaccurate when he commences his refutation of Saint-German's *Diuision* by denying one of its principal theses, namely, the existence of a significant amount of dissension between the clergy and the laity (*Apologye*, p. 60). There is a large body of evidence that the dissension was every bit as acute as Saint-German claimed. First there is the letter which Richard Fitzjames, Bishop of London, sent to Wolsey, requesting him to intercede on behalf of Dr. Horsey who was accused of murdering Richard Hunne:

> . . . for assured am I, if my chancellor be tried by any twelve men in London, they be so maliciously set, 'in favorem haereticae pravitatis' that they will cast and condemn any clerk, though he were as innocent as Abel. . . .[26]

In *Colyn Cloute* Skelton says:

> For, as farre as I can se,
> It is wronge with eche degre:
> For the temporalte

Accuseth the spiritualte;
The spirituall agayne
Dothe grudge and complayne
Vpon the temporall men: (ll. 59–65)[27]

The Spanish envoy to the court of Henry VIII reported to his master that nearly all the people in England hated the priests,[28] while Colet's sermon to Convocation bears testimony to the same fact. Turning to the judgment of several students of the period, Seebohm,[29] Taylor,[30] Mallet,[31] and Trevelyan[32] all support Saint-German's description of the situation.

More is wide of the mark on another occasion when he tells Saint-German that so far as complaints against the clergy are concerned, "the matters haue late been examined, and the trueth hath been playnly proued contrary" (*W*, p. 1004). More is referring to the Complaint of the Commons and the Supplication against the Ordinaries, and certainly neither the Commons, nor Henry, who rejected Convocation's reply,[33] would agree with More's version of the proceedings. On this point More was not supported even by the very clergy he was defending, for Convocation, in answer to the Supplication against the Ordinaries and hoping thereby to stave off further attacks, inaugurated a program to reform the abuses, the existence of which was no longer denied.[34]

Another kind of inaccuracy occurs in More's response to Saint-German's accusation that his words dealing with the partiality of clerical judges were misconstrued. More denies any misrepresentation and asserts that when Saint-German quoted his own words he slyly left out a "therefore" on which the whole matter depended and that Saint-German did not originally say "they haue punished many persones," but "therefore they haue punished manye persones" (*W*, p. 954). Thus, says More, the accusation that the clergy seek to punish anyone who dares to criticize them is not from hearsay at all but comes from Saint-German himself. However, More's version of what Saint-German said is incorrect; the latter did not leave out anything when in *Salem and Bizance* he quoted what he had said before in the *Diuision* (*SB*, fols. 36r-36v).

Saint-German's charge that More was inconsistent is not entirely unjustified. For instance, More argues that ex officio trials are necessary because without them people, anticipating reprisal, would be afraid to accuse heretics (*W*, p. 970), but he later says that no powerful person whom people need fear was ever accused of heresy (*W*, p. 978).

Another kind of inconsistency occurs when More, defending the imposition of penance on persons not proved guilty of heresy but merely accused, says that anyone who lives in such a way as to make his neighbors think him guilty of heresy "is well worthy me thynketh to do some penaunce for that maner of byhauour, wherby he geueth all other folke occasyon to take hym for so noughtye" (*Apologye*, p. 148). It is ironic that he should advocate punishment[35] on the evidence of hearsay in the same book in which he objects to Saint-German's accusations from hearsay. The fact that the same punishment is meted out for greater and lesser crimes does not disturb More, who calls it an "vnresonable reaso*n*" to complain of this situation (*W*, p. 1029). Yet it was the same situation of which he strongly complained in the *Utopia*, in which he argued that to punish alike greater and lesser crimes served only to increase the incidence of all crime.[36]

Looked at more broadly, one interesting and puzzling feature of this controversy is the ambiguous attitude which More displays toward his opponent. While he is at times quite certain that Saint-German is writing with malevolent intent and that his claims to impartiality are merely part of his controversial technique, there are other occasions when More forgets the harsh things he said and credits his adversary with basically good intentions such as he never allowed to any other opponent. For instance, on one occasion after he has examined some of Saint-German's points in the *Diuision*, More calls a halt and says that he will not touch any other points his opponent has made because some of them could be answered by every wise man in the reading, and some are very true (*Apologye*, p. 108). After refuting Saint-German's first chapter, More is still of the opinion that his opponent means well (ibid., p. 146), which, strangely enough, does not prevent More from calling him a liar on numerous occasions afterward (*W*, pp. 931, 940, 962). As he nears the end of his *Debellacyon*, More reiterates the conviction that his opponent means well; his is merely a case of having been misled, thinks

More (*W*, p. 956). Toward the end of what he has to say about *Salem and Bizance*, More tells his readers that there are some parts of that book which he likes very much, especially those parts which deal with the sacraments (*W*, p. 1030).

One could, of course, assume that this occasional praise of his opponent is part of More's controversial technique, that he has taken to heart the criticisms of the harshness characterizing his previous controversial works and has determined that an occasional display of graciousness might work just as well as constant vituperation. On the other hand, the fact that More was disputing not against a heretic but a fellow Catholic also probably influenced him, so that he could afford to have his opponent be wrong in only part of what he said, instead of in law, grammar, logic, rhetoric, theology—everything.

VII

Conclusion

The main techniques employed by the Reformers in their attack on the Church were the polemical use of secular and ecclesiastical history and the Scriptures.

Their use of history probably played some part in preparing public opinion to accept the assault on clerical wealth and power that Henry embarked on for his own purposes. At least that was the expectation of the government, which attempted to secure the services of Tyndale and which actually recruited Barnes. Henry's favorable reception of Fish and his pamphlet is further evidence of the Crown's appreciation of Protestant historical propaganda. The Reformers' references to ecclesiastical history to demonstrate the nonprimitive origins of Catholic doctrine and practice must be regarded as good strategy, and their citing of actual or imagined incidents of clerical immorality from the chronicles in their criticisms of clerical celibacy and monasticism would have been effective on a popular level.

Tyndale's translation of the New Testament changed many of the terms the clergy had used to claim scriptural support for their position, while his marginal notes were intended to ensure for the

214

new text an interpretation favorable to the Reformers. Thus on two counts his version was made a vehicle for propaganda. Furthermore, the Reformers' repeated claims that Catholics were afraid of an open Bible—and the reluctance of the clergy to provide such a Bible—implied strongly that neither the behavior nor the doctrine of the Catholic clergy could stand to be measured by the yardstick of the Scriptures.

Looking more broadly at the Reformers' campaign, we find that certain similarities are, of course, apparent between More's technique and that of his opponents. After all, they shared the same educational background so that their use of the disciplines of logic and rhetoric, for instance, is essentially the same. The differences are to be found, I think, in the form of their works, in their use of Scripture, and in their use of history.

Most important to note is that Protestant strategy was a strategy of attack—More's of defense—and that the strategy of attack dictated the form of the works the Reformers wrote. Of this strategy Tyndale was the leading exponent, and his works became prototypes for subsequent Protestant polemics. (Since in all three areas to be discussed—form of work, use of Scripture, and use of history—Tyndale was indebted to Luther,[1] Luther may be regarded as the ultimate source of early Tudor Protestant strategy.)

Tyndale pioneered the two genres on which the Reformers relied: the short treatise of exposition, often of a scriptural passage, such as the *Mammon* and the *Obedience*, descendants of which are Barnes's treatise on the Church, Frith's work on the Eucharist, Joye's exposition of Daniel; and the short, selective analysis of an opponent's work, such as Tyndale's answer to More, in which tradition are Frith's work on purgatory, Barnes's answer to More, and Joye's book against More.

Tyndale's use of Scripture—apart from his translation—again laid the groundwork for subsequent Protestant technique. His insistence on the primacy of Scripture combined with his use of what I have called a "pliable" Bible provided him with a very convenient document. (His "manipulation" of the Bible was really no different from his "manipulation" of the chronicles; in both instances, in effect, he provided his own source.) And in his "infallible" approach to the Scriptures he was followed by most early and mid-century Protestant polemicists—by Barnes, less by Frith, by Joye, by Turner, by Becon, and, above all, by Bale.

And Tyndale's "new" history, written ultimately, as has been pointed out, by himself, which made the double point that all medieval history had to be "corrected" by Protestant interpretation and that Catholics were historically treasonous, not only had a tremendously damaging effect on the fortunes of the Catholic clergy in England in Tyndale's own day, but was also the "history" adopted by Fish, Barnes, Becon, and especially by Bale, who used Tyndale's historical theories in both his prose works and in *King Johan*, the first Protestant history play.

It is curious that More did not make a greater effort to rebut the Reformers' allegations from history. His attempts in this area were mostly confined to his book against Fish, whose polemical use of history was, however, less extensive and more accurate than that of Tyndale and Barnes. Perhaps More thought it wiser to say as little as possible about the Reformers' historical assertions, which were so favorably received by Henry.

More's most outstanding technique was his use of the dialogue form. Thus in his *Dialogue concernynge heresyes* he was able to present a favorable picture of his own side and an unfavorable one of the Reformers through the creation of a character for himself and for his interlocutor. A similar technique was used against Barnes, for whom an unfavorable character was created and who was defeated by More's spokesmen. The dialogue form also permitted More to return repeatedly to points he wished to treat at some length, without being as obviously repetitious as he was in later works written as straightforward treatises. And More's genius for dialogue and character produced the eloquent souls of his *Supplicacion*, who were in themselves intended as dramatic proof of that work's main thesis.

More's use of humor must also be numbered among his most successful techniques. Enlivening sometimes lengthy doctrinal debate, its earthy quality must have contributed to whatever popular appeal More's polemics enjoyed. That some of More's humor was directed at the foibles of the Catholic clergy, especially in his *Dialogue*, probably enhanced the picture he tried to present of himself as an independent layman who was not a hireling of the clergy. Occasionally, humor served More as a substitute for discussion and, as used against his opponents generally, it implied that there was something ludicrous about both the men and their arguments.

Any attempt to decide who was the victor in the controversy between More and his opponents is a difficult task. The question certainly cannot be answered, as it too often is, according to the particular religious belief of the writer, nor on the basis that in England the cause of Protestantism was ultimately victorious. The triumph of Protestantism was the result of many factors, only one of which was the polemical acumen of its advocates.

However, the fact that almost the entire burden of answering the Reformers in the vernacular was placed on the shoulders of one man —More—hardly helped the Catholic cause, and there can be little doubt that this situation adversely affected the quality of the overlengthy polemics More evidently felt obliged to write after 1529, when he had no leisure for polishing—and pruning—his controversial works. The dearth of English Catholic propaganda in the early and middle Tudor periods is a problem which bears investigation.

More carried out his commission to champion the Church quite brilliantly at first, in his *Dialogue* and in most of his *Supplicacion*. The dramatic devices these works contain make their arguments persuasive and immediate. But More's later defenses, written hastily and under enormous pressure of work, lack force. We know that the prolixity of his *Confutacyon* lost him readers, and the highly technical legal discussions in his works against Saint-German must have had the same effect. In a treatise such as the *Debellacyon*, the "simple and unlearned men" whom More was commissioned to address seem to have been forgotten. Merely on the ground that they failed in their primary function of attracting readers, More's later polemics must be judged poor propaganda.

For on the Protestant side lay all the advantage of attack, in that exposés of abuses usually attract more readers than do defenses of the *status quo*. That Tyndale, Frith, and Fish were widely read— especially Fish—must in a large measure be attributed to the fact that what they had to say was of popular interest. But to the inherent advantage of their position they added the virtue of terseness; they produced "many shorte treatyses"—a deliberate tactic, More thought, and he was probably right.

Thus Protestant propaganda presented a difficult problem, to which More's strategy of exhaustive rebuttal was surely not the correct solution. In this situation, perhaps More should not have attempted a reasoned defense at all, but should have devoted himself instead exclusively to counterattack, possibly in the style of Murner's *Von dem Grossen Lutherischen Narren.*

A few comments should be made about the literary quality of More's polemical works as compared to that of his noncontroversial works.

Since, as mentioned, the bulk of More's polemical work was written in great haste under tremendous pressure, and since most of his nonpolemical works were written at greater leisure, one obvious difference is that the latter, as a group, tend to be more polished. Obviously, also, More would make greater efforts to achieve literary polish in the nonpolemical category, since the exhibition of literary elegance would be one of the main objects of the work. Good examples are his *Richard the thirde*, his epigrams, and his *A dialoge of comfort*, written during his imprisonment in the Tower. The one polemical work to which More had time to give some finish is his *Dialogue concernynge heresyes*, the careful construction of which has already been discussed. It stands in sharp contrast to the piecemeal and formless character of all his other polemics, including the *Supplicacion of soules*, the first book of which contains the central dramatic device of the "souls" but lacks total structure.

More's noncontroversial works also tend to be somewhat less repetitious than the polemical, again chiefly for the reason that when the former were written, More had time to edit what he wrote. *Richard the thirde* and *Utopia* are not at all repetitious, and it should be remembered that the prolix More of the later polemics was at one time master of the concise epigram. The *Dialogue concernynge heresyes* is repetitious, but here the repetition is still controlled and, as was pointed out, should be regarded as part of More's polemical technique. It is in the *Supplicacion of soules* that he begins to lose control and weary his readers with unnecessary repetition. Evidently the habit carried over later to the noncontroversial *Comfort*[2] which, of course, More wrote under a different kind of pressure.

Understandably, the tone of the polemics is sharp—except the work against Frith—while that of the nonpolemical works is not. Yet in the area of tone the two categories tend to blend, for some of the wonderful satire of *Richard*, the *Utopia*, and the epigrams is essentially the same as the kind of satire More used against his opponents. There is the same masterful characterization and dramatization, as well as the same keen eye for the ridiculous—such as in the Anemolian ambassadors section of the *Utopia* and the picture of Barnes or the David-Bathsheba section in the *Confutacyon*, where More ridicules Tyndale's distinction between sinning and not sinning.

What has been said probably exhausts the points of difference between More's style in the polemical and the nonpolemical works. Essentially, just as the More of the Latin polemics is the More of the English polemics, so the picture of More we get from his works of controversy is not substantially different from the impression of him we get from his other works. For instance, More's flair and penchant for dramatization are evident in everything he wrote. The dramatic structure of the *Dialogue* against Tyndale, of the *Supplicacion*, and of parts of his other polemical works is no less brilliant than that of the *Richard*, the *Utopia*, or the *Comfort*. In fact, as dramatic creation I would put More's "souls" second only to his picture of Richard III —and ahead of any of his Utopian characters, who lack the life of More's "Luther" and "Barnes" as portrayed in the dramatic sketches of the *Responsio* and the *Confutacyon*.

And, of course, More's humor—really inseparable from his dramatizations—runs through all his works. The same keen eye which pierces the pretensions of humanity in the *Utopia* and the epigrams is focused on the self-importance of Luther and Barnes, the specious arguments of Fish, and the claims to impartiality of Saint-German. Essentially, More's humor consists of the ability to detect the ludicrous and to dramatize it, to make it come alive before our eyes, and then to draw it out to its logical—or rather absurd—conclusions.

Not too surprisingly, again, all of More's methods of argumentation analyzed by Leland Miles in his edition of the *Dialoge of com-*

fort, such as scriptural barrage, strategically placed anecdote, homey analogy, alliteration, metaphor, wordplay, and merry tales are, as I hope this study has not too tediously demonstrated, common to all of More's works. The fact requires no comment; personality does not vary with genre, and style is the man.

The controversy affected more than just the immediate issues. The Reformers' polemical use of the Scriptures, which included their demand for a vernacular version, led their opponents eventually to produce an English Bible, the Douay Version. But the most important consequence was, of course, the translation made by Tyndale. It has been estimated that the Authorized Version of 1611 is ninety per cent Tyndale's,[3] and the influence of that version on subsequent English thought and literature is too well appreciated to require elaboration.

The polemical use of history affected the discipline of history itself. The use made of history by both Reformers and Catholics helped to stimulate interest in history generally and to produce history with a point,[4] replacing the more or less aimless compilations of the medieval chronicles. "Pointed" history is hardly the modern ideal, but such a history was a necessary bridge between the medieval annals and the "historical revolution" of the late sixteenth and the seventeenth centuries.[5]

The need for a logic suited to polemics led Ramus to revise the entire discipline, and the new Ramist logic was adopted by English textbooks on the subject.[6]

The religious dispute profoundly influenced English language and literature. So far as vocabulary is concerned, the controversy added a whole host of words and phrases to the language, many of which are in use today.[7]

The most influential of the polemical techniques was the use of certain rhetorical forms, such as the polemical dialogue, which helped shape polemical drama. The dialogue's technique of making the opposition condemn itself by its own words was an intermediate step to the self-condemnatory speeches and actions of the "evil" characters in polemical drama,[8] as in Bale's *King Johan*—the first English history play and ultimately the source of Shakespeare's drama[9]—

whose technique is essentially that of self-condemnation by the opposition and a polemical use of history derived directly from Tyndale.[10] It is surely not stretching the point to suggest that this technique of making opponents proclaim their own evil intentions influenced the assigning of self-incriminatory speeches to villains in Tudor and Stuart drama.

Finally, Protestant vernacular polemics and Bible translations forced Catholic apologists to abandon Latin for English. It was, then, in the area of language that Reformation polemics made their greatest impact, and there can be little doubt that discussions in the vernacular by learned and respected men on both sides of questions considered to be of vital importance played a part in elevating the status of English as a fit medium for the expression of serious thought.[11]

BIBLIOGRAPHY

Primary Works

Aeneas Sylvius. *Aeneae Sylvii Piccolominei Senensis, qvi post adeptvm pontificatvm, Pivs eivs nominis secvndvs appellatus est, opera.* Basel: Henricpetrinus, 1571.

Antoninus, Saint. *Opus . . . hystoriarum . . . Antonini.* Lugduno: Nicolaus Wolff, 1512.

Aristotle. *The "Art" of Rhetoric.* Ed. and trans. John H. Freese. London: Loeb Classical Library, 1947.

Augustine, Saint. *Opera Omnia.* 16 vols. (*Patrologia Latina,* XXXII-XLVII). Ed. J.P. Migne. Paris: Garnier Brothers, 1864-1877.

Bale, John. *Acta Romanorum Pontificum.* N. pl., n. pr., 1558.

——. *The Actes of Englysh Votaryes.* Wesel: n. pr., 1546 (*STC* 1270).

——. *The Apology of Iohan Bale agaynste a ranke Papyst.* London: J. Day, 1555 (*STC* 1275).

——. *A Brefe Chronycle Concernynge . . . Oldecastell.* Antwerp?, n. pr., 1544 (*STC* 1277).

——. *The Epistle Exhortatorye.* Antwerp?, n. pr., 1544 (*STC* 1291).

——. *The first two partes of the Actes . . . of the Englysh votaryes.* London, T. Raynalde and A. Vele, 1548-1551 (*STC* 1271).

——. *Illvstrivm Maioris Britanniae Scriptorvm.* Ipswich: J. Overton, 1548 (*STC* 1295).

——. *The Pageant of Popes.* London: T. Marshe, 1574 (*STC* 1304).

——. *Yet a course at the Romyshe foxe.* Zurik: O. Iacobson, 1543 (*STC* 1309).

Barlowe, Jerome [= William?]. *A dyaloge descrybyng the orygynal ground of these Lutheran faccyons.* London: W. Rastell, 1531 (*STC* 1461).

——. [or William Roy] *A proper dyaloge/ betwene a Gentillman and a husbandman/ eche complayninge to other their miserable calamite/ through the ambicion of the clergye.* Antwerp?: H. Luft, 1530 (*STC* 6813).

——. *Rede me and be nott wrothe.* Ed. Edward Arber. London: Edward Arber, 1871.

Barnes, Robert. *A supplicatyon . . . vnto the most excellent and redoubted prince kinge henrye the eyght.* Antwerp: S. Cock, 1531 (*STC* 1470).

——. *A supplicacion vnto the most gracyous prynce H. the .viij.* London: J. Byddell, 1534 (*STC* 1471).

——. *Vitae Romanorum Pontificum, quos Papas vocamus, diligenter & fideliter collectae.* Wittenberg: J. Clug, 1536.

Becon, Thomas. *The Relikes of Rome.* London: J. Day, 1560? (*STC* 1754).

Bibliothek Älterer Schriftwerke der Deutschen Schweiz. 9 vols. Ed. Jakob Baechtold and Ferdinand Vetter. Frauenfeld: J. Huber, 1877-1892.

Brewer, J.S. and J. Gairdner, Eds., *Letter and Papers, Foreign and Domestic, of the Reign of Henry VIII.* 21 vols. London: Longmans, Green, Reader & Dyer, 1862-1910.

Brinklow, Henry. *Henry Brinklow's Complaynt of Roderyck Mors.* Ed. J.M. Cowper. London: Early English Text Society, 1874.

The Brut or The Chronicles of England. 2 vols. Ed. Friedrich W.D. Brie. London: Early English Text Society, 1906-1908.

Bugenhagen, Johann. *Epistola J. Bugenhagii Pomerani ad Anglos.* Wittenberg: N. Schirlentz, 1525.

Capgrave, John. *The Chronicle of England.* Ed. F.C. Hingeston. London: Great Britain, Public Record Office, Chronicles and Memorials, No. 1, 1858.

Cicero, Marcus Tullius. *De Inventione Rhetorica.* Ed. and trans. H.M. Hubbell. London: Loeb Classical Library, 1949.

——. *De Oratore.* 2 vols. Ed. and trans. E.W. Sutton and H. Rackhaus. London: Loeb Classical Library, 1948.

Coverdale, Miles. *A confutacion of that treatise/ which one Iohn Standish made agaynst the protestacion of D. Barnes.* Zurich: C. Froshauer, 1541? (*STC* 5888).

Erasmus, Desiderius. *Opus Epistolarum Des. Erasmi Roterodami.* Ed. P.S. Allen et al. 11 vols. Oxford: Clarendon Press, 1906-1947.

Fabyan, Robert. *The New Chronicles of England and France.* Ed. Henry Ellis. London: F.C. & J. Rivington, 1811.

Fisher, John. *Assertionis Lutheranae Confutatio.* Cologne: P. Quentell, 1523.

——. *Defensio Regie assertionis contra Babylonicam captiuitatem . . . ad maledicentissimum Martini Lutheri libellum.* Cologne: P. Quentell, 1525.

——. *Sacri sacerdotii defensio contra Lutherum.* Cologne: P. Quentell, 1525.

Four Supplications. Ed. F.J. Furnivall. London: Early English Text Society, 1871.

Foxe, John. *The Acts and Monuments of John Foxe.* Ed. Stephen R. Cattley. 8 vols. London: R.B. Seeley and W. Burnside, 1837-1841.

Frith, John. *An other boke against Rastel named the sybsedye or bulwark to his fyrst boke.* Antwerp: M. deKeyser, 1533? (*STC* 11385).

Froissart, Jean. *The Chronicle of Froissart.* 6 vols. Trans. Sir John Bourchier, Lord Berners, 1523-1525. Ed. W.P. Ker. London: David Nutt, 1901-1903.

Gardynare, German. *A letter of a yonge gentylman . . . wherin men may se the demeanour & heresy of Iohn Fryth.* London: W. Rastell, 1534 (*STC* 11594).

Gayangos, Pascual De, et al., Eds. *Calendar of Letters, Despatches, and State Papers, Relating to the Negotiations between England and Spain, Preserved in the Archives at Simancas and Elsewhere.* 13 vols. London: Longman & Co., 1862-1954.

Gwynneth, John. *A manifeste detection of the falshed of J. Friths boke.* London: T. Berthelet, 1554 (*STC* 12559).

——. *A Playne Demonstration of Iohn Frithes lack of witte.* London: T. Powell, 1557 (*STC* 12560).

Hall, Edward. *The Triumphant Reign of King Henry VIII.* 2 vols. Ed. Charles Whibley. London: T.C. & E.C. Jack, 1904.

Hardyng, John. *The Chronicle of John Hardyng.* Ed. Henry Ellis. London: F.C. & J. Rivington, 1812.

Harpsfield, Nicholas. *The Life and death of Sr. Thomas Moore.* Ed. Elsie V. Hitchcock and R.W. Chambers. London: Early English Text Society, 1932.

Harvey, Gabriel. *The Works of Gabriel Harvey.* 3 vols. Ed. Alexander B. Grosart. London: The Huth Library, 1884-1885.

Henry VIII. *Assertio septem sacramentorum aduersus Martinum Lutherum, aedita ab inuictissimo Angliae & Franciae Rege et Do. Hyberniae Henrico eius nominis octauo.* N. pl., n. pr., 1523.

——. *A copy of the letters, wherin . . . kyng Henry the eyght made answere vnto a certayn letter of Martyn Luther.* London: R. Pynson, 1526 (*STC* 13086).

——. *Literarum, quibus . . . Henricus octauus . . . respondit, ad quandam epistolam Martini Lutheri.* London: R. Pynson, 1526 (*STC* 13084).

Higden, Ranulph. *Polychronicon of Ranulph Higden.* Ed. Rev. J.R. Lumby. London: Great Britain, Public Record Office, Chronicles and Memorials, No. 41, Part 8, 1882.

Hoveden, Roger De. *The Annals of Roger De Hoveden.* 2 vols. Trans. Henry T. Riley. London: H.G. Bohn, 1853.

Hutten, Ulrich von. *Auserlesene Werke.* 3 vols. Ed. and trans. Ernst Münch. Leipzig: N. pr., 1822-1823.

Joye, George. *An Apology made by George Joy, to satisfy, if it may be, W. Tindale.* Ed. Edward Arber. London: Edward Arber, 1882.

——. *The Exposicion of Danielle the Prophete.* London: J. Daie and W. Seres, 1550 (*STC* 14824).

——. *The refutation of the byshop of Winchesters derke declaration.* London: J. Herford, 1546 (*STC* 14827).

——. *The Subuersion of Moris false foundacion.* "Emdon: Iacob Aurik," 1534 (*STC* 14829).

Luther, Martin. *D. Martin Luthers Werke.* Ed. J.K.F. Knaake et al. Weimar: H. Böhlau, 1883-.

More, Thomas. *The Apologye of Syr Thomas More, Knyght.* Ed. Arthur I. Taft. London: Early English Text Society, 1930.

——. *The Complete Works of St. Thomas More.* Ed. Richard S. Sylvester et al. New Haven: Yale University Press, 1961-.

——. *The Correspondence of Sir Thomas More.* Ed. Elizabeth F. Rogers. Princeton: Princeton University Press, 1947.

——. *A Dialogue of Comfort.* Ed. Leland Miles. Bloomington, Ind., and London: Indiana University Press, 1965.

——. *Eruditissimi viri G. Rossei opus . . . quo . . . refellit . . . Lutheri calumnias quibus . . . Angliae . . . regem Henricum . . . octauum . . . insectatur.* London: R. Pynson, 1523 (*STC* 18089).

——. *The Latin Epigrams of Thomas More.* Ed. and trans. Leicester Bradner and Charles A. Lynch. Chicago: University of Chicago Press, 1953.

——. "St. Thomas More's Letter to John Bugenhagen," Trans. Mother M.A. Sinclair. Unpublished dissertation. Loyola University of Chicago, 1957.

——. *Thomae Mori Angliae qvandam cancellarii Opera Omnia, qvotqvot reperiri potuerunt ex Basileensi Anni MDLXIII, et Lovaniensi Anni MDLXVI.* Frankfurt am Main and Leipzig: C. Genschius, 1689.

——. *A Translation of St. Thomas More's "Responsio ad Lutherum"* by Sister Gertrude J. Donnelly. Washington: The Catholic University of America Press, 1962.

Nashe, Thomas. *The Works of Thomas Nashe.* 5 vols. Ed. R.B. McKerrow. London: A.H. Bullen, 1904-1910.

Nauclerus, Johannes. *D. Iohannis Navcleri . . . Chronica.* Cologne: P. Quentell, 1544.

Nisard, Charles. *Les Gladiateurs de la République des Lettres.* 2 vols. Paris: N. pr., 1860.

Platina, Bartolomeo. *B. Platinae Cremonensis de vita & moribus summorum Pontificum historia.* Cologne: Eucharius Ceruicornus, 1529.

Quintilian, Marcus Fabius. *The Institutio Oratoria of Quintilian.* 4 vols. Ed. and trans. H.E. Butler. London: Loeb Classical Library, 1953.

Rastell, John. *A new boke of Purgatory.* London: John Rastell: 1530 (*STC* 20719).

Rhetorica ad C. Herennium. Ed. and trans. Harry Caplan. London: Loeb Classical Library, 1954.

Roper, William. *The Lyfe of Sir Thomas Moore, knighte.* Ed. Elsie V. Hitchcock. London: Early English Text Society, 1935.

Roy, William. See Barlowe.

Saint-German, Christopher. *The addicions of Salem and Byzance.* London: T. Berthelet, 1534 (*STC* 21585).

——. *A dialogue betwixte . . . Salem and . . . Bizance.* London: T. Berthelet, 1533 (*STC* 21584).

——. *A Tretise Dyers articles whiche haue bene a speciall cause of the diuision that is betwyxte the spiritualtie and the temporaltie in this realme.* See More, *Apologye,* ed. Taft.

Satirische Feldzüge wider die Reformation. Vol. III of *Deutsche Literatur. Sammlung literarischer Kunst- und Kulturdenkmäler in Entwicklungsreihen.* Reihe Reformation. 8 vols. Ed. Arnold E. Berger. Leipzig: Peter Reclam, Jr., 1930-1942.

Sherry, Richard. *A Treatise of Schemes & Tropes.* London: J. Day, 1550 (*STC* 22428).

Skelton, John. *The Poetical Works of John Skelton.* 2 vols. Ed. Rev. Alexander Dyce. London: T. Rodd, 1843.

The Statutes at large, from Magna charta, to the . . . [forty-first] year of the reign of King George the Third, inclusive. 14 vols. Revised, corrected, and continued by Charles Runnington. London: Eyre & Strahan, 1780-1800.

Turner, William. *A nevv booke of spirituall Physik.* Basel?: M.A. Constantius, 1555 (*STC* 24361).

——. *The Rescvyng of the Romishe fox.* Zurich?: C. Froshauer?, 1554 (*STC* 24355).

Tyndale, William. Trans. *The Beginning of the New Testament Translated by William Tyndale 1525. Facsimile of the Unique Fragment of the Uncompleted Cologne Edition.* Oxford: Clarendon Press, 1926.

——. *Expositions and Notes on Sundry Portions of the Holy Scriptures, together with The Practice of Prelates.* Ed. H. Walter. Cambridge: Parker Society, 1849.

——. Trans. New Testament. Worms: P. Schoeffer, 1526 (*STC* 2824).

——. Trans. New Testament. Antwerp: M. DeKeyser, 1534 (*STC* 2826).

Volterra, Raphael of. *Commentariorvm Vrbanorum Raphaelis Volaterrani.* Basle: J. Froben and N. Episcopius, 1544.

Wendover, Roger of. *The Flowers of History.* 2 vols. Trans. Rev. J.A. Giles. London: H.G. Bohn, 1849-1892.

Westminster, Matthew of. *The Flowers of History.* 2 vols. Trans. C.D. Yonge. London: H.G. Bohn, 1853.

Wilson, Thomas. *Wilson's Arte of Rhetorique, 1560.* Ed. G.H. Mair. Oxford: Clarendon Press, 1909.

——. *The rule of reason.* London: R. Grafton, 1552 (*STC* 25809).

Secondary Works

Atkins, J.W.H. *English Literary Criticism: The Renascence.* London: Methuen, 1951.

Baldwin, Charles S. *Medieval Rhetoric and Poetic.* Gloucester, Mass.: Peter Smith, 1959.

Bennett, H.S. *English Books and Readers, 1475-1557.* Cambridge, Cambridge University Press, 1952.

Bone, G.D. "Tindale and the English Language," *The Work of William Tindale.* Ed. S.L. Greenslade. London: Blackie & Son, 1938.

Bridgett, T.E. *Life and Writings of Blessed Thomas More.* London: Burns Oates & Washbourne, 1935.

Burnet, Gilbert. *History of the Reformation of the Church of England.* 7 vols. Oxford: Clarendon Press, 1865.

Butterworth, Charles C. and Allan G. Chester. *George Joye 1495?-1553, a Chapter in the History of the English Bible and the English Reformation.* Philadelphia: University of Pennsylvania Press, 1962.

The Cambridge History of English Literature. 15 vols. Ed. A.W. Ward and A.R. Waller. Cambridge: Cambridge University Press, 1908-1931.

Cargill Thompson, W.D.J. "The Sixteenth-Century Editions of *A Supplication Unto King Henry The Eight* by Robert Barnes D.D.: A footnote to the History of the Royal Supremacy," *Transactions of the Cambridge Bibliographical Society,* III (1960), 133-142.

——. "Who Wrote 'The Supper of the Lord'?" *Harvard Theological Review,* LVIII (1960), 77-91.

Cecil, Algernon. *A Portrait of Thomas More, Scholar, Statesman, Saint.* London: Eyre and Spottiswoode, 1937.

Chambers, R.W. *Man's Unconquerable Mind*. London: Jonathan Cape, 1939.

——. *Thomas More*. London: Jonathan Cape, 1935.

Clebsch, William A. *England's Earliest Protestants 1520-1535*. New Haven: Yale University Press, 1964.

——. "More Evidence That George Joye Wrote The Souper of the Lorde," *Harvard Theological Review*, LV (1962), 63-66.

Cooper, Charles H., Ed. *Athenae Cantabrigienses*. 3 vols. Cambridge: Deighton, Bell & Co., 1858-1913.

Crane, W.G. *Wit and Rhetoric in the Renaissance*. New York: Columbia University Press, 1937.

Delcourt, Joseph. *Essai sur la Langue de Sir Thomas More d'après ses oeuvres anglaises*. Montpellier: Roumégons, 1913.

Delcourt, Marie. "L'Amitié d'Erasme et de More entre 1520 et 1535," *Bulletin de l'Association Guillaume Budé*, XIV (January, 1936), 7-29.

Demaus, Robert. *William Tyndale. A Biography. A Contribution to the Early History of the English Bible*. London: Religious Tract Society, 1871.

Dickens, A.G. *The English Reformation*. London: B.T. Batsford, Ltd., 1964.

——. *Thomas Cromwell and the English Reformation*. London: The English Universities Press, 1959.

Doernberg, Erwin. *Henry VIII and Luther*. London: Barrie & Rockliff, 1961.

Elson, John. "Studies in the King John Plays," *Joseph Quincy Adams Memorial Studies*. Washington: Folger Shakespeare Library, 1948, pp. 183-197.

Fife, R.H. *The Revolt of Martin Luther*. New York: Columbia University Press, 1957.

Fines, J. "The Post-Mortem Condemnation of Richard Hunne," *English Historical Review*, 76 (July, 1963), 528-531.

Flesseman-van Leer, E. "The Controversy about Scripture and Tradition between Thomas More and William Tyndale," *Nederlands Archief voor Kerkgeschiedenis*, New Series, XLIII (1959), iii, 143-165.

Fussner, F. Smith. *The Historical Revolution*. New York: Columbia University Press, 1962.

Gairdner, James. *The English Church in the Sixteenth Century*. London: Macmillan & Co., 1902.

——. *Lollardy and the Reformation in England*. 4 vols. London: Macmillan & Co., 1908-1913.

Gasquet, Francis A. *Henry VIII and the English Monasteries*. 2 vols. London: John Hodges, 1888-1889.

Grisar, Hartmann. *Luther.* 6 vols. Trans. E.M. Lamond. Ed. Luigi Cappadelta. London: Kegan Paul, Trench, Trübner & Co., 1913-1917.

Harris, J.W. *John Bale, A Study in the Minor Literature of the Reformation.* Urbana: University of Illinois Press, 1940.

Hay, Denys. *Polydore Vergil.* Oxford: The Clarendon Press, 1952.

Howell, Wilbur S. *Logic and Rhetoric in England 1500-1700.* Princeton: Princeton University Press, 1956.

Hughes, Philip. *The Reformation in England.* 3 vols. London: Hollis and Carter, 1950-1954.

Hunt, Ernest W. *Dean Colet and His Theology.* London: Society for Promoting Christian Knowledge, 1956.

Hutton, W.H. *Sir Thomas More.* London: Methuen & Co., 1895.

Joachim, Erich. *Johannes Nauclerus und seine Chronik.* Göttingen: N. pr., 1874.

Kautsky, Karl. *Thomas More and His Utopia.* London: A. & C. Black, Ltd., 1927.

Kernan, Gerald. "Saint Thomas More, Theologian," *Thought,* XVII (June, 1942), 281-302.

Krapp, George P. *The Rise of English Literary Prose.* New York: Oxford University Press, 1915.

Krodel, G.G. "Luther, Erasmus and Henry VIII," *Archiv für Reformationsgeschichte,* LIII (1962), 60-78.

Lewis, C.S. *English Literature in the Sixteenth Century Excluding Drama.* Oxford: Clarendon Press, 1954.

Lucas, Henry S. *The Renaissance and the Reformation.* New York: Harper & Brothers, 1934.

Lupton, J.H. *A Life of John Colet.* London: George Bell & Sons, 1887.

McGiffert, Arthur C. *Martin Luther, The Man and His Work.* New York: The Century Company, 1912.

Mackie, J.D. *The Earlier Tudors.* Oxford: The Clarendon Press, 1952.

Mackinnon, James. *Luther and the Reformation.* 4 vols. New York: Russell & Russell, 1962.

Mallet, Charles E. *A History of the University of Oxford.* 3 vols. London: Methuen & Co., 1924-1927.

Mann, Horace K. *The Lives of the Popes in the Early Middle Ages.* 19 vols. London: Kegan Paul, Trench, Trübner & Co., 1902-1932.

Marc'hadour, Germain. *L' Univers de Thomas More.* Paris: J. Vrin, 1963.

Marti, Oscar A. *Economic Causes of the Reformation.* New York: The Macmillan Company, 1929.

Maynard, Theodore. *Humanist as Hero, the Life of Sir Thomas More.* New York: The Macmillan Company, 1947.

Milsom, S.F.C. "Richard Hunne's 'Praemunire'," *English Historical Review,* 76 (January, 1961), 80-82.

Mozley, J.F. *John Foxe and His Book*. London: Society for Promoting Christian Knowledge, 1940.

——. "The Supper of the Lord, 1533," *Moreana*, X (May, 1966), 11-16.

——. "Tyndale's 'Supper of the Lord'," *Notes and Queries*, CLXXXIII (November, 1942), 305-306.

——. *William Tyndale*. London: Macmillan & Co., 1937.

Mullinger, James B. *The University of Cambridge*. 3 vols. London: Longmans, Green, & Co., 1873-1911.

Nugent, Elizabeth M., Ed. *The Thought and Culture of the English Renaissance, An Anthology of Tudor Prose 1481-1555*. Cambridge: Cambridge University Press, 1956.

Ogle, Arthur. *The Tragedy of the Lollard's Tower*. Oxford: Pen-in-Hand Publishing Co., 1949.

Ong, Walter J. *Ramus and Talon Inventory*. Cambridge, Mass.: Harvard University Press, 1958.

——. *Ramus: Method, and the Decay of Dialogue*. Cambridge, Mass.: Harvard University Press, 1958.

Owst, Gerald R. *Literature and Pulpit in Medieval England*. Cambridge: Cambridge University Press, 1933.

Pastor, Ludwig von. *The History of the Popes*. 40 vols. Ed. R.F. Kerr et al. London: Kegan Paul, Trench, Trübner & Co., 1891-1953.

Pineas, Rainer. "The English Morality Play as a Weapon of Religious Controversy," *Studies in English Literature*, II (Spring, 1962), 157-180.

——. "John Bale's Nondramatic Works of Religious Controversy," *Studies in the Renaissance*, IX (1962), 218-233.

——. "Thomas More's *Utopia* and Protestant Polemics," *Renaissance News*, XVII (Autumn, 1964), 197-201.

——. "William Tyndale's Influence on John Bale's Polemical Use of History," *Archiv für Reformationsgeschichte*, LIII (1962), 79-96.

Pollard, A.F. *Henry VIII*. London: Goupil & Co., 1902, 1951.

——. *Wolsey*. London: Longmans, Green & Co., 1929, 1953.

Pollard, A.W. *Records of the English Bible*. London: Oxford University Press, 1911.

Rashdall, H. *Universities of Europe in the Middle Ages*. Ed. F.M. Powicke and A.B. Emden. Oxford: The Clarendon Press, 1936.

Reed, A.W. *Early Tudor Drama*. London: Methuen & Co., 1926.

Reynolds, E.E. *The Trial of St. Thomas More*. New York: P.J. Kenedy, 1964.

Ribner, Irving. "Morality Roots of the Tudor History Play," *Tulane Studies in English*, IV (1954), 21-43.

Rogers, Elizabeth F. "Sir Thomas More's Letter to Bugenhagen," *The Modern Churchman*, XXXV (March, 1946), 350-360.

Routh, E.M.G. *Sir Thomas More and His Friends*. London: Oxford University Press, 1934.

Rupp, E. Gordon. *Studies in the Making of the English Protestant Tradition*. Cambridge: Cambridge University Press, 1949.

Schaff, David S. *John Huss. His Life, Teachings, and Death After Five Hundred Years*. New York: C. Scribner's Sons, 1915.

Schoeck, R.J. "Common Law in England on the Eve of the Reformation," *Medieval Studies*, XXV (1963), 125-147.

——. "The Meaning of 'Ex Officio' in the Sixteenth Century," *Notes and Queries*, New Series, VII (October, 1960), 365-366.

Schorn, Georg J. *Die Quellen zu den Vitae Pontificum Romanorum des Bartolommeo Platina*. Rome: Armani & Stein, 1913.

Seebohm, Frederick. *The Oxford Reformers of 1498*. London: Longmans, Green & Co., 1867.

Smith, H. Maynard. *Henry VIII and the Reformation*. London: Macmillan, 1948.

Smith, Preserved. *The Life and Letters of Martin Luther*. New York: Houghton Mifflin, 1911.

Strype, John. *Ecclesiastical Memorials, Relating Chiefly to Religion . . . Under King Henry VIII. King Edward VI. and Queen Mary I.* 6 vols. Oxford: Clarendon Press, 1820-1840.

Sylvester, Richard S. "John Constable's Poems to Thomas More," *Philological Quarterly*, XLII (October, 1963), 525-531.

——. "The 'Man for All Seasons' Again: Robert Whittington's Verses to Sir Thomas More," *Huntington Library Quarterly*, XXVI (February, 1963), 147-154.

Taylor, Henry O. *Thought and Expression in the Sixteenth Century*. 2 vols. New York: The Macmillan Company, 1920.

Thurston, H. "Pope Joan," *The Month*, CXXIII (1914), 450-463.

Trevelyan, George M. *English Social History*. London: Longmans, Green & Co., 1944.

Vertu, Mora. "Le Chancelier sur la Sellette: More Accusé par William A. Clebsch," *Moreana*, V (1965), 107-114.

Watson, Foster. *The English Grammar Schools to 1660*. Cambridge: Cambridge University Press, 1908.

White, Helen C. *Social Criticism in Popular Religious Literature in the Sixteenth Century*. New York: The Macmillan Company, 1944.

Wood, Anthony À. *Athenae Oxonienses*. 5 vols. Ed. Philip Bliss. London: F.C. & J. Rivington, 1813-1820.

Zeeveld, W. Gordon. See Nugent.

NOTES

The following abbreviations have been used throughout the notes:

$W = The\ Workes\ of\ Sir\ Thomas\ More\ Knyght,\ sometyme\ Lord\ Chaun-$
cellour of England, wrytten by him in the Englysh tonge, ed. William Rastell (London, 1557), *STC* 18,076.
$Ww = The\ Whole\ workes\ of\ W.\ Tyndall,\ Iohn\ Frith,\ and\ Doct.\ Barnes,$
*three worthy Martyrs . . . collected and compiled in one Tome
togither*, ed. John Foxe (London, 1573), John Daye, *STC* 24,436.

Each of the three books has its own pagination. The page references,
therefore, are to the section written by the particular author cited.

Preface

1. For example, the entire body of John Bale's polemics is dismissed
with the remark, "Of Bale's works as a controversialist, perhaps the less
one says the better," J.W. Harris, *John Bale* (Urbana, Ill., 1940), p. 13,
while the standard biography of Thomas More spares only four pages for
all of More's works of religious controversy; see R.W. Chambers, *Thomas
More* (London, 1935), pp. 252-255. William Tyndale's biographer says
of his subject's most powerful polemic, *The practyse of Prelates*, that it is

the most expendable of all Tyndale's works and that he would gladly exchange it for another Old Testament book translated by the Reformer; see J.F. Mozley, *William Tyndale* (London, 1937), p. 169.

2. For instance, T.E. Bridgett, *Life and Writings of Blessed Thomas More* (London, 1935), 3rd ed., on the Catholic side, and William A. Clebsch, *England's Earliest Protestants* (New Haven, 1964), on the Protestant.

3. For instance, George P. Krapp, *The Rise of English Literary Prose* (New York, 1915) and C.S. Lewis, *English Literature in the Sixteenth Century* (Oxford, 1954).

1. Lutheran Controversy

1. See, for instance, Bridgett, p. 210; Theodore Maynard, *Humanist as Hero, The Life of Sir Thomas More* (New York, 1947), p. 140; Algernon Cecil, *A Portrait of Thomas More* (London, 1937), pp. 193-194.

2. *Assertio septem sacramentorum aduersus Martinum Lutheru*m (n. pl., 1523), sig. *2^r.

3. See below, pp. 53 ff., 121 ff., 152 ff.

4. See Luther, *Werke*, ed. J.K.F. Knaake et al. (Weimar, 1883-), X, ii, 198.

5. See, for instance, *Assertio*, sig. B2^r.

6. *Assertio*, sigs. A1^r, A1^v, B4^v, C1^r, C3^v, F2^r, G3^v.

7. For Tyndale and Barnes, see below, pp. 53 ff. and 121 ff. For Bale, see my article, "William Tyndale's Influence on John Bale's Polemical Use of History," *Archiv für Reformationsgeschichte*, LIII (1962), 79-96.

8. For general treatments of Luther as a polemicist, see Arthur C. McGiffert, *Martin Luther, The Man and His Work* (New York, 1912), pp. 150-155; James Mackinnon, *Luther and the Reformation* (New York, 1962), II, 28, 158, 217, 334, III, 122-140; Erwin Doernberg, *Henry VIII and Luther* (London, 1961), pp. 31-39.

9. See, for instance, More, below, pp. 17, 27.

10. On this, even Luther's enemies could not deny that he was a true prophet! Unless stated otherwise, all translations throughout this study are mine.

11. See, for instance, the Protestant polemical morality play *New Custome* (1573), *STC* 6150.

12. See below, p. 27.

13. For Henry, see above, p. 5; for More, see below, p. 25.

14. *Werke*, X, ii, 188. Cf. the German version of Luther's reply to Henry, ibid., pp. 233-234, 236.

15. To achieve the same purpose, Henry had used the charge of inconsistency against Luther; see above, p. 5.

16. For a discussion of this and other figures of rhetoric as used in polemics, see below, pp. 69, 174.

17. See below, p. 170.

18. See above, p. 5.

19. See below, pp. 22-23.

20. While More used the form in his *Utopia*, his polemical use of dialogue dates from his answer to this passage of Luther's. He does not really use modified dialogue throughout the *Responsio*, as has been claimed by Sister Gertrude Donnelly in her *A Translation of St. Thomas More's "Responsio ad Lutherum"* (Washington, 1962), pp. 30-31; his answers to Luther's quotations are too long; see below, pp. 15-16.

21. See Richard Sherry, *A treatise of Schemes & Tropes* (London, 1550), p. 69; *Rhetorica ad Herennium*, IV, xliii. 55. The technique is used in both polemical dialogue and polemical drama.

22. For contemporary commentary on the technique of distortion in polemics and its classical source, see Erasmus' letter to Dorp in *Opus Epistolarum*, ed. P.S. Allen et al. (Oxford, 1906-1947), II, 102-103.

23. *Werke*, X, ii, 210-211; cf. *Assertio*, sig. C3^r.

24. Cf. More, *Ervditissimi viri Guilelmi Rossei opus . . . quo . . . refellit . . . Lutheri calumnias* (London, 1523), sig. DD3^r. Hereafter cited as *Responsio*.

25. Cf. Joye's comment on More's work, that More thought "whan he wrote these blasphemyes that ye laye peple shuld rede onely his bokis neuer to se what shulde be answered: for that the answers were so strayghtlely forboden to be brought in to the lande/ and therfore he lyed as him lysted and wrote what he wolde," *The Subuersion of Moris false foundacion* (Emdon, 1534), sig. E7^v. Actually, More was exceptional in that he went out of his way to provide readers with extensive and usually accurate quotations from his opponents.

26. Cf. *Responsio*, sig. A4^r, and see below, p. 21, where More makes it clear that he thinks his work will be read by Lutherans as well as Catholics. Also, in his *Apologye* More cites the complaints of the "brethren" about the length of his books; see below, p. 21.

27. For a biography, see Chambers.

28. See his letters to Edward Lee, to Dorp, and to a monk in *The Correspondence of Sir Thomas More*, ed. Elizabeth F. Rogers (Princeton, 1947). Hereafter cited as *Correspondence*.

29. *Correspondence*, pp. 212-239. See also More's epigrams against Brixius in *The Latin Epigrams of Thomas More*, ed. and trans. Leicester Bradner and Charles A. Lynch (Chicago, 1953), Nos. 170, 171, 172, *et passim*.

30. *The apologye of Syr Thomas More, Knyght*, ed. Arthur I. Taft (London, 1930), p. 52. Hereafter cited as *Apologye*.

31. See Donnelly, p. 32.

32. Other fictional settings occur in the *Utopia*, *A Dialogue concernynge heresyes*, and *A dialogue of comfort*.

33. *Responsio*, sigs. A2^r-A2^v.

34. See below, pp. 85 and 158.

35. See Clebsch's criticism of the effectiveness of this technique of More's, especially in vernacular works, pp. 33 and 287. See also, on this technique, Miles Coverdale, *A confutacion of that treatise/ which one Iohn Standish made agaynst the protestacion of D. Barnes* (Zurich, 1541?), sigs. a7^r-a7^v.

36. See above, p. 4 and below, p. 27.

37. Chambers, p. 193.

38. Cf. G.G. Krodel, "Luther, Erasmus and Henry VIII," *Archiv für Reformationsgeschichte*, LIII (1962), 60-78. Whatever More meant by his remark, he did not mean that he had prepared an index, as some writers have supposed (see Taft, *Apologye*, pp. 271-272n). There is no index to the *Assertio*.

39. More also refers to the *Assertio*'s arguments quite frequently in his other polemical works. Taft thinks More's purpose in these references is to remind Henry publicly of his previous support of the papacy; see *Apologye*, p. xxxvi.

40. More's English works were commissioned to be written for "simple and unlearned men" (see below, p. 39), and perhaps it was the terms of the commission which caused Clebsch (pp. 259, 287, 289, 295) to consider these works less learned than the Latin. But surely the "simple and unlearned" would have found More's treatises against Saint-German, for instance, rather rough going; see below, p. 192 ff.

41. *Responsio*, sig. F3^v; cf. *Assertio*, sig. G3^v.

42. See below, pp. 101-102.

43. See below, pp. 190-191.

44. Krapp, p. 44.

45. See below, p. 180.

46. For further examples of More's use of logical fallacies, see below, p. 103.

47. See Luther, *Werke*, X, ii, 201.

48. See Luther, *Werke*, X, ii, 195.

49. *Responsio*, sig. L2^r; see Luther, *Werke*, VI, 561.

50. See Sherry, p. 69.

51. The assigning of speeches to characters for the purpose of expressing his own views and the creation of an entire dramatic framework had, of course, been used by More for nonpolemical purposes in his *Utopia*.

52. See above, p. 12.

53. See below, p. 93.

54. See my article, "The English Morality Play as a Weapon of Religious Controversy," *Studies in English Literature*, II (Spring, 1962), 157-180.

55. See Luther, *Werke*, X, ii, 186.

56. See above, pp. 12-13.

57. See Luther, *Werke*, X, ii, 191.

58. *Responsio*, sig. TT3ᵛ; Luther, *Werke*, X, ii, 188.

59. See *Assertio*, sig. C3ʳ.

60. See below, pp. 169, 197.

61. *Responsio*, sig. H10(d)ʳ. One of the techniques of the polemical dialogue; see below, p. 90.

62. See above, p. 11 f.

63. *Responsio*, sig. DD3ʳ. More is correct.

64. E.g., *Responsio*, sig. FF1ʳ. For other accusations of lying against Luther, see ibid., sigs. II1ᵛ, SS1ᵛ.

65. See below, pp. 98, 176.

66. See J.S. Brewer and J. Gairdner, eds., *Letters and Papers, Foreign and Domestic, of the Reign of Henry VIII* (London, 1862-1908), III, i, ccccxxix, and W.H. Hutton, *Sir Thomas More* (London, 1895), p. 198.

67. E.g., *Responsio*, sigs. H10(b)ᵛ-H10(c)ʳ. See Luther, *Werke*, VI, 202-276; Tyndale, *Ww*, pp. 61-62.

68. For instance Fisher, in his 1526 sermon; see Clebsch, p. 29; also Saint-German, below, pp. 194-195.

69. Clebsch, pp. 36-37.

70. Ibid., p. 37; Doernberg, p. 53.

71. *A copy of the letters, wherin . . . kyng Henry the eyght made answere vnto a certayn letter of Martyn Luther* (London, 1526), sig. A5ʳ.

72. See below, pp. 99, 103, 108, 163.

73. *Literarum, quibus . . . Henricus octauus . . . respondit, ad quandam epistolam Martini Lutheri* (London, 1526), sigs. C1ʳ-C1ᵛ.

74. See below, p. 34.

75. "leude Leeman" is the English version (*A copy*, sigs. E2ʳ-E2ᵛ); cf. below, p. 103, where More uses the same term for Luther's wife.

76. Clebsch, p. 12.

77. H.S. Bennett, *English Books and Readers 1475-1557* (Cambridge, 1952), p. 33.

78. H. Maynard Smith, *Henry VIII and the Reformation* (London, 1962), p. 299.

79. J.D. Mackie, *The Earlier Tudors* (Oxford, 1952), p. 345.

80. Clebsch, p. 25.

81. *Correspondence*, p. 325.

82. It was also answered by Cochlaeus.

83. Elizabeth F. Rogers, "Sir Thomas More's Letter to Bugenhagen," *The Modern Churchman*, XXXV (March, 1946), p. 351; Mother M.A. Sinclair, "St. Thomas More's Letter to John Bugenhagen," unpublished dissertation (Loyola University of Chicago, 1957), p. 16.

84. *Correspondence*, pp. 325-326.

85. See above, p. 16.

86. He does the same in his letter to Dorp, *Correspondence*, p. 30, and in *The Confutacyon of Tyndales answere;* see below, p. 109.

87. See below, p. 115.

88. See below, pp. 34-35.

89. *Correspondence*, p. 336. Cf. using the opponent's form of argument against him, below, p. 320.

90. See Thomas Wilson, *The Arte of Rhetorique*, ed. G.H. Mair (Oxford, 1909), pp. 183-184.

91. *Correspondence*, pp. 328, 331. See Rogers, p. 352; Sinclair, p. 8; Preserved Smith, *The Life and Letters of Martin Luther* (New York, 1911), pp. 157, 164.

2. William Tyndale

1. See A.W. Reed, *Early Tudor Drama* (London, 1926), p. 165; Germain Marc'hadour, *L'Univers de Thomas More* (Paris, 1963), p. 376.

2. James B. Mullinger, *The University of Cambridge* (London, 1873), I, 80-82.

3. For a biography, see Mozley, *Tyndale*.

4. *W*, p. 1037.

5. By Constitution VII of the Synod of Oxford (1407). See Reed, p. 162.

6. A.W. Pollard, *Records of the English Bible* (Oxford, 1911), p. 135; Bennett, p. 35.

7. Mackie, p. 345. How unsuccessful the attempts were to keep Tyndale's works out of England is acknowledged by William Barlowe, *A dyaloge descrybyng the orygynal ground of these Lutheran faccyons* (London, 1531), sigs. t4ʳ-t4ᵛ.

8. Mullinger, I, 571, 578.

9. In *The Poetical Works of John Skelton*, ed. Rev. Alexander Dyce (London, 1843), I, 206-224.

10. Ibid., p. 206.

11. Skelton does not name the two scholars. The identification is made by Mullinger in his *Cambridge*, I, 607-608.

Thomas Bilney was born ca. 1495. He attended Cambridge and was ordained in 1519. He embraced the doctrine of justification by faith and became one of the leaders of a group of young Reformers at Cambridge.

However, on most other points, such as the power of the Church and of the Pope and the doctrine of the Eucharist, Bilney remained orthodox. He was examined by Wolsey in 1526 for preaching against pilgrimages and the worship of saints, but was let off when he swore that he did not hold Luther's doctrines. In 1527 he preached against images, for which he and Arthur were made to do public penance. In 1531 Bilney was again charged with preaching heresy and was executed as a relapsed heretic. See John Foxe, *Acts and Monuments*, ed. S.R. Catley (London, 1837-1841), IV, 619-628.

The date of Arthur's birth is unknown. He was educated with Bilney at Cambridge. See Foxe, IV, 619-628.

12. See below, pp. 85-86.

13. The translation is that of Bridgett, pp. 281-282. The Latin text is in *Correspondence*, pp. 387-388.

14. See Edward Hall, *The Triumphant Reign of King Henry VIII*, ed. Charles Whibley (London, 1904), I, 159. On More's reputation for eloquence in English, see also Richard S. Sylvester, "The 'Man for All Seasons' Again: Robert Whittington's Verses to Sir Thomas More," *Huntington Library Quarterly*, XXVI (February, 1963), 147-154, and "John Constable's Poems to Thomas More," *Philological Quarterly*, XLII (October, 1963), 525-531.

15. See Nicholas Harpsfield, *The Life and death of Sr. Thomas Moore*, ed. Elsie V. Hitchcock and R.W. Chambers (London, 1932), p. 20; also William Roper, *The Lyfe of Sir Thomas Moore, knighte*, ed. Elsie V. Hitchcock (London, 1935), pp. 67-68.

16. In this More goes beyond Skelton, who in his *Replycacyon* agrees that Bilney and Arthur were shown too much leniency, but thinks it would have been sufficient if they had been made to recant their heresies publicly in all the places where they had preached, and if they had been warned that any relapse into heresy would put them in danger of execution.

17. For discussion of the Hunne case, see below, p. 166.

18. Clebsch, on the basis of Joye's statement that "Frith wrote tindals answers to More for tindale" (*Apology*, ed. Arber, p. 33), thinks Frith wrote that part of the *Answere* which comes under the heading of "The solutions and answeres vnto M.Mores [books]" (pp. 95-97). His main reason for so thinking is that the citations from Scripture in this section do not agree with Tyndale's translation of the New Testament, and "Tyndale, in his undisputed writings and translations, naturally preferred the readings of his own 1526—and later the 1534—New Testament" (p. 95). Curiously, Clebsch later says that Tyndale "set little store by his own first translation" (p. 143), which would seem to be somewhat of a contradiction.

Actually, Tyndale was not in the habit of quoting from his own translations, nor was faithfulness to any one version a common practice of the
time. Compare, for instance, the translations in Tyndale's *An exposicion
vppon the v. vi. vii. chapters of Mathew* (ca. 1532) with those in his 1526
New Testament. See also Butterworth and Chester, *George Joye* (Philadelphia, 1962), pp. 82-83, 107, and Mozley, *Tyndale*, p. 203.

19. The form of this work was dictated by the form of Tyndale's
Answere, in that More painstakingly cites chapter after chapter of Tyndale and appends his own comments.

20. See *W*, p, 816.

21. For discussion of the length of More's works, see below, pp. 188,
208-209.

22. See J.F. Mozley, "Tyndale's 'Supper of the Lord'," *Notes and
Queries*, CLXXXIII (November, 1942), 305-306, and "The Supper of the
Lord, 1533," *Moreana*, X (May, 1966), 11-16. Cf. the arguments of Cargill
Thompson and Clebsch for Joye's authorship, in *The Harvard Theo-
logical Review*, LIII (1960), 77-79, and ibid., LV (1962), 63-66.

23. Like the *Confutacyon*, the *Answere* is a chapter-by-chapter refutation of Tyndale.

24. Possibly because of government harassment; Marc'hadour, p. 489 ff.

25. For Tyndale as a translator, see Mozley, *Tyndale*; G.D. Bone,
"Tindale and the English Language" in S.L. Greenslade, *The Work of
William Tindale* (London, 1938); R.W. Chambers, *Man's Unconquerable
Mind* (London, 1939).

26. See E. Flesseman-van Leer, "The Controversy about Scripture
and Tradition between Thomas More and William Tyndale," *Nederlands Archief voor Kerkgeschiedenis*, New Series, XLIII (1959), iii,
143-165.

27. See More, *W*, pp. 151-152.

28. For an indication of the laity's feelings toward the clergy at the
time Tyndale wrote, see below, p. 192 ff.

29. For Tyndale's change of attitude toward interpretation of Scripture, see Clebsch, pp. 172, 197.

30. *Ww*, pp. 166-167; New Testament (1534), sig. *.ii.^{r}.

31. The same can be said of the Reformers' treatment of the medieval
morality play: the established villain of the pre-Reformation plays, the
Vice, was identified as a Catholic in post-Reformation Protestant morality
drama.

32. This is the main technique employed by Christopher Saint-
German; see below, p. 197.

33. On Tyndale's annotations, see Mozley, *Tyndale*, pp. 146 and 200.

34. See More's epistles to Edward Lee, to Dorp, and to a monk in
Correspondence, pp. 27-74, 137-154, 165-206.

35. It is highly probable that Tyndale's polemical use of history influenced John Bale to expand the material Tyndale touched on; see my article on Tyndale's influence on Bale.

36. *Ww*, p. 181. It is just possible that by "the Chronicles of England" Tyndale means a specific chronicle of this name printed by Caxton. However, the capitalization of the word "chronicles" is in itself no indication of a specific reference since Tyndale often capitalizes this word.

37. *Ww*, p. 374 (misnumbered for p. 362). Ranulph Higden's *Polychronicon*.

38. The major chronicles dealing with English history in print by 1536 were: *The Brut* or *The Chronicles of England* (1480), *Polychronicon* (1482), Robert Fabyan's *The New Chronicles of England and France* (1516), *The Chronicle of Froissart* (1523). It is unlikely that Tyndale on the Continent saw John Rastell's *The Pastime of People* (1529) before publishing the bulk of his assertions about English history in *The practyse of Prelates* (1530). Polydore Vergil's *Historia Anglica* (1534) was published one year after Tyndale's last polemical work.

39. See fns. 55, 56, and 57.

40. *A Brefe Chronycle Concernynge . . . Oldecastell* (1544), *The Actes of Englysh Votaryes* (1546), *Acta Romanorum Pontificum* (1558), trans. in 1574 as *The Pageant of Popes*.

41. Bale also uses this technique; see *Pageant*, sig. B4^v and *Votaryes*, sigs. A5^r-A5^v.

42. For a discussion of Tyndale's attitude toward tradition, see E. Flesseman-van Leer.

43. Cf. Bale's *The second part . . . of the English votaries* (1551), sigs. A3^r-A4^v, where he holds the Roman Church responsible for the actions of such Roman Emperors as Nero, on the basis of the common name "Roman."

44. *Ww*, p. 351. For a discussion of Tyndale's use of historical sources, see below, p. 61 ff.

45. *Ww*, p. 129. A reference to the case of Richard Hunne, for which see below, p. 166 ff.

46. See A.F. Pollard, *Wolsey* (London, 1953), p. 177 and note.

47. *Ww*, pp. 114-115. A reference to Wolsey's alliance with the Emperor against the French and subsequent alliance with the French against the Emperor. See Pollard, *Wolsey*, pp. 99-164.

48. See More, *W*, pp. 304, 313.

49. *Ww*, p. 155. Bale makes the same point about confession; see his *Yet a course at the Romyshe foxe* (1543), sig. C6^v and *The Epistle Exhortatorye* (1544), sig. B1^r.

50. Henry's French campaign in 1522. See A.F. Pollard, *Henry VIII* (London, 1951), pp. 119-126.

51. *Ww*, p. 181. See fn. 46.

52. See *Ww*. pp. 231, 251, 269.

53. *Ww*, pp. 102, 116, 391. The same points are made by Simon Fish and Christopher Saint-German; see below, pp. 156 and 198.

54. See Pollard, *Wolsey*, pp. 121-123.

55. See, for instance, *The Annals of Roger De Hoveden*, trans. Henry T. Riley (London, 1853), I, 35-36; Roger of Wendover, *The Flowers of History*, trans. Rev. J.A. Giles (London, 1849), I, 178; Matthew of Westminster, *The Flowers of History*, trans. C.D. Yonge (London, 1853), I, 396-397; Ranulph Higden, *Polychronicon*, ed. Rev. J. R. Lumby (London, 1876), VI, 277-279; *The Brut or The Chronicles of England*, ed. Friedrich W.D. Brie (London, 1906-1908), I, 103-104.

56. See Wendover, I, 330-331; *Polychronicon*, VII, 239; Robert Fabyan, *The New Chronicles of England and France*, ed. Henry Ellis (London, 1811), p. 235.

57. The Rev. H. Walter's note on this passage in his edition of Tyndale's works is: "William of Malmesbury confirms part of this statement, though he does not say on what ground the money was to be paid." *Expositions and Notes*, Parker Society (Cambridge, 1849), p. 295.

58. See Wendover, II, 254-255; *The Brut*, I, 158; Fabyan, p. 316.

59. Tyndale regards a rebellion against John as evil since in his eyes John was England's first "Protestant" hero.

60. See Fabyan, p. 568; *The Brut*, II, 359; *The Chronicle of John Hardyng*, ed. Henry Ellis (London, 1812), pp. 349-350.

61. *The Brut*, II, 511; Fabyan, pp. 616-617.

62. The only evidence Rev. H. Walter can cite in support of Tyndale's claim that Edward IV's proposed marriage was broken off by the clergy through the instrumentality of Friar Bungay is as follows: "In the first edition of Fabian's Chronicle after relating the events of the battle of Barnet in 1471, he says: 'Of the mists and other impediments which fell upon the lord's party by reason of the incantations of friar Bungay, as the fame went, we list not to write.' fol. ccxxiii." *Expositions and Notes*, p. 304. It is evident that here once again Tyndale has "filled out" the chronicler's account.

63. For Skelton's attacks on Wolsey, see Pollard's index under "Skelton," *Wolsey*, p. 389.

64. *Ww*, p. 137. Saint-German expresses the same views; see below, p. 196.

65. Cf. Saint-German's *Diuision* in Taft's edition of More's *Apologye* and More, *W*, pp. 285-286.

66. More, *W*, pp. 969, 982.

67. *Ww*, p. 180. Cf. Fish, below, p. 157.

68. Henry is reported to have said of Tyndale's *Obedience*, "This is

a book for me and for all kings to read." John Strype, *Ecclesiastical Memorials* (Oxford, 1820-1840), I, i. 173.

69. See Henry Brinklow, *Complaynt of Roderyck Mors*, ed. J.M. Cowper (London, 1874), pp. 56-57.

70. In 1531 Henry instructed Cromwell to win Tyndale to the royal cause. In his attempt Cromwell was unsuccessful, but he did manage to secure for the Crown the services of such polemicists as the Reformers Robert Barnes and John Bale, as well as Christopher Saint-German. See Mozley, *Tyndale*, p. 187 ff.; A.G. Dickens, *Thomas Cromwell* (London, 1959), pp. 22, 156; McCusker, *Bale*, p. 75; W. Gordon Zeeveld in *The Thought and Culture of the English Renaissance*, ed. Elizabeth M. Nugent (Cambridge, 1956), p. 245.

71. By the Submission of the Clergy, 1532.

72. *The Statutes at Large*, Runnington edition (London, 1876), II, 166.

73. See Pollard, *Henry VIII*, p. 221.

74. *CHEL* (1950), IV, 321-322.

75. See W.G. Crane, *Wit and Rhetoric in the Renaissance* (New York, 1937), p. 49; W.J. Ong, *Ramus and Talon Inventory* (Cambridge, Mass., 1958), p. 395; *CHEL*, III, 424.

76. Cicero does not deal with sarcasm as such, but he does discuss various devices which could easily be considered as sarcasm; see *De Oratore*, ed. and trans. E.W. Sutton and H. Rackhaus (London, 1948), I, 415-419. Quintilian is not enthusiastic about the use of sarcasm; see *The Institutio Oratoria of Quintilian*, ed. and trans. H.E. Butler (London, 1953), II, 457. Cf. *CHEL*, III, 23.

77. *Ww*, p. 150. See also Ulrich von Hutten's ridicule of the loosing and binding power claimed by the Pope, *Werke*, ed. Ernst Münch (Leipzig, 1822), I, 297.

78. See Aristotle, *The "Art" of Rhetoric*, ed. and trans. J.H. Freese (London, 1947), pp. 467, 469; Cicero, *De Oratore*, I, 395-396, 403-405; Quintilian, *Institutio Oratoria*, II, 475; cf. *CHEL*, III, 23.

79. See below, p. 92.

80. This device appears *ad nauseam* throughout the nondramatic polemical works of John Bale. It serves a more sophisticated purpose in his polemical morality plays, as it does in other Protestant moralities, in which it is used to reveal the Catholic Vice's evil nature to the audience; see my article, "John Bale's Nondramatic Works of Religious Controversy," *Studies in the Renaissance*, IX (1962), 218-233, and my article on the polemical morality play.

81. See fn. 75.

82. See Mozley, *Tyndale*, p. 14; also H. Rashdall, *Universities of Europe in the Middle Ages* (Oxford, 1936), ch. 14.

83. See *Ww*, p. 176. In his *Dialogue concernynge heresyes* More makes his interlocutor, who leans toward the Reformers, declare, "I take reason for playne enmye to faith" (*W*, p. 148).

84. *Ww*, pp. 280, 288. A number of the techniques of religious controversy used by the polemicists studied in this work are discussed in Thomas Wilson's *The rule of reason* (1551) which, although published some years after the present controversies, is really the logic of Aristotle and Rudolphus Agricola illustrated from contemporary religious problems. Wilson's treatise on logic is thus an interesting source book for sixteenth-century techniques of religious controversy. One of the techniques recommended by Wilson is challenging the form of the opposing argument (*Rule* [1552], sig. R6^r).

85. See Wilson, *Rule*, sig. F1^r ff.

86. See Chambers, *More*, p. 175.

87. *Ww*, p. 251. Erasmus often translated the Greek "ecclesia" by the Latin "congregatio." See, for instance, II Corinthians i.2 and Colossians iv.16.

88. See his epistles to Edward Lee and to a monk in *Correspondence*.

89. New Testament (Cologne, 1525), sigs. G2^v-G3^r.

90. For Erasmus' influence on Tyndale, see Robert Demaus, *William Tyndale* (London, 1925), pp. 54 and 69.

91. *Ww*, p. 304. Some works had been erroneously attributed to the authors Tyndale mentions; for an instance of such incorrect attribution, see Frederick Seebohm, *The Oxford Reformers* (London, 1867), p. 54. However, Tyndale is stretching the point when he claims that such errors were deliberate deceptions on the part of the clergy.

92. See More, *W*, pp. 315-316.

93. *Ww*, p. 250; cf. "church," *OED*, B.

94. See p. 75.

95. See below, p. 85.

96. See below, p. 93.

97. Cf. More's treatment of quotations from Luther, above, pp. 23-24.

98. *Ww*, p. 254. What prompted Tyndale's charge was not only More's elevation to high political office—a reward, as he mistakenly thought, for More's services to the clergy—but also the news that the English clergy took up a collection to reward More for his writings defending the Church. What Tyndale evidently did not know was that More refused the money; see Roper, p. 48, and More, *W*, p. 867.

99. *Ww*, p. 293. The "Cardinall" is Wolsey.

100. See Nos. 53, 160, 186, 187.

101. At the suggestion of More or Stokesley, says Rupp, but cites no evidence for his statement; see *Studies in the Making of the English Protestant Tradition* (Cambridge, 1949), p. 60.

102. See Anthony À Wood, *Athenae Oxonienses*, ed. Philip Bliss (London, 1813), I, 366-367. The portion of the *Dyaloge* to which reference is made is on sigs. F4^v-G1^r.

103. "Barlous" is given as one of More's pseudonyms in a summary of a 1536 letter in *LP*, X, 232-233. I am indebted for this information to Prof. James P. Lusardi of Wesleyan University.

104. See William Turner, *A nevv booke of spirituall Physik* (Basel?, 1555), sig. F8^v.

105. See below, p. 87.

106. *Opera Omnia*, ed. J.P. Migne (Paris, 1841), Vol. I (*Patrologia Latina*, XXXII).

107. For instance, by Wycliffe.

108. In *Werke*, Vol. I.

109. *Bibliothek Älterer Schriftwerke der deutschen Schweiz*, ed. J. Baechtold (Frauenfeld, 1878), Vol. II.

110. Ibid.

111. Ed. Edward Arber (London, 1871); see Rupp, p. 55 ff. on Jerome and William Barlowe.

112. In Hutten, *Werke*, Vol. II.

113. In *Satirische Feldzüge wider die Reformation*, ed. Arnold E. Berger (Leipzig, 1933).

114. In Charles Nisard, *Les Gladiateurs de la République des Lettres* (Paris, 1860), I, 31-33.

115. Ibid., pp. 94-95.

116. *Werke*, Vol. II.

117. Outside the dialogue form, the most notable work in which the opposition is condemned by its own words is *Epistolae Obscurorum Virorum*, written by Hutten and others, in which this is the principal satiric technique.

118. See Donnelly, pp. 14-15.

119. See *Correspondence*, p. 437.

120. *Opus Epistolarum*, II, 502, and in various other epistles.

121. E.g., *W*, pp. 204, 276.

122. James Gairdner, *Lollardy and the Reformation in England* (London, 1908), I, 511-512.

123. See, for instance, his *Utopia* and *A dialogue of comfort*.

124. See Harpsfield, pp. 84-87.

125. See Helen C. White, *Social Criticism in Popular Religious Literature of the Sixteenth Century* (New York, 1944), pp. 32-33.

126. Under the term "humor," I have included various devices which have as their object ridicule, i.e., "the act of exciting laughter at a person or thing" (*OED*, Sect. 3). Since humor is defined as "that which excites amusement" (*OED*, Sect. 7a), of which laughter is a product, ridicule

may be defined as that which excites amusement at a person or thing. Therefore ridicule is a subclass of humor.

127. For his "merry tales" More had a precedent in the humorous anecdotes of the medieval *exempla*. See Gerald R. Owst, *Literature and Pulpit in Medieval England* (Cambridge, 1933), pp. 163-167. For a discussion of More's indebtedness to medieval preaching and devotional writing, see R.W. Chambers, "The Continuity of English Prose," in Harpsfield.

128. For discussion, see below, p. 166.

129. *W*, p. 198. Arthur I. Taft, in the introduction to his edition of More's *Apologye* (London, 1931), says that More never used the device of humor or ridicule as the only answer to an argument. The only evidence Taft offers for this conclusion is what he terms More's "seriousness of purpose" (p. lvii). I believe I have sufficiently demonstrated that More does, in fact, occasionally use humor to avoid a difficult situation and as the only answer to an argument. Taft also says that "If More's chapter could not be satisfactorily refuted, Tyndale was not unwilling to dismiss it with a scoff" (p. xxviii). Are we to understand by this that Tyndale had less "seriousness of purpose" than More? Actually Tyndale never dismisses an entire chapter of More's *Dialogue* with a scoff for purposes of avoiding refutation. The three chapters in the *Dialogue* which Tyndale does ridicule contain no doctrinal points whatsoever. In the first, More gives an imaginative account of how he came to write the *Dialogue*, in the second, he relates some obscene practices carried on at an "abbey" in France, and in the third, More asserts that Luther wrote a book glorifying himself and his deeds at Worms, but in such a manner as to make people think that he himself was not the author. This assertion Tyndale labels as "poetry." (The book was written by one of Luther's friends; see R.H. Fife, *The Revolt of Martin Luther* [New York, 1957], pp. 655-656. More's chapters are Bk. I, 1; Bk. II, 10; and Bk. IV, 4. Tyndale's comments are contained in *Ww*, pp. 279, 299, and 327.)

130. See Bradner and Lynch's edition, pp. xxvi-xxvii.

131. Ibid., p. 126.

132. *Opera Omnia* (1689), pp. 258-259.

133. See *W*, p. 127.

134. See Erasmus' comment, *Opus Epistolarum*, IV, 21, and Budé's in *Utopia*, ed. Edward Surtz, S.J., and J.H. Hexter, *The Complete Works of St. Thomas More*, (New Haven, 1965), IV, 12.

135. See *The History of King Richard III*, ed. Richard S. Sylvester, in *The Complete Works of St. Thomas More* (New Haven, 1963), vol. II; and *A Dialogue of Comfort Against Tribulation*, ed. Leland Miles (Bloomington, Ind., 1965).

136. *Ww*, p. 68. See below, p. 176, and Joye, *The refutation of the byshop of Winchesters derke declaration* (London, 1546), fol. 59ʳ.

137. For an estimate of More as a theologian, see Gerald Kernan, "Saint Thomas More, Theologian," *Thought*, XVII (June, 1942), 281-302. When appealing to patristic authority, More almost always quotes the Father in question and supplies references.

138. See *Opera Omnia*, VIII (*Patrologia Latina*, XLII), 176.

139. *W*, pp. 1056, 1058, 1065, 1067. These passages certainly do support More's position—just as the passages Tyndale cites, often from the same Fathers, support his position. Polemicists on both sides of the controversy were able to find patristic statements which seemed to uphold their particular point of view.

140. John Colet, Dean of St. Paul's Cathedral and founder of St. Paul's School, in his Oxford lectures on St. Paul's epistles departed from the scholastic method of expounding isolated texts and adopted an approach to the Pauline epistles which attempted to explain them in the light of what they had meant to the people to whom they were written. See J.H. Lupton, *A Life of John Colet* (London, 1887), pp. 59-74, and Ernest W. Hunt, *Dean Colet and His Theology* (London, 1956), pp. 88-103.

141. See below, p. 101.

142. See below, p. 105.

143. *W*, pp. 628-634, 649-650.

144. *W*, pp. 220-221.

145. See, for instance, "Pierce's supererogation" and "The trimming of Thomas Nashe," in *The Works of Gabriel Harvey*, ed. Rev. Alexander Grossart (London, 1885), II, 27-331, III, 1-73; "Have With You to Saffron-Walden," in *The Works of Thomas Nashe*, ed. R.B. McKerrow (Oxford, 1904), III, 1-141.

146. See Nisard, *passim*.

147. "A bishop then must be blameless, the husband of one wife. . . ."

148. Luther, "Von den guten Werken," *Werke*, Vol. VI, and Tyndale, *Ww*, pp. 61-62.

149. That there is no deliberate attempt at deception on More's part here, however, is indicated by the fact that he gives the Latin.

150. I Corinthians xi.23.

151. When More was writing, the Hussite movement was split into three separate factions: the Taborites, the Calisetines, and the Bohemian Brethren. There were Hussite priests, not ordained by Rome, who administred the sacraments. See David S. Schaff, *John Huss* (New York, 1915).

152. See Hartmann Grisar, *Luther*, ed. Luigi Cappadelta (London, 1914), I, 35, 75, 105n., 324.

153. *W*, p. 255. More probably was told these things by some of Luther's German enemies, such as Cochlaeus, with whom More was corresponding in the year he wrote the *Dialogue*. See fn. 129.

154. See Henry S. Lucas, *The Renaissance and the Reformation* (New York, 1934), p. 455.

155. "Eine treue Vermahnung zu allen Christen," "Von weltlicher Oberkeit," and "Ermahnung zum Frieden," *Werke*, Vols. VIII, XI, XVIII.

156. See Ludwig von Pastor, *The History of the Popes*, ed. R.F. Kerr et al. (London, 1908), IX, 361, 398.

157. Ibid., p. 400.

158. Mozley, *Tyndale*, p. 231.

159. See below, p. 209 ff.

160. *Werke*, VI, 561.

161. See, for instance, *W*, p. 175.

162. MS. Cotton Titus D. IV.

163. Cf. Taft, *Apologye*, p. xxxvi.

164. See his letter to Brixius, *Correspondence*, pp. 212-239.

165. The same would hold true in the Brixius dispute, in which More was defending the honor of England.

166. See above, p. 106.

167. *W*, pp. 149-150, 163. It is interesting to note that at the end of the *Utopia* More says that it is pride alone that leads man to prefer the unjust laws under which he lives to the just laws of the Utopians; see *Utopia*, pp. 242-244.

168. See Nos. 53, 160, 186, 187.

169. See More's letter to Dorp, *Correspondence*, pp. 27-74.

170. "And as they sinne not, so they erre not. And on the other side as they sinne, so they erre: but neuer vnto death and damnation" (*Ww*, p. 258).

171. See above, pp. 96-97.

172. See above, p. 80.

173. For instance, Karl Kautsky, *Thomas More and His Utopia* (London, 1927).

174. For instance, E.M.G. Routh, *Sir Thomas More and his Friends* (London, 1934); C.S. Lewis, *English Literature in the Sixteenth Century* (Oxford, 1954); E.E. Reyonolds, *The Trial of St. Thomas More* (New York, 1964).

175. *Correspondence*, p. 188.

176. See fn. 134.

177. *Utopia*, p. 247.

178. *Correspondence*, pp. 27-74, 165-206.

3. Robert Barnes

1. See Rupp, p. 40.

2. See W.D.J. Cargill Thompson, "The Sixteenth-Century Editions of *A Supplication Unto King Henry The Eight* by Robert Barnes D.D.:

A footnote to the History of the Royal Supremacy," *Transactions of the Cambridge Bibliographical Society,* III (1960), 133-142; Clebsch, pp. 60-73.

3. See Dickens, *Cromwell,* pp. 22-23; cf. More, *W,* p. 761.

4. For the similarity between Tyndale's and Barnes's approaches to history, see, for instance, Tyndale, *Ww,* p. 366, and Barnes's section of the same work, pp. 193-194.

5. In the 1531 *Supplicatyon* Barnes says that it would be "to longe a processe" to prove clerical subversion from the chronicles (sig. A8ʳ), and it is therefore possible that he merely found more time later to expand his work.

6. *Vitae Romanorum Pontificum* (Wittenberg, 1536), sig. F6ᵛ. Hereafter cited as *Vitae.* See Clebsch, p. 73.

7. *Vitae,* sig. H4ᵛ. For a general discussion of Barnes's accuracy in his use of the chronicles, see p. 134 ff.

8. For Barnes's treatment of the bishop's oath, see below, pp. 126-127.

9. See Zeeveld, pp. 244-246.

10. The 1534 Act of Succession (26 Henry VIII, c. 2) made it treason to deny the legality of Henry's marriage. Thus arguments such as those of Barnes were not necessary to induce formal acquiescence in Henry's action; the intent would rather be to illustrate the inconsistency of the Catholic position. Barnes is, of course, committing the fallacy of equating the pre-Henrican clergy with the Henrican clergy.

11. Discussion and text of the two oaths is in Gilbert Burnet's *History of the Reformation of the Church of England* (Oxford, 1865), I, i, 249-251.

12. In 1530 Henry had accused the entire English clergy of breach of praemunire in that they had recognized Wolsey as legate; see Mackie, pp. 353-354.

13. See below, p. 194 ff.

14. So did Bale; see my article on his nondramatic works.

15. See Georg J. Schorn, *Die Quellen zu den Vitae Pontificum Romanorum des Bartolommeo Platina* (Rome, 1913), pp. 44-45; also the article on Platina in *The Catholic Encyclopedia.*

16. See Horace K. Mann, *The Lives of the Popes in the Early Middle Ages* (London, 1902-1932), VII, v, 216.

17. For instance, Johannes Nauclerus was not; see Erich Joachim, *Johannes Nauclerus und seine Chronik* (Göttingen, 1874), p. 9.

18. *Vitae,* sigs. K5ᵛ-K6ʳ. For the Joan legend, see H. Thurston, "Pope Joan," *The Month,* CXXIII (1914), 450-463.

19. *Vitae,* sig. M6ᵛ. But cf. Mann, IV, 136.

20. *Ww,* p. 328; *Vitae,* sigs. L1ᵛ-L7ᵛ.

21. See *B. Platinae Cremonensis de vita & moribus summorum Ponti-*

ficum historia (Cologne, 1529), p. 60, and *Commentariorvm Vrbanorum Raphaelis Volaterrani* (Basle, 1544), fol. 250ᵛ.

22. See *D. Iohannis Navcleri . . . Chronica* (Cologne, 1544), fol. 672; Aeneas Sylvius, *Abbreviatio supra Decades Blondi*, in *Opera* (Basle, 1571), pp. 200-201; *Opus . . . hystoriarum . . . Antonini* (Lugduno, 1512), ii, fols. 183ʳ-183ᵛ.

23. See Fabyan, p. 255.

24. See Platina, p. 90; Nauclerus, fol. 607; *Rapsodie historiarum Enneadum Marci Antonij Coccij Sabellici* (Paris, 1509), fol. 54ᵛ.

25. Platina, p. 108.

26. Antoninus, ii, fol. 186ᵛ.

27. See, for instance, Wendover, I, 330-331; *Polychronicon*, VII, 239; Fabyan, pp. 235, 568; Hardyng, pp. 349-350; *The Brut*, II, 359.

28. See fn. 24, above.

29. See *The Chronicle of Froissart*, ed. William P. Ker (London, 1901-1903), III, 460-467.

30. Platina, p. 136.

31. Becon cites Barnes as one of his authorities for his *The Relikes of Rome* (London, 1560?), sig. A8ᵛ.

32. Bale, *Votaryes* (1546), sig. G2ᵛ.

33. The 1539 Act of Six Articles (25 Henry VIII, c. 14).

34. See *Ww*, pp. 295-296.

35. See, for example, *W*, p. 736.

36. See *W*, p. 352.

37. For other examples of the mock creed, see Murner's creed for Luther in *Von dem Grossen Lutherischen Narren* and Bale's creed for the Mass in *The resurreccion of the masse*.

38. For polemical drama, see my article on the polemical morality play.

39. Probably boys, kept for sexual purposes. The accusation was a common one among Reformers.

40. Barnes is referring to Clement VII who was thought to be illegitimate; see the account of his life in von Pastor.

41. See H. Maynard Smith, pp. 63-64.

42. *Ww*, p. 235. For other examples of Barnes's use of polemical *exemplum*, see *Ww*, pp. 238, 263, 264.

43. For instance, Taft, *Apologye*, p. xxxi.

44. See below, p. 190.

45. *W*, p. 736; see also *W*, p. 343.

46. See above, p. 13.

47. See, for instance, Bale, in my article on his nondramatic polemical works.

48. For discussion, see below, p. 149 ff.

49. More charges throughout that Barnes tries to keep himself and

his intentions in the dark and that he tries to "blind" his readers; see, for instance, *W*, pp. 750, 796.

50. See Mozley, *Tyndale*, p. 231.

51. See the similar use of this device by Frith against More, below, pp. 186-187.

52. Krapp (p. 100) makes the amazing statement that More did not use many rhetorical devices and that he especially avoided alliteration, the incorrectness of which claim becomes apparent from even a casual reading of More.

53. *W*, p. 739. See the similar charge against Fish, below, pp. 169-170.

54. *W*, pp. 742, 772, 775, 797, 808-809.

55. See above, p. 88.

56. This passage was obviously written after Barnes had left England.

57. *W*, pp. 343, 761. Cf. Frith, *Ww*, p. 156; Joye, *The Exposicion of Danielle the Prophete* (London, 1550), sig. K8ʳ.

58. *W*, p. 769. More claims the charge was bawdry and that she "receiued two nunnes in by night . . . & suffred .ii. men to resort . . . to the*m*. . . . for the furtheraunce of loue betwene the brethren and the sistren of the euangelycall secte . . ." (*W*, p. 769). However, it is unlikely that the Lord Chancellor would be interested in a case of simple bawdry. More always regarded marriage between former nuns and former friars as illicit, and his words make it probable that the people involved were married renegade religious. The situation is, of course, pictured as one of bawdry to discredit the Reformers. The real charge, therefore, was probably that of harboring renegade religious "of the euangelycall secte."

4. Simon Fish

1. In *Four Supplications*, ed. F.J. Furnivall (London, 1871). All references are to this edition.

2. Foxe, IV, 656-666; *DNB*.

3. Most of Fish's accusations are echoed in two other contemporary diatribes: Roy and/or Barlowe's *A proper dyaloge* (1530) and Tyndale's *The practyse of Prelates* (1530).
diatribes: Roy

4. See below, p. 197 ff.

5. See More's comment, below, p. 163 ff.

6. Pp. 4-5. Cf. Tyndale and Barnes above, pp. 57 and 126.

7. See above, p. 59.

8. See A.F. Pollard, *Henry VIII*, p. 11.

9. Pp. 12-13. For the Hunne case, see below, p. 166.

10. See below, p. 192.

11. See Mackie, p. 372n.

12. All estimates of English clerical wealth at the time of the Dis-

solution have to be of a tentative nature, since they are all based on the inexact data compiled in the *Valor Ecclesiasticus* of Henry VIII and the records of the Court of Augmentation (Oscar A. Marti, *Economic Causes of the Reformation in England* [New York, 1929], p. 19). Based on these sources, figures for the annual income of all English religious houses range from a minimum of £131,609 (Burnet) to a maximum of £171,313 4s. 5d. (Speed). Using the data provided by Speed, who lists the annual income of each friary of the five mendicant orders mentioned by Fish, we get an annual income for all the English friaries of £2,216 16s. 11d. (History of Great Britain [London, 1650], pp. 799-828).

Gasquet's treatment of this subject is invalid, since he misreads Fish's figure of £43,333 6s. 8d. as £436,333 6s. 8d. (*Henry VIII and the English Monasteries* [London, 1888], I, 33).

13. The population was about 3 million (Hughes, *Reformation in England*, I, 4), of which 1/400 is 7,500. But there were 9,407 secular livings alone (Marti, p. 21), to which number must be added approximately 9,000 for the inmates of the monasteries (Mackie, p. 373), as well as an indeterminate number of mendicants and those in minor orders. Fish's figure, therefore, is in error by well above 50 per cent.

14. Henry Brinklow's *Complaynte of Roderyck Mors* and the anonymous *A Supplication of the poore commons*.

15. See above, pp. 85-86.

16. This device of More's is brilliantly turned against him by Roy and/or Barlowe, with the claim that, since he was unable to answer Fish by himself, More had to get supernatural help from purgatory—another of More's inventions along with his *Utopia;* see *A proper dyaloge,* sigs. B1^r-B1^v.

17. See Fish, p. 13.

18. It is thought that Barlowe wrote this without Roy's assistance. See J.F. Mozley, *The Times Literary Supplement,* No. 2412 (April 24, 1948), p. 233.

19. The veracity of all of More's statements noted in this section will be discussed below, p. 167 ff.

20. Mackie, pp. 291-292; Foxe, IV, 191.

21. See Wendover, II, 238-246, 269; Fabyan, pp. 319-320; Matthew of Westminster, II, 116; *The Brut,* I, 162-164.

22. See Mackie, pp. 292-293; Arthur Ogle, *The Tragedy of the Lollard's Tower* (Oxford, 1949), p. 47.

23. *Utopia,* p. 66; see also p. 333.

24. Fabyan, pp. 574-576; cf. John Capgrave, *The Chronicle of England,* ed. F.C. Hingeston (London, 1858), p. 297. For More's relationship to Fabyan, see Richard S. Sylvester's edition of More's *The History of King Richard III* in *The Complete Works of St. Thomas More* (New Haven, 1963), II, lxxiii-lxxv.

25. Fabyan, p. 578; see also *The Brut*, II, 495.

26. Fabyan, p. 602.

27. IV, 198. James Gairdner in *The English Church in the Sixteenth Century* (London, 1904) uncritically makes More his final authority for the Hunne case and rejects the genuineness of the letter—for which Foxe is the only source—on the basis that "it is so utterly opposed to what More tells us of the king's conviction of Horsey's innocence . . ." (p. 39). For Foxe's reliability, see J.F. Mozley, *John Foxe and His Book* (London, 1940), pp. 153-185.

28. Ogle, pp. 3-4, 9, 55. On the Hunne case, see also S.F.C. Milsom, "Richard Hunne's 'Praemunire'," *English Historical Review*, 76 (January, 1961), 80-82, and J. Fines, "The Post-Mortem Condemnation of Richard Hunne," *English Historical Review*, 78 (July, 1963), 528-531.

29. See Frith, *Ww*, p. 64, and German Gardynare, *A letter of a yonge gentylman* (London, 1534), sig. C5^r.

30. See C.S. Lewis, pp. 61, 306-307; F. Watson, *The English Grammar Schools to 1660* (Cambridge, 1908), p. 440; J.W.H. Atkins, *English Literary Criticism: The Renascence* (London, 1951), p. 18; W.S. Howell, *Logic and Rhetoric in England 1500-1700* (Princeton, 1956), pp. 64, 106, 123; but cf. W.J. Ong, *Ramus: Method, and the Decay of Dialogue* (Cambridge, Mass., 1958), pp. 253, 283.

31. These were somewhat the same terms John Skelton had used in his *Replycacion* to characterize the background of two other Reformers, Bilney and Arthur:

> A lytell ragge of rethorike
> A lesse lumpe of logyke,
> A pece or a patche of philosophy. . . .
> > Dyce, I, 208.

32. See *W*, p. 448.

33. Frith, *Ww*, pp. 34-35.

5. John Frith

1. Foxe, V, 1-15; *Athenae Oxonienses*, I, 47; *Athenae Cantabrigienses*, ed. Charles H. Cooper (Cambridge, 1858), I, 47-48.

2. Fisher's *Assertionis Lutheranae Confutatio*, More's work against Fish, and Rastell's *A new boke of purgatory* (1530). Of the three, only Rastell replied to Frith's criticism, in a nonextant work, listed in Bale as *Apologia ad Ioannem Frith* (*Illust. Maj. Brit. Script. Summarium* [1548], sig. KKk2^r). Frith, in turn, answered Rastell's reply in *An other boke against Rastel* (1533?), and, according to Foxe (V, 9), converted his opponent.

3. See *Ww*, pp. 107-108.

4. See *Ww*, p. 108.

5. For Bale's use of rhetoric, see my article on Bale's nondramatic polemical works.

6. After Frith's execution for heresy in 1533, his writings were attacked in a series of dialogues by the Catholic polemicist John Gwynneth (for whom see *DNB*) and in a single pamphlet by German Gardynare, a nephew of Bishop Stephen Gardiner. The latter especially emphasizes Frith's intellectual arrogance; see *A letter of a yonge gentylman* (1534), sigs. A3ʳ, A6ᵛ-A7ʳ, B4ᵛ; also William Turner, *The Rescvynge of the Romishe fox* (Zurich?, 1545), sig. C1ʳ.

7. *Ww*, p. 66. Unless stated otherwise, the rhetorical figures mentioned will be found in Cicero, *Orator*, xxxix. 135-xli. 40.

8. See Sherry, p. 28; Wilson, *Arte*, p. 187.

9. *Ww*, p. 54. A technique reminiscent of More's, as are many of Frith's polemical devices. Whether Frith deliberately patterned his polemical technique on that of his great opponent is impossible to determine, but in reading Frith, one is often reminded of More's style as exhibited in his earlier polemics.

10. See Wilson, *Arte*, pp. 144, 149.

11. See Sherry, p. 46; Wilson, *Arte*, p. 151.

12. See More, *W*, pp. 179, 656, 716.

13. An example of the polemical use of proverbs; see Sherry, p. 45; Wilson, *Arte*, p. 119.

14. See Sherry, pp. 45-46; Wilson, *Arte*, p. 146.

15. In his 1512 address to Convocation, Colet attributed "all the decaye of the churche" to "the couvetousnes of prestes." As the prime example of this covetousness, Wolsey was attacked some years later by Skelton in poems such as *Colyn Cloute* and *Why come ye nat to courte*, while clerical covetousness was one of the main reasons cited by Saint-German for the prevalence of anticlerical feeling among the laity; see below, p. 199.

16. See *Rhetorica ad Herennium*, IV. xxviii. 38.

17. *Ww*, p. 66. A synonym for lie.

18. See Wilson, *Arte*, p. 180; cf. More, *W*, pp. 262, 282.

19. See Sherry, p. 59; Wilson, *Arte*, p. 188.

20. Cf. *Rhetorica ad Herennium*, II. viii. 12. For discussion of the rumor technique, see below, p. 197 ff.

21. See Wilson, *Arte*, p. 181.

22. See Charles S. Baldwin, *Medieval Rhetoric and Poetic* (Gloucester, Mass., 1959), pp. 152, 155, 166; Watson, pp. 91, 93.

23. *Ww*, p. 126. The reference is to Henry's attempt to "divorce" Catherine of Aragon. Frith's point is that if Catherine according to divine law is actually Henry's wife, the English clergy err in attempting to obtain an annulment of a valid marriage for Henry, and that if the marriage never was valid, the clergy erred in originally permitting it.

Both Clebsch (p. 124) and one of his reviewers (*Moreana*, V, 112) misunderstand Frith's point. Frith is not talking about "the inerrancy of the Church," and certainly not about papal infallibility, but about the English clergy. His dilemma seeks to prove that they are not "the Church [which] can not erre," a point made by all the Reformers (see p. 42). That Frith's dilemma is based on a number of errors in both fact and logic would detract little from its effectiveness in popular polemics.

24. Recommended by Wilson, *Rule*, sig. R6^r.

25. Cf. Wilson, *Rule*, sig. R6^r.

26. Frith was himself accused of sophistry; see Gwynneth, *A manifeste detection of the falshed of J. Friths boke* (London, 1554), sigs. D4^r-D4^v, E1^r-E3^r; Gardynare, *A letter*, sig. C5^r.

27. By Constitution VII of the Synod of Oxford (1407). The officially commissioned champion of the Church, More did not regard the Scriptures themselves as heresy; see *W*, p. 241 ff.

28. It does not, of course, since it is not a true syllogism, in that the major premise does not lead to the conclusion.

29. Gwynneth comments that Frith "doothe exclame and crie against sophisters and sophistrie almoste in euery corner of his booke, and yet plaieth none other, but the same parte hym selfe" (*Detection*, sig. D4^v).

30. *Ww*, pp. 34, 45. See More, *W*, p. 324. Charges that his patristic citations omit key words unfavorable to him are made against Frith by Gwynneth, *A Playne Demonstration of Iohn Frithes lacke of witte* (London, 1557), sigs. C4^v-D4^r, and Gardynare, *A letter*, sig. C5^r.

31. *Ww*, pp. 4, 12, 13. Rastell probably derived the technique from More.

32. See my article, "Thomas More's *Utopia* and Protestant Polemics," *Renaissance News*, XVII (Autumn, 1964), 197-201.

33. More used the same technique against Barnes; see above, p. 145.

34. Among the accusations made against More at his trial two years later was that of speaking with evil intent. He was charged with having made statements *maliciously* against the King, i.e., in a sense meant to "depresse hys prerogatiue." For an account of More's trial, see Harpsfield and E.E. Reynolds, *The Trial of St. Thomas More*.

35. *Apologye*, p. 7.

36. *Correspondence*, p. 440.

37. Cf. Marie Delcourt, "L'Amitié d'Erasme et de More entre 1520 et 1535," *Bulletin de l'Association Guillaume Budé*, XIV (January, 1936), 25n.; Clebsch, p. 287.

38. For instance, by Rogers, *Correspondence*, p. 439, and Bridgett, p. 292.

39. See Mozley, *Tyndale*, p. 197.

40. *Correspondence*, p. 450. Throughout *The souper of the Lorde*, More is ridiculed for this passage; see, for instance, *Ww*, p. 466.

41. *Studies*, p. 199.

42. See Wilson, *Arte*, p. 201; Sherry, p. 47.
43. See Wilson, *Arte*, p. 201.

6. Christopher Saint-German

1. Mackie, p. 357.
2. Strype, I, i, 198.
3. Mackie, p. 354.
4. For discussion, see R.J. Schoeck, "The Meaning of 'Ex Officio' in The Sixteenth Century," *Notes and Queries*, New Series, VII (October, 1960), 365-366; see also the same author's "Canon Law in England on the Eve of the Reformation," *Medieval Studies*, XXV (1963), 125-147.
5. Gairdner, *The English Church*, pp. 114-115.
6. Printed in Taft's edition of More's *Apologye*. Hereafter cited as *Diuision*. Taft's edition is cited for More throughout this chapter.
7. *Illvstrivm Maioris Britanniae Scriptorvm* (Ipswich, 1548), sig. Sss3^r.
8. *A dialogue betwixte . . . Salem and . . . Bizance* (London, 1533), fol. 44^v. Hereafter cited as *SB*.
9. *The Addicions of Salem and Byzance* (London, 1534), fols. 63^r-64^r; cf. ibid., fol. 16^r. Hereafter cited as *Addicions*.
10. These thirty-nine chapters are similar in form to More's *Confutacyon* and *Answere*. More quotes portions of the *Diuision* and then comments.
11. Cf. Taft, p. xlii.
12. See above, p. 115.
13. For a discussion of the form of this dialogue, see below, pp. 201-202. Salem (Jerusalem) represents the canon, and Bizance (Constantinople), the common law. These names were chosen possibly because Jerusalem, as the Holy City, was associated with the claims of the spiritual or clerical law, while Constantinople, because of the caesaropapism of Emperor Justinian I and his codification of Roman law, was associated with the claims of secular law.
14. The entire *Debellacyon* is in the form of a chapter-by-chapter refutation of *Salem and Bizance*.
15. For discussion of the form of the *Addicions*, see below, p. 201.
16. *Poetical Works* (Dyce), I, 315-322.
17. *Diuision*, p. 206. The same charge was made by Skelton in *Colyn Cloute*.
18. *SB*, fols. 34^v-35^r. See More, *Apologye*, p. 110.
19. *SB*, fols. 37^v-38^r. Both Saint-German and More are using "as of a policie" in an unfavorable, and "politic" in a favorable, sense.
20. See below, p. 207.
21. *Apologye*, p. 67. Actually More was himself an expert in the use

of the "some-say" device. For instance, he introduced his discussion of the Bilney case by remarking that "this that I shall tell you, haue I harde reported, how be it I will not warrant it for trouth" (*W*, p. 207); he closed the discussion by admitting that he had heard the matter from others, "men of more worship and troueth therto, then that any man I wene, wold mistrust their tale" (*W*, p. 215).

22. See *SB*, fol. 38ʳ.

23. *Apologye*, p. 6. Joye refers to "Moris longe bablynge . . . bokis" (*Subuersion*, sig. A8ᵛ).

24. Ibid., p. 9. Thus the plan of the *Confutacyon* is quite different from the one in the *Dialogue*, in which More built up to a single conclusion over the course of many chapters. For instance, most of Book I of the *Dialogue* is devoted to establishing the single point that the Catholic Church is the church of Christ.

25. See *Diuision*, p. 224.

26. Foxe, IV, 196.

27. *Poetical Works* (Dyce), I, 313.

28. *Calendar of Letters, Despatches, and State Papers*, ed. Pascual De Gayangos et al. (London, 1879), IV, i, 367.

29. *Oxford Reformers*, p. 232.

30. Henry O. Taylor, *Thought and Expression in the Sixteenth Century* (London, 1924), I, 178.

31. Charles E. Mallet, *A History of the University of Oxford* (London, 1924), II, 59.

32. George M. Trevelyan, *English Social History* (London, 1944), p. 48.

33. Mackie, p. 354.

34. Ibid.

35. While penance was not usually thought of as "punishment" for sin, it was More himself who chose to regard it in that light, in order to demonstrate that the procedure in heresy cases was no more unfair than that adopted in felony cases; see *W*, pp. 959, 986, 992, 998, 1029.

36. *Utopia*, p. 74.

7. Conclusion

1. See A.G. Dickens, *The English Reformation* (London, 1964), pp. 73–74; Clebsch, pp. 137–155, 170, 195–197; Mackinnon, II, 123, 127.

2. See Miles's edition, pp. c–ci.

3. Mozley, *Tyndale*, p. 108.

4. Other factors involved were nationalism and humanism. For instance, More's *Richard the thirde*, not a work of religious polemics, is also "pointed history." On humanist histories, see Denys Hay, *Polydore Vergil* (Oxford, 1952), pp. 145–157.

5. See F. Smith Fussner, *The Historical Revolution* (New York, 1962), pp. 17-25.

6. See Howell, pp. 11, 219, 229.

7. See, for instance, More's contribution from his English polemics in Joseph Delcourt, *Essai sur la Langue de Sir Thomas More* (Montpellier, 1913), pp. 402-461.

8. See my article on the English morality play.

9. See John Elson, "Studies in the King John Plays," *Joseph Quincy Adams Memorial Studies* (Washington, 1948), pp. 183-197, and Irving Ribner, "Morality Roots of the Tudor History Play," *Tulane Studies in English*, IV (1954), 37n.

10. See my article on Tyndale's influence on Bale.

11. See also Krapp, p. 152.

INDEX